Home Country

Peter C. Newman

Home Country

PEOPLE, PLACES, AND POWER POLITICS

INTRODUCTION BY HUGH MACLENNAN

McCLELLAND AND STEWART LIMITED
MACLEAN-HUNTER LIMITED

BY THE SAME AUTHOR:

FLAME OF POWER
Intimate profiles of Canada's
greatest businessmen

RENEGADE IN POWER
The Diefenbaker Years

THE DISTEMPER OF
OUR TIMES
Canadian Politics in Transition:
1963-1968

HOME COUNTRY
People, Places, and Power
Politics

The Canadian Publishers
McClelland and Stewart Limited
25 Hollinger Road, Toronto

Maclean-Hunter Limited

0-7710-6756-9

Printed and bound in Canada by
T. H. Best Printing Company Limited,
Don Mills, Ontario

Contents

FOR *Christina,*
my love,
my colleague

Acknowledgements

Most of the articles in this book were first published, in slightly different form, by either the *Toronto Star* or *Maclean's* Magazine. I am grateful to their publishers, Beland Honderich and Lloyd Hodgkinson respectively, for allowing me to reproduce the material here. The chapter called *Noises from the Attic* first appeared in the *New York Times* and the final selection in the book is a condensed version of an article written for Norman Cousins of the *Saturday Review*.

Introduction

FOR MOST WRITERS THERE OCCURS a moment in childhood which determines the direction of their minds when they grow older.

"I was in Prague on the morning of March 15, 1939, and saw through excited nine-year-old eyes the panzer troops pouring into the city, heralded by bombers. Motorcycles, gun carriers, tanks, armoured cars with ice on their running-boards [only a child would notice such a symbolic detail], roared through the misty morning. The first soldiers were young and nervous, fodder for the resisting guns that were never fired; then came the veteran officers, in shiny Mercedes, and, like crows of ill-omen, the black-uniformed Gestapo."

So wrote Peter Newman about the land of his birth, which in 1968 suffered still another panzer invasion, this time from the East. I had often wondered why I have felt a peculiar affinity of spirit with Peter Newman and this paragraph gave me the answer. At the age of nine, he had witnessed the first invasion of World War II. At the same age, twenty-two years earlier, I had witnessed the biggest single explosion before Hiroshima. He had been born in a small country, I in a small province, and we both loved Canada. I had been haunted by the feeling that technological man is so addicted to explosions (once it was over, Halifax was very proud of its Great Explosion) that not even in peace time can he do without them. Newman has been haunted by the terrible damage that can be done by politicians and has become an artist among journalists, his insights and illuminations even more important than his analyses.

Every Czech knew, and now the whole world knows, that the Hitler war would never have happened if democratic politicians had understood the nature of the challenge they faced in the twentieth century. It is simply this: technological society changes so fast that a policy or a leader perfect for one crisis becomes obsolete for the next. Peter Newman's early experience must have seared this knowledge into his brain cells.

He sees modern politics as the explorer Stanley saw his journey down the Congo River: one cataract after another. John Diefenbaker seemed right for 1957; three years later, only his fighting spirit kept him afloat in the whirlpools. In the early sixties, Mike Pearson was the only leader willing to face the crisis caused by the Quebec separatist movement; by the time he had navigated that cataract, he and his ship were so battered they needed a new captain and officers. Newman recorded both voyages without fear or favour and many called him cruel to Diefenbaker and Pearson. But his love for Canada was fierce.

The sense of urgency never leaves him. In 1972 he wrote that "the Diefenbaker years of Canadian history seemed as distant as the Boer War." I stared at the sentence and whispered, "My God, he's right!" For when Diefenbaker reached power in 1957, not even sputnik had appeared. Since then, in addition to the moon landings and the indisputable proof that we humans are direct descendants of weapon-bearing animals, the volume of scientific and technological knowledge has doubled itself.

If Newman is the most personal of our serious journalists, it is because he sees the personality of a nation's leader as more important than most North Americans have hitherto believed. He may be right, for North America today is at least as sick as was Europe (outside Nazi Germany) in 1939. In childhood he knew that World War II had been caused by personalities, not by peoples: Adolf Hitler, a criminal psychopath; Joseph Chamberlain, an out-dated Victorian business man; Léon Blum, a Victorian ideologue, for years out of touch with reality; Josef Stalin, a barbarian of paranoiac genius. All these men made fateful decisions within the prison cells of their own characters and backgrounds, the very areas in which journalism is traditionally weak and art is supreme.

Anyway, Newman's journalism pays far more attention to the man than to his policies. Consider this, written from Washington: "I saw Richard Nixon close only once this week, at his press conference in the East Room of the White House. Impeccably dressed and made up, he resembled nothing so much as a headwaiter in a once-great restaurant that no longer has a first-class chef, nervously greeting diners with the hope that a patina of charm will hide his underlying insecurity. . . . I kept watching Nixon, searching for some glimmer of human response under the careful television mask he wore. . . . Then, our glances briefly locked, he noticed me looking at him, and just for an instant – a frozen flutter of time – I caught the real Nixon. In that small stillness of insight, I recognized a man so terrified – his breath and muscles seemed as taut as a pole-vaulter's – that he could barely keep himself under control. Wild gooseberry eyes looked out at me with the plea of a man who had spent a lifetime being snubbed, begging for belief."

This is not journalism; this is art. To make you hear, feel, and see – this above all. So said Conrad and left it at that. But the historian's art is forever frustrated by intruding facts, and the enormous fact that intrudes here is that three years after Newman described Nixon – and I'm sure the description is perfect – Nixon won an overwhelming mandate from the American people. European pros were talking of him in awed tones. Then, abruptly, what Peter Newman had detected in the man was revealed to the entire world with the Watergate scandals.

In Israel, where Newman went into the firing line along the Suez Canal to see for himself, he also had lunch with Moshe Dayan, and guess what? Dayan reminded him of Pierre Trudeau. "Dayan and Trudeau are about the same height, equally bald, nearly the same age. Most important of all, you feel that indefinable quality at work which allows both men to create space around themselves, so that neither friends nor enemies feel they can really touch them." Has anyone ever offered a more apt description of Trudeau's personal essence? And put it into perspective by linking it with Dayan's?

In this book Newman finally had to deal with Trudeau's election debacle in the fall of 1972 without being able to know whether or not Trudeau could recover from it. Once more he concentrates on the personality, and never was it more essential to do so. He describes the election as "a referendum on Trudeau which Trudeau lost." According to Newman, he lost it because he had previously lost touch with the Canadian people. As few public men I ever met had such sensitive antennae as Trudeau possessed, what is important here is how this happened. According to Newman, Trudeau was surrounded by a little group of high-minded intellectuals, in spirit somewhat like John F. Kennedy's team of think-tankers, who not only isolated their chief from the people but apparently did not believe that public opinion mattered much.

At the time I write this, I have no idea of Canada's immediate politi-

15

cal future. I can only say that if Pierre Trudeau's rejection by English-Canadian voters outside Quebec is a permanent one, then once more Peter Newman's vision of modern politics has been proved accurate. When Trudeau took power, the cataract before him was in full spate; it was the Quebec separatist movement. He was elected by both English Canada and the majority of Quebeckers to steer the ship down the cataract, and this he did with the utmost courage. The measure of his success was confirmed by the overwhelming support given to him by Québecois at the time of the FLQ crisis in 1970; it was further endorsed by his landslide victory in Quebec in the election of 1972, in which nearly all Anglophone voters stood together with their Francophone *concitoyens*. But in 1972, apparently, the Anglophone provinces concluded that the last rapids were passed, that it was an entirely new river and they wanted a change of captains.

Though the United States is still technically a democracy, it has in fact become a highly organized empire. Canada, on the other hand, remains an actual democracy and its voting pattern has become so volatile that it well may be that in this world of violent change democracy is compulsively frustrating its own aims.

This is the kind of disturbing thought that Peter Newman's book leaves me with; and that is the essence of his craft. He disturbs, stimulates, enlightens – he makes you see, feel, hear and care.

Hugh MacLennan

Foreword

SOMETIME IN 1965 OR 1966 – I'VE FORGOTTEN the exact month, those wild years run together now like city lights in a rainstorm – on the morning after I'd broken a story about one of the many splits within the Pearson cabinet, the Prime Minister began a meeting with his ministers by inveighing against me and my kind. He ended his lecture by saying he was fed up with reading about his government's intimate deliberations before they were cold on his tongue and that he was imploring his ministers not to talk to Newman, not to allow their assistants to talk to Newman and not even to talk to their wives who might conceivably talk to Newman. One of Pearson's senior privy councillors, who had himself been burned by the fires of journalistic fervour but was possessed of more wit than most, remarked with a straight face that it might be a kindness to give me a chair. "It must be pretty uncomfortable for Peter to have to crouch under the table while the Cabinet's in session," he said, and burst into laughter when two of his colleagues looked surreptitiously under the table to see if I was really there.

I never did get to hide under that piece of hallowed furniture, of course, but I've always held on to the image that small exchange conjures up as somehow symbolic of my craft: there sits the journalist, ever the outsider, hunched over, discomfited, suspect, fascinated and feverishly scribbling. It's a mad trade and I love it.

Most of the pieces in this collection of journalism – and pieces is an accurate description since they are really only fragments – were written against a deadline of a few days or, more frequently, a few hours. They are footnotes to history recorded on the run and represent only a small fraction of the approximately one and a half million words I filed during

17

a hectic dozen years as a reporter and editor for the *Toronto Star* and *Maclean's* Magazine.

As I read the printer's galleys just before writing this foreword, I remembered the times and places and people I had written about and realized the distance we've all travelled since.

During the interval covered by this collection Canada virtually re-invented itself. The psychological climate of the country seemed to change as we walked in it. From being self-satisfied facsimile Americans living in a quiescent, still faintly backward society, we became ardent if slightly neurotic Canadians reaching out for modern new forms and a future modelled, for the first time, on our own rather than imported values. The Protestant Ethic, that sombre view of life which worships moderation (not just as a safe course between extremes but as the one essential ingredient of social change) was still with us, but in its purest form it had become as rare as the Sunday suit that symbolized it. Our quarter-century-old admiration of all things American exhausted itself in the blazing villages of Viet Nam, the dark labyrinth of Watergate, and the long overdue realization that the U.S. was crowding out not just our industries but our way of life. It was an uproarious time and most of the pieces in this book reflect the exhilaration of changing values and dying shibboleths.

This collection makes no attempt to reconstruct the politics of the Sixties. Many columns describing people and ideas crucial to that time were incorporated, in different form, into two other books, *Renegade In Power* and *The Distemper of Our Times,* though for the sake of balance I have included a couple of articles on the chief protagonists of the era, Lester Pearson and John Diefenbaker. Many other pieces contained such intensely specific references to events in progress that they would require footnote explanations almost as long as the columns themselves; some stories that made headlines and seemed so important at the time have long since lost their relevance. So instead of a compendium, the book is a variation on several themes.

Part I reflects the first of these – my conviction that the definition of ourselves so many of us were earnestly seeking in the period, was made more possible by the simple act of looking back at the country from foreign shores. For me, journeys to Czechoslovakia, Israel, Laos, Sweden and especially Richard Nixon's America, turned into catalytic experiences that made me realize, among other things, that the colonization of a country is never an isolated act but an ongoing process. Conquest requires surrender and the contests that really matter are not fought on battlefields or even in business boardrooms but in the souls of a people and the minds of their leaders.

Part II contains a selection from dozens of articles about Pierre Elliot Trudeau, reflecting the initial rush of promise many of us felt when he first appeared, the dilution of that hope as it became painfully clear his brand of politics was little more than technique without compassion and finally, the realization that in modern times no man on a horse, no leader however miraculous he may appear, can provide a nation with its *raison d'être*.

Sections III and VII are profiles, for the most part, of men who had their moments of power, who were important in my life or the life of their country and exercised their authority or projected their ideas in a manner that enlarged their contexts. Eras are remembered by the names of their leaders but sometimes can be more clearly defined through the quality of their supporting casts.

The most visible Canadian political issue of the Sixties was a series of confrontations, at unequal intervals and of unpredictable intensities, between Quebec and the rest of the country. The ultimate compromise remains to be discovered but the search for some workable antidote to the toxins of revolution occupied the minds and hearts of a generation of French Canadians whose leaders I talked to in those years.

For me the most exhilarating assignments have always been election campaigns. I remember particularly those incredible journeys on the Diefenbaker trains, lying awake in a roomette, blinds open, hearing the miles click by and seeing the lights of Prairie towns like blinking fireflies in the distance. It was a politics that died with the last huff of the last engine of the last of those trains as it pulled into Prince Albert on election eve in 1965 to await the results of its long odyssey.

In Part VIII, I've tried to describe my love affair with Canada, an emotion that's endured for more than thirty years. This may be the only country in the world where even a mild display of open affection immediately makes you a curiosity. Since I became known as a nationalist, I have continuously been asked a series of peculiar questions, the oddest of them being, Why are you so anti-American?, as though a feeling for Canada could be defined only in negative terms. The truth is that my response to Canada was formed long before I gave much thought to the vagaries, economic or otherwise, of the United States. It was a feeling born directly out of a central experience of my life.

I was born in Vienna and spent my early childhood in Breclav, a Czech border town where my father ran a sugar factory. We lived the protected existence of the privileged bourgeoisie of pre-war Europe, in a house full of music and books, where tennis was played on a private court and meals were served with ritualistic grace. Holidays in the Austrian Alps and on the Italian Riviera were planned for and embarked on with the sure knowledge that they would be as languorous as last year in Marienbad or the year before in Gstaad. The whole period had a dream-like quality that was abruptly shattered by the Nazi invasion of the Sudetenland in the late fall of 1938. The following eighteen months were a jumble of arrivals and departures, a time of exodus and survival. We crossed borders on forged papers, joined the fleeing mob on the refugee-choked highways leading out of Paris that German fighters machine-gunned for target practice while returning from more serious missions, and retreated across the beautiful fields of France just ahead of Hitler's tanks, desperately trying to find the right official to bribe so we could get yet another worthless exit visa. But what I recall most vividly is the memory of my experience as a boy of ten during a long night spent lying in a field beside a dock, just south of Bordeaux where we hoped to find passage to England, and being dive-bombed at irregular intervals by black Stukas silhouetted against the cool moon. Sometime before morning, I was possessed of the absolute certainty that my world had come to an end. And next day when the Czech army in exile, to which we had attached ourselves, commandeered a Belgian freighter called the *Ville de Liège* and we finally sailed away from the continent, I knew I would never be a European again.

And so, in the late summer of 1940, I came to Canada. It was the only place that would take us in and because of that acceptance, which literally saved our lives, I immediately felt for the country the direct, unaffected passion of a child. It's a feeling that's with me still.

We came as immigrant farmers, though none of us had ever done a day's work on a farm in our lives, because that was the only permissible category for immigrants of non-British stock in those days. For the next five years, my mother, father and aunt worked fifteen acres of vegetables near Freeman, Ontario while I finished my studies. By the time I went to university, I'd attended eighteen schools and been taught in five different languages.

It may be that this early impermanence fuelled a youthful search for stability – for causes and individuals who would authenticate experience so that my world and identity would never come to an end again. But the arena of politics in which I decided to work as a journalist seemed to be populated by men and ideas with short lives, leaving me with an uneasy sense of discontinuity.

I went to Ottawa at the age of 28 just as John Diefenbaker was assuming power. I left at 39 just before the public's disillusionment with Pierre Trudeau began to set in, having had what amounted to an intensive post-graduate course in the art of the possible. Like most journalists, I was accused on different occasions of being partial to one party or another, depending on the speaker's bias. Politicians are often angered by the "power" of the press. But the truth is that only the idiots among journalists think they have power. All the reporter has is some limited influence which is tempered by the restrictions put on him by his editor and his publisher. At the same time no reporter escapes – or should want to – developing attitudes through which he perceives events. He is, after all, a sharer in the experiences of his times. The best service he can render readers is to let them know what his prejudices are.

Having voted at one time or another for all the parties except Social Credit, I find myself in early middle age not so much searching for new causes as reaching for an ideological position that's open and free from cant. To my surprise, I now harbour a suspicion of the automatically assumed beneficence of change. I have come to believe in the value of tradition, especially as it allows us to preserve the relatively gentle society which still exists on this side of the 49th parallel. But if I am aware of how much there is to lose, I also realize how far there is to go.

Perhaps my real ideological swing has been away from a blind acceptance of the "small-l" liberalism of the Fifties to a strongly-felt nationalism. In retrospect, it seems to me that liberalism perhaps never really had that much hold on the Canadian consciousness; it was more an American ideal, enshrined within the u.s. constitution and unwittingly imported into Canada during the period when we were entranced with the American dream. The primary thread in Canadian intellectual and social history is becoming a kind of cautiously progressive, tenaciously pragmatic individualism which rejects the American assumption that more is better; that progress, efficiency and gain are the ultimate goals of human activity.

This trend – the revolutionary-sounding idea of returning at least some decision-making authority to communities of people, as opposed to exercising it, however benignly, on their behalf – has yet to penetrate the upper reaches of Canadian political leadership. When it does, the issues that matter will become much more tangible and far less amenable to the arithmetic of compromise. It will signal the end of the old-style politics which has often seemed little more than the art of

21

exchanging favours, with the parties in power translating the demands of Canada's various voting blocks into federally-sponsored benefits, while granting high office to the power brokers who keep the system flowing most smoothly.

Looking back on the period covered by this book, it seems to me that it was a time of redefinition, of deciding who we are, why we are here and what we want to be. Old authorities and institutions kept breaking down as we swung from a preoccupation with values as the ground of experience, to experience as the ground of values. The great thing about Canada today is the excitement of the sudden expansion of possibilities, potentials and concerns. It's like a thaw after a hard winter. It's not that we've suddenly become an interesting country. It's that we finally realize this has always been true.

It is far too much to claim for *Home Country* that it's the chronicle of a time. But it is the chronicle of a political education, my own. And what I've learned is not to believe in magical leaders any more; that character and compassion are more important than ideology; and that even if it's absurd to think you can change things, it's even more absurd to think that it's foolish and unimportant to try.

Peter Newman

PART ONE   *Places*

Czechoslovakia

I

I WAS GOING BACK TO CZECHOSLOVAKIA this summer, after thirty years, to visit Prague and a little border town called Breclav, where my father was once the president of an industrial complex and I was a much-protected and happy little boy. I had been thinking of it as that most sentimental of journeys, the native's return, and had hoped to indulge myself in spirit and in print in a reprise of a whole life style that had been kept alive in my memory by my relatives who loved their country, Czechoslovakia, as fiercely as I love my own, Canada.

When I saw Prague last it was March, 1939, that sad winter after Munich, and the tanks the Czechs were gazing at were German tanks. We had stayed far too long, months after many of my parents' friends had fled the country. But my father, Oskar Newman, was a politically active nationalist, an economic adviser to the Benes government, "a true Czech," as such men were called to differentiate them from the Sudetenland Germans. He was filled with a naïve optimism that, despite everything, the Western alliance would not let the Czechs down and it was only the fact that his wife and child were candidates for Nazi concentration camps that persuaded him to leave at all. To him, and to the thousands of Czech patriots like him who saw their young country as a bastion of freedom in Central Europe, the Munich pact of 1938 between the English, the French, the Italians, and the Germans was a betrayal of the human spirit. Still, he believed that the agreement, under which Czechoslovakia gave up its fortified frontiers for the sake of "peace in our time," would sate the Germans' lust for *Lebensraum*.

Even though we lived in the Sudetenland, we stayed on. At the end of September, after being bombed, we left the Breclav house, which the

Nazis soon occupied and turned into a gambling casino, and took refuge with my grandparents in the capital. So I was in Prague on the morning of March 15, 1939, and saw through excited nine-year-old eyes the panzer troops pouring into the city, heralded by bombers. Motorcycles, gun carriers, tanks, armoured cars with ice on their running-boards, roared through the misty morning. The first soldiers were young and nervous, fodder for the resisting guns that were never fired; then came the veteran officers, in shiny Mercedes, and, like crows of ill-omen, the black-uniformed Gestapo.

Prague was full of strangers that day. Trade fairs the week before had been infiltrated by hundreds of Germans who now lined the streets, cheering, to give newsreel cameramen the impression that Czechs were welcoming the invasion. Three thousand German students had enrolled the year before in Prague universities, and now they had uniforms on and were marshalling the crowds. Czechs walked by the tanks with averted eyes; civil disobedience was not a creed then, and the Czech army, denied its fortifications, had crumbled without a fight. In the marketplace, women sat amidst the stalls of goose-liver pâtés and fresh sweet butter, crying.

We were all outfitted with gas masks in long grey canisters that were made in Japan, didn't work, and looked like Hallowe'en toys. The stores were selling flashlights with blue glass for the blackouts. The affluent were trying desperately to convert money into negotiable assets. (My father bought sheets of valuable stamps which I was supposed to smuggle out of the country in the guise of a child's stamp collection. But I traded them off to another boy for a cap pistol to shoot Germans. When my father discovered this as we crossed the border on falsified passports, he was too anguished even to care.)

The newspapers were still free that one final day (and until the last few months, for only one three-year period in thirty years have they ever been free again) and published black-bordered editions. There were a thousand rumours. The Germans were supposed to be confiscating onions by the kilo to make poison gas. It was a measure of our innocence that nothing more horrible than World War I style gassings was imaginable. Ambulances screamed across the city and were said wryly to be carrying German officers sick on whipped-cream cakes from the coffee shops. Jews were committing suicide. All was lost in twenty-four hours.

It was a sad capitulation, not in the country's tradition. Czechoslovakia had been united only two decades earlier out of a nervous conglomeration of Germans, Moravians, Slovaks, and Rusyns added to the Bohemian heartland. The various nations that formed the new Czechoslovakia had been sturdily resisting oppression for a thousand years. But it was the Czechs' geographical misfortune to block the path to Russia and the Balkans from easy access by the Germans, who were ever mindful of Bismarck's dictum: "Whoever controls Bohemia, controls Europe."

The character of the Czech people has always had two strains. As a beachhead of Western culture in Eastern Europe, they are imbued with both the Western tradition of liberal humanism and with a Slavic fatalism which allows small men to make prudent adjustments to overwhelming realities.

The Czech ambiance is far more difficult to capture than that of the flamboyant European races – the French, the Italians, the Hungarians. But there was something of its grace exhibited at Expo in 1967 and it was caught beautifully in the prize-winning film *Closely Watched Trains,* in which the anti-hero, the young trainman, gives up his life in resistance to the Nazis but as a throwaway gesture, bravely but unemotionally – dying absurdly in the midst of full life. The Czechs are courageous but careful. De-Stalinization was begun in the country only in 1963, seven years after Khrushchov's anti-Stalin speech had cleared the way for the Hungarian uprising of 1956.

Young Czechs may have found the fumes of freedom heady this year, but Alexander Dubcek himself never intended to launch a revolution. Men of his generation are by nature unwilling to go too far because they know that their country has been betrayed three times before by the free West – in 1938 at Munich; in 1945, when the Americans allowed Russia to occupy Prague; and in 1948, when the world watched the Communist takeover in February.

It is a bad joke among Czechs that Western statesmen are forever saying, "Of course we sympathize with you, but we can't do anything." Even in this context, Mitchell Sharp's initial lukewarm response to the Russian invasion as being "disappointing" or maybe even "regrettable" seemed a hell of a way to write off the freedom of a people.

Still, no words, however stirring, will help the Czechs now and those among them with long memories must be saying again, as the paper *Lidove Novidny* did in its lead article on the day of the Nazi invasion so long ago: "We wanted to sing with the angels but now we must howl with the wolves."

[1968]

27

II

SPRING STEALS RELUCTANTLY INTO THIS ANCIENT, threadbare but still bewitchingly beautiful city without stirring the hopes that usually mark the end of winter. This is Prague two years after the Czechs reached out for freedom with an impulse that spread like bushfire, only to be extinguished by the Russian invasion of 1968. The interval has been a time without seasons, a sad span of endurance with a scarcely bearable present and no obvious future.

The Czechs have little left to sustain them now except the characteristic black humour that has always baffled their invaders. "Which country has the highest mountains in the world?" a taxi driver will ask over his shoulder, and then answer ruefully, through the side of his mouth: "Czechoslovakia. After all, we've been going downhill for thirty years." A man in a beer hall will lean over and recount a favourite aphorism: "There really are only two ways left to get rid of the Russians: the natural way, with the Angel Michael descending from heaven to drive them out with his flaming sword, or the supernatural way, with the Supreme Soviet ordering them to climb back into their tanks and toddle off home."

This kind of wit springs from a depth of political cynicism so remote from the North American experience that it is almost impossible to grasp. Detachment from one's environment can strengthen the human spirit only if it is based on some timeless conviction, and the Czechs are fortifying their souls with the belief that their little country, which managed to survive three centuries of Hapsburg despotism and six years of Nazi occupation, can outlast the Russian empire as well. "We are not born to be governed easily," they boast, asserting their national destiny through inner rebellion, like existential heroes in a novel by Camus. The Czechs' determination to outlive and, if possible, to outwit the Russians bears little relationship to the situation as it exists.

The dismemberment of Alexander Dubcek's brave dreams of a humane communism is almost complete – censorship has been reimposed, the borders have been resealed, and there are constant rumours of mass arrests and possible show trials.

At the moment, there is a struggle for power within the first circle of the Czech Communist party and the very real fear of a purge in party ranks. All 1,600,000 members of the party – out of a total population of about 14,500,000 – have had to turn in their red cloth cards. Only those deemed sufficiently loyal to the Soviet Union (or able to

28

prove they were "misled" by "Dubcek's counter-revolutionary tendencies") will be reinstated. Having a party card can mean the difference between being able to practise your profession or being forced into manual labour, educating your children or sending them into factories, getting a new apartment or sharing a single room.

These and other punitive measures would seem to indicate a final Russian triumph over Czech liberalism. But in Czechoslovakia these days, truth is not always the sum of the ascertainable facts. Having tasted liberty, the Czechs have become aware of the difference between freedom and power. Having tried and failed to make their brand of communism more progressive, they are set on a carefully contrived course of passive resistance which could, in the long run, prove more effective than their short-lived revolt. Their natural effervescence long gone, the Czechs are instinctively functioning as a silent, passive majority by deliberately opting out of political involvement. This "internal migration" is evident among workers, students, and intellectuals alike and amounts to a nationwide lethargy that threatens to ruin an already fragile economy.

It is a tactic without leadership but not without cunning, based on the theory that only by returning some of the freedoms withdrawn since August, 1968, will the Czechoslovak government be able to ensure the kind of economic performance from their people being demanded by the Russians. The Czech version of passive resistance takes many subtle forms and can be seen in the faces of hundreds of people all over Prague – in the swift passage of a smile curving the lips of a postman as he watches two Russian officers trying to find their way through a maze of narrow alley-ways, in the mechanical tone of an official government spokesman, parroting the party line while his hands drum lightly on a table top, sending out a wordless message as if to say, "Don't pay too much attention to this canned crap. After all, I do not control the mysteries of life. I am only part of them, and all the world knows the truth about the Russians."

The longer Prague remains an occupied city, the more this spirit of silent rebellion grows. Most of the seventy thousand Russians still stationed on Czech soil stay out of sight in armouries and suburban barracks. But occasionally, and always in pairs, Russian officers can be seen, briefcases firmly in hand, stomping through the streets or standing in the lobby of the Hotel Yalta. A midnight ride through the deserted city shows that the only building surrounded by policemen with glistening sub-machine-guns is the headquarters of the Czechoslovak-Soviet Friendship Society. "We have to guard it because people are always trying to throw bricks through the windows," a Czech policeman explains, with grave decorum and dancing eyes.

It is somehow incongruous that this drama of human repression and resentment should be happening in Prague, which is still, quite simply, the most beautiful city in the world. The magnificent sweep of Hradcany Castle dominates the skyline, managing to combine the best of Romanesque, Gothic, renaissance, and baroque architecture, the gleaming spires of St. George's Basilica (which have been looking down on Prague since 1142), the ancient Charles Bridge, whose sculptured supports slope down to the whispering weirs of the Moldau – all these and the city's many other wonders now seem museumlike, detached from the harsh realities of the moment.

The light comes to Prague these spring mornings as it might come into the boudoir of a once very beautiful, now very old, woman, living on memories and gallantry. Spontaneous gaiety is so rare that when it happens, passers-by stop and stare – at dogs frolicking in a churchyard, at a student, handsome in an ancient fur hat, making jokes about a group of East German tourists standing stolidly to watch the statues of saints emerge out of the old town hall clock as it strikes the hour. There is little traffic except for taxis, aged coal trucks, and the black, chauffeur-driven Tatras owned almost exclusively by party functionaries. The cars' rapacious snouts make them look like schools of sharks as they cruise the streets between government ministries.

It is a city of wild contrasts. The tourist hotels smell of sweat and old pork fat, but they serve drinks in exquisite Czech crystal glasses. Office workers eat, in the buffets off Wenceslas Square, hors d'oeuvre made of goose-liver pâté or caviar frosted with swirls of mayonnaise, while standing upright at plastic-topped tables in fifteen-year-old overcoats.

People find their only emotional outlet in the city's cultural life. Prague has five symphony orchestras and twenty-eight theatres, most playing every week night. This month alone it is possible to see performances of plays by Shakespeare, Anouilh, Christopher Fry, Edward Albee, and Peter Ustinov, operas by Smetana, Tchaikovsky, Strauss, and Bizet as well as ballets, pantomimes, and art exhibitions. At one concert, which featured the Prague symphony playing Vivaldi's *Four Seasons* with a young Czech violinist as soloist, the vivacity of the crowd was astonishing. Everyone looked shabby – to be anything else is an affront to humanity in Prague – but almost everybody was full of the kind of joyful anticipation you see in North America only on the faces of five-year-olds watching a magician. People were there for a good time, and they found not just pleasure in the music but hope – and for some the hopefulness was too much. By the end of the performance, their faces were wet with tears.

[1970]

III

HE LOOKED SOMEHOW LIKE A CAPTIVE CHIPMUNK – shrewd, with darting eyes, clawing at a world he had helped to make and now wanted to destroy. One of the middle-aged journalists who had supported Alexander Dubcek's liberalization in 1968, he had been forced out of his profession. But I had been told where to find him, and now he was expressing some of the thoughts he could no longer publish himself.

We met at the back of a large beer hall in Prague's Old Town. During an hour's conversation he sat hugging himself, as though the warmth of the tavern were some precious contraband that could be smuggled out, hoarded against the cold March wind rattling the windows. At the beginning, our conversation was halting, as stylized as a burlesque routine – a systematic progression of disclosures, with the journalist guarding against spontaneous reactions. But gradually the taut bonds of nervousness dissolved, and he talked freely about how he had burned away his youth and half his mature life in support of the communist ideal, and how it had been shattered by the Russian invasion.

"What you don't realize, you and other western reporters," he said, "is that nearly 90 per cent of Czechoslovaks were loyal Communists. Certainly we wanted to change the style and the meaning of communism, to make it less inhuman, to create a new society in Czechoslovakia which would allow ordinary people to realize their aspirations. But we never intended for a moment to swing the country back towards capitalism or even to take any steps that might be considered anti-Russian. When the Kremlin claimed it had to invade us to prevent the overthrow of the Communist party, it was a lie, because we never wanted to do that."

He went on to describe how, if the Dubcek initiative had been allowed to flourish, communism might have evolved into a genuinely popular political movement instead of a new form of dictatorship which concentrates power in the hands of party functionaries, how it

31

could have pioneered an effective synthesis between the scientific revolution of our time and true socialism.

"And what happens now?" he asked. "For twenty-five years Czech thought and Czech journalism were concentrated on the notion that our country's future was bound up with our allies, the Russians. Will people ever again believe anything they read in the papers or hear from the politicians? Who will convince the next generation that there is any hope, any point to following the communist dogma?"

He reminisced about the spring of 1968, the exciting experience of being able to publish for the first time in his working life exactly what he thought, to read a free exchange of opinions. "The Russians have been claiming that the underground radio and television stations which stayed on the air after August 21, 1968, were part of a West German plot to take over Czechoslovakia," he said. "Some of the equipment was German, all right, but it consisted of ancient emergency transmitters left over from World War II, and stockpiled on Russian orders in the event of an invasion from the West. Of course, the irony that they should be used to fight an invasion from the East would be lost on the Russian mind; to appreciate irony, a people must be civilized."

After some more anti-Russian talk, he got up to go, suddenly impatient with me, himself, exhausted ideas, futile hopes, and vain heroics. "Most of us have left journalism now, because if we can't write the truth we don't want to write at all. Our slogan has become: 'Optimism equals lack of information.' But a few of the Dubcek followers are still trying to change things. After all, what can the Russians do except put them in prison? They can't invade us twice."

[1970]

IV

A HARSH PRESENCE, WITH EYES AS BARREN AS POTHOLES, Gustav Husak, who succeeded Alexander Dubcek as first secretary of the Czechoslovak Communist party in April, 1969, does not comfortably fit the crucial role into which history has cast him. For Husak, described in the tortuous lexicon of Marxist ideology as "a moderate dogmatist," has become the only collateral the Czechs possess against a return of their country to the darkness of neo-Stalinist oppression. He is certainly the best and probably the only chance the Czechs have of saving anything out of the Dubcek liberalization program and bringing their country back to something like economic health.

An austere, bespectacled bear of a man who raps out his sympathy for Czech nationalism and his disapproval for anything that departs from communist orthodoxy in the same sharp tones, Husak finds himself caught between two conflicting purposes. He must retain Russian support by persuading the Kremlin that he has permanently quashed the Dubcek progressives, while at the same time he must win acceptance among the Czechs by convincing them that he is not uncompromising in his anti-reform policies.

To gain the precious time he needs to achieve this delicate balance, Husak has been busy stroking the Czech populace with conciliatory words while acting tough enough to placate the Russians. In all his pronouncements, Husak is careful to differentiate between Dubcek's "romanticism" and his own "realism." He seems bent on leading his country by stealth into the modified liberalization achieved by Janos Kadar in Hungary. "Husak is just as concerned about people's duties as about their rights. But unlike the real hard-liners, he does remember that people still have rights," says one observer of Czech politics. "Certainly he's an orthodox Communist but so many liberals have been eliminated from the party's ruling circle here that of the survivors, Husak is well to the left of centre." Husak's most overt support of the Kremlin came last August when he put down riots marking the first anniversary of the Russian invasion by sending armed troops to dispel student protesters in Wenceslas Square. Immediately afterward, he was invited to Moscow, was awarded an Order of Lenin, and has been apparently carrying out Russian directives ever since.

The main reason he retains some degree of sympathy among the Czechs is that he was himself a victim of the kind of oppressive measures the Russians are now trying to impose on his country. Born in 1913 near the Slovak capital of Bratislava, he joined the Communist party at twenty, fought the Nazis as a member of the Czech underground, and advanced in the postwar Communist hierarchy until 1950, when he was arrested on a charge of "bourgeois nationalism." Sentenced to life imprisonment, he was tortured, released only in 1960, and not allowed to return to active politics until 1967, when his Stalinist enemies in the Czech communist movement were on the run.

An early supporter of Dubcek, Husak became first secretary of the Slovak Communist party, and it was only after the dramatic events of August, 1968, that he turned against the reformers, calling the Russian invasion "an acceptable way out of the situation which will give us an opportunity to solve basic economic and national problems." Despite his orthodox communism, Husak's prison experience left him committed to supporting a framework of legality that will prevent the imprisonment of citizens without just cause. "We are not butchers and our party is not a slaughterhouse. It will never lower itself to contrived trials and contrived accusations – not even against political adversaries," he says.

But Czech intellectuals remain cynical. Though they doubt whether Husak will stage show trials based on confessions extracted by torture, he is quite capable, they think, of strangling party opponents in a web of petty legalisms. Husak's main problem at the moment is to surround himself with enough like-minded, relatively moderate followers so that he can go before next year's party congress (the 160-member ruling circle of the party) with a unified program that will have some chance of acceptance by both the Czechs and the Russians. His chief rival is Lubomir Strougal, who recently replaced the progressive Oldrich Cernik as the Czechoslovak premier. Strougal was one of the first Czechs to be sent to Moscow for secret-police training after the Communists took power in 1948, and he became minister of the interior in the Stalinist regime of Antonin Novotny. He later broke with Novotny and at one memorable central committee meeting, when Novotny chided him for his reputation as a ladies' man, Strougal shouted back, "It's true that these hands have held many a woman's behind. But they aren't bloody like yours."

Walking among Prague's old palaces, now occupied by the various communist ministries, you get a sense of intelligences at work behind their baroque facades but little feeling about the actual policies Czechoslovakia intends to follow in the future. Czechoslovakia's only hope now is for some form of long-term liberalization within the Kremlin itself which would be reflected in allowing part of Dubcek's program to be revived. But that seems at least a generation or so away. With the present too unbearable to think about, the Czechs live in the vague hope that tomorrow is bound to be better than today.

[1970]

V

THE CZECHS HAVE NEVER CONFUSED LOVE OF COUNTRY with love of glory. They are the most ardently patriotic nationalists in central Europe, but they don't see much point in fighting wars they can't win. Throughout history (in 1848, 1938, 1948, and 1968) they have allowed their country to be invaded or taken over by outsiders but then

34

confused their enemies with a subtle brand of insurrection that amounts to survival without heroics, collaboration without surrender.

The Czechs are very unsatisfactory subjects. There is at the moment in the Prague law courts, for example, a case being fought by a group of Czech lawyers who are demanding compensation from the Russians for the wooden traffic signs knocked over by their invading tanks two years ago. Because such audacity is not something the Russians know how to deal with, the Kremlin is rumoured to have agreed to pay a small indemnity. "When we win the case," one of the lawyers is being quoted around Prague, "we will, of course, give 220 roubles back to the Russians. That will take care of the return airplane fare for Dubcek from Moscow in 1968. After all, it was supposed to be a one-way ticket."

This mixture of quiet levity and relentless obstructionism, when practised on a national scale at every level of political and economic activity, can be devastatingly effective. "The victim suspects you are having him on, but he can't prove it," writes the American sociologist Milton Mayer in a recent study of the Czech character. "He has a monopoly on violence. But to be baited into using it, then crushing the joker, is to confess that he has nothing else. If the Czechs carry their serene imbecility too far and the Russians return to the cities shooting, they will convert their disaster into a cataclysm."

The Czechs do not subscribe to the Gandhian injunction of putting "one's whole soul against the will of the tyrant." Theirs is a much more subtle tactic. It is the art of what they call *pod fousky* which means "laughing under your moustache."

Heroism is something the Czechs have learned to outgrow. Their model is the Good Soldier Schweik, whose motto was: 'Always try to outlive the enemy: dying will get you nowhere.' Schweik was a fictitious batman in the Austro-Hungarian imperial army, the master creation of the Czech novelist Jaroslav Hasek. His misadventures make hilarious reading, but they reflect Schweik's supreme concern: to stay alive. He achieved such stunning success in keeping himself away from frontline fighting that, by the end of Hasek's book, he managed to be taken prisoner by his own army.

Schweikism is a kind of creative apathy which offers co-operation without actually delivering it. Obedience is loudly pledged but orders are invariably misunderstood. Schweik is always eager to comply with any and all demands made on him, but the net effect is the bafflement and confusion of his oppressors.

35

"Do you admit everything?" an angry Austrian officer asks the hapless Schweik.

"If you want me to admit it, sir, then I will. It can't do me any harm. But if you were to say: 'Schweik, don't admit anything, I'll argue to the point of my last breath.' "

At another interrogation, Schweik sums up his defence by solemnly and proudly declaring: "I'm no malingerer. I'm feeble-minded, fair and square. You just ask them in the Ninety-First Regiment."

Though the Russians make Schweik's Austrian superiors look pretty benign, the Czechs have successfully adapted the Good Soldier's spirit to their present circumstances. In one current anecdote, a street cleaner comes up to a Russian soldier during a visit to Prague by Soviet Premier Kosygin, just as the Czech guard of honour is firing a twenty-four-gun salute. The street cleaner innocently asks, "What's this – another war?"

"No, you imbecile. We have a v.i.p. visitor – Premier Kosygin."

"In that case, what's wrong with our soldiers? They fired twenty-four rounds and missed him every time."

Where Schweikism has become a serious threat to Czechoslovakia's Communist party is in the factories, on whose output the economy depends. Workers are staging deliberate slowdowns by misunderstanding orders and ostracizing those colleagues who want to fulfil production quotas. Absenteeism (always backed up by elaborate excuses) is running so high that the economy is now on a kind of unofficial three-and-a-half-day week.

The government of party secretary Gustav Husak has moved stringently against industrial malingering by sponsoring a new labour code that covers "abuses of the socialist economy, working discipline and parasitism," with a year's imprisonment for those found guilty. In true Schweikian fashion, workers are pledging their allegiance to Husak but not getting back to work. In union elections, they are placing silly loudmouths in important jobs while protecting their real leaders.

The Czechs have used these tactics to survive the colonialism of the Hapsburgs, the capitalist republicanism of Masaryk, the tyranny of the Nazis, and now the domestic socialist dictatorship of the Communists. Their will to survive has become their governing ideology, and it is as far as they want to commit themselves. Their spirit is a way of living out the Czech proverb that "No man can tell in what faith he will die."

[1970]

Israel

I

ALL DAY THE WIND BLOWS ACROSS THE SINAI. It fans in from the Mediterranean or swings southerly and comes howling down arid-hot from the Egyptian plains, raising the temperature twenty degrees in an hour. It whips up sandstorms that pummel the body and obliterate the horizon, providing cover for Egyptian and Israeli raiding parties to cross the Suez. The canal itself seems like a small, silty, remarkably benign river, as I crouch in a fortified Israeli bunker, less than ten feet from its eastern shore. I can't spot any Egyptians on the other bank, but the Israeli army captain beside me says: "Stick your head up and you're a dead man." I take his word for it.

There is a sudden glint of sunshine against metal from across the canal and the Israeli private on the other side of me tightens his rifle-grip. He is nineteen years old and his name is Jacob. He wears thick glasses, is pudgy, has a shy smile, and has killed ten Egyptian snipers in six days from this bunker. As I watch Jacob and we discuss the war, I realize that here, with this army, the Israelis have overcome the traditional view of Jewishness. The sorrow associated with being Jewish has gone out of the eyes of these young fighters and it has been replaced by pride and toughness. Instead of being inward-looking and fearful, they are fierce and forward-looking; instead of being contemplative intellectuals, they are courageous activists. Instead of saying "next year in Jerusalem," they are saying "this year in Sinai."

I ask the army captain who has accompanied me from Tel Aviv how being a good soldier fits in within the Jewish tradition. "What's not to understand?" he says. "Look in the Old Testament. It's right there in black and white. When we had to fight, we always did it well." The captain and I had left Tel Aviv at four o'clock that morning in a Volkswagen. As we crossed the Gaza Strip into the Sinai, I could see the burned-out skeletons of Egyptian and Israeli tanks, reminders of the Six-Day War fought here twenty-eight months ago. Twelve thousand men died in this desert during some of the war's fiercest battles and part of the highway is fenced in because unexploded mines still litter the sand.

At El Arish we stop for gas and I buy a shell necklace from a shy Arab girl. I pay her twice what she asks, but it still costs only twelve cents, though it must have taken her days to make it. The captain reminds me that El Arish has an interesting history. It used to be called Rhinokokura (the City of the Cut Noses) when it was an Egyptian colony populated by mutilated slaves.

We drive on through the Sinai. This is Lawrence of Arabia country, a place of shifting dunes punctured by a few palm groves. We pass the occasional huddle of Bedouins tending palm trees. Until you're right up close to them, you're never really certain whether they are holding a hoe or a rifle. The captain beside me unostentatiously cocks the sub-machine-gun on his lap. About twenty miles from the canal we come to our first Israeli checkpoint. "I'm sorry," says one of the sentries, "you won't be allowed to wet your feet in the canal today. The water is a bit polluted." It is obviously a line he has used before, but everybody at the little outpost laughs and we are told to report to the local commander's hut.

A girl sergeant brings us some delicious orange juice and a lieutenant-colonel begins to brief us on the situation. The Egyptians have been unusually quiet today; there is an almost daily exchange of mortar and artillery fire; Egyptian planes have raided his camp but their aim is lousy; he does not anticipate any major attacks. "The Egyptians have surrounded us again," he says. Then adds: "The poor bastards."

The mood of the army camp is informal. Nobody salutes anybody else. Soldiers sit on jeeps, cleaning their rifles. The girls in uniform look like Song of Solomon maidens, unaccountably done up in khaki. A half-truck rumbles out, manned by a dozen men with sub-machine-guns at the ready.

We drive on to the canal. Cairo is only eighty-five kilometres away now. The captain blandly informs me that we are within range of

Egyptian artillery. We drive fast. The road has many potholes and the captain answers my question before I ask it. Yes, the potholes were made by artillery shells. We pass through the abandoned town of Kantara, past its burned-out railway station and a tottering mosque. On one street I spot a child's abandoned doll, always the saddest mark of war. Then suddenly, there is a line of trees and we are at the canal. "That's Suez," says the captain.

We slither into the bunker which lines the shore. The only vehicle in sight is a captured Egyptian truck. Its Russian markings are plainly visible. Inside the bunker, two off-duty soldiers are playing cards. A radio is on, tuned to Paul Desmond taking a cool saxophone solo on "Moonlight in Vermont." We spend an hour looking across the canal at Egypt and nothing much happens.

This is the way things are at Suez these days. Men on both sides sit, daring each other to fire first, knowing that whatever the politicians may say a war is on and they are fighting it.

[1969]

II

THIS IS ELECTION DAY IN ISRAEL, but the talk is more of war than of politics.

With Golda Meir's Labour Front coalition sure to be returned, both the people and the government of Israel seem less concerned with details of the voting than with somehow controlling the sudden escalation of events before they lead to another armed conflict. In Jerusalem, the cabinet met yesterday to discuss its post-election response to the Lebanese crisis. In Bethlehem, a garage that housed terrorists' trucks was discovered and dynamited. In Haifa, a voluntary civil defence guard was being organized and the British liner *Carmania* decided not to call, "due to the political situation." In Gaza, an Arab guerrilla, dressed as a woman, was arrested because the grenades he was carrying in his brassiere looked too lumpy to an observant policeman. Danny Kaye has left the country after entertaining the troops. Here, in the Upper Galilee, far from the civilization of Israel's Mediterranean coastline, you can smell war, like a forest fire which you taste in the air long before you see it. The landscape is floodlit by a violent sun, its unrefracted rays giving every scene the stark, super dimensions of a Cinerama film.

Among the tumbling foothills of the Gilead, on the Jordanian border, Israeli armoured cars glide along the asphalt frontier roads being built to replace the dirt tracks, which were too easy to mine. At Beit Yosef, within a hundred yards of Jordan, civilians are piling sandbags around doorways. Yellow watchtowers with spotlights and platforms for nighttime machine-gunners have been erected at strategic infiltration points. At Gesher Kibbutz, Centurion tanks squat in the cotton fields with their guns pointed at Jordan, and in the kibbutz itself, trenches have been dug for protected access to shelters. The kibbutz dining-hall is being repaired after a recent hit by a Syrian artillery shell.

There is a bunker here dug out for the kibbutz children; it is air-conditioned and hermetically sealed against poison gas. The children are put to bed here every night, because the shells come in without warning.

There is barbed wire everywhere. I drive down to Tiberias, on the Sea of Galilee, where King Herod once ruled. The daily special at the local restaurant is St. Peter's fish and it's delicious, but a fly keeps trying to climb up my nose, spoiling the meal.

"That is a Syrian fly," an Israeli sitting opposite me remarks. "It is quite true. That is certainly a Syrian fly," he earnestly repeats. "You see, in Israel we have undertaken a large disinfectant program. The Syrians, they have done nothing."

This is fairly typical of the Israeli attitude towards themselves and the Arabs. The Arabs are incompetent wastrels, while Israel is the land of permanent miracles. Everywhere I go, kibbutz managers point out acre after acre of land reclaimed from the malaria-infested swamps that once covered this valley.

After lunch, I drive to Metulla. Its hotels are closed, watchtowers crowd the plum orchards, a truck crew is hurriedly pouring cement into a new anti-shrapnel bunker. For three nights now the citizens of Metulla have watched the Lebanese army trying to flush out *Al Fatah* border positions. First come the flares, then the mortar and machine-gun fire.

I spend the night in a guest house at a border kibbutz and, after dinner, several of us sit around in front of the dining-hall with jugs of lemon squash. The muted phosphorescence of the evening seems a little too tranquil, as if the land was holding its breath in the expectation of violence. The soft scent of the eucalyptus trees and the vibrating splash of the sprinklers give the scene a measure of false reality.

Next morning I drive around the Golan Heights, taken by the Israeli army during some of the Six-Day War's fiercest fighting. Kibbutz farmers are plowing around the wreckage of Russian-built tanks. At the end of the day, I go back to the Lebanese border. Where it dips into the sea, small cable cars run down to the grottos of Rosh Hanikra. The instructions in each cabin read: *"In Case of Emergency, Open Window and Wait for Instructions."*

It seems like a good idea.

[1969]

III

MOSHE DAYAN SLOUCHES THROUGH THE OPEN VESTIBULE of the Yarden Hotel at Tel Aviv and conversation stops. He is dressed in army fatigues with no insignia and has just flown in by helicopter from the marketplace at Deir el Balah, where terrorist hand grenades killed two farmers. Involuntarily, I turn to look at the eyepatch which has become his symbol. But it is Dayan's good eye that reaches out and grips you, fascinates you, holds you in its unblinking stare, demanding: "What have you done for Israel lately?"

We spend an hour lunching together, and as I watch and listen to Israel's minister of defence, he reminds me for some curious reason of Pierre Elliott Trudeau. It seems like an absurd comparison. One man is a professional soldier whose desert warfare strategy has made military history, the other an intellectual lately come to politics who has never fought for his country. Yet the similarities persist. Dayan and Trudeau are about the same height, equally bald, nearly the same age. Most important of all, you feel that indefinable quality at work which allows both men to create space around themselves, so that neither friends nor enemies feel they can really touch them. Such response fosters their individual legends, the romantic remoteness that sets them apart from lesser politicians.

In their different ways, they are both courageous and compelling statesmen, their flamboyant success satisfying the romantic child in all of us; both touched by a seismic sensitivity that helps them react to events faster than their contemporaries. They share impatience with routine encounters, desperate boredom with protocol, and unconcern for the moods and feelings of others. There is even some resemblance in their mannerisms, though Dayan somehow manages to shrug with his eye instead of his shoulders. They both grew up in cultural minorities but are operating outside the tradition of their backgrounds. Dayan is a very non-Jewish kind of Israeli, just as Trudeau is a very non-French-Canadian kind of Quebecker.

It is pointless to stretch the comparison very far (for one thing,

41

Dayan is much more passionate about his country than Trudeau will ever be), but as I sit there listening to Dayan and thinking about Trudeau I remember what Yall Dayan, the young novelist, has written about her father: "He is a lonely man who holds the key to his soul in his own hand, and he himself directs the traffic of people and ideas trying to reach him."

It is a description that fits Pierre Trudeau perfectly.

Just as Trudeau becomes most agitated when discussing the value of the French fact in Canada's future, Dayan's animation grows as he talks about his own heritage. "A Jew," he says, "is a very specific human being, different from others by religion, language, history, and philosophy. And the problem for us is to maintain that uniqueness. I have more in common with the Jews in Miami Beach than with the Arabs in the next village from here."

The words balloon out from him now, punctuated by swift hand gestures, precise in their emphasis as though each limb movement was timed by a stopwatch. He talks with great compassion about fighting, about war and about survival, and when I ask him why Israelis are such good soldiers, he answers: "They are not good soldiers. They are good fighters. They're very bad at parades and that sort of thing."

Not really expecting an answer, I ask Dayan to rank Canada's army. "If I had to choose a non-Israel army to fight with," he says, "it would be the Canadian commandos, because they are all volunteers. Of course, I wouldn't want to spend my evenings with the Canadians. For that, I would choose the Italian commandos."

A doer in a nation of talkers, a politician-general who puts decisiveness ahead of consensus, Dayan is easily the most controversial man in Israel today. There is endless speculation about whether he will eventually succeed Golda Meir as prime minister. He has many enemies, but, paradoxically, one of his greatest handicaps in getting the top job is that most Israelis do not want him to leave the defence portfolio. His picture is everywhere. American tourists line up for posters of Dayan and buy medallions glorifying his deeds.

Dayan spends most days criss-crossing the country by helicopter, personally dealing with outbreaks of violence in the border areas and occupied territories. Admired for being a hawk who beat the Arabs, he is now being criticized for attempting to integrate, with some moderately enlightened methods, the inhabitants of the regions taken by Israel during the Six-Day War. When realistic peace treaties are signed, Dayan says that he would like to see Moslems now living on the west bank of the Jordan River maintain their Jordanian citizenship, creating a kind of autonomous Arab region that would include Israeli military bases.

That is hardly a practical suggestion at the moment, but it does illustrate Dayan's essential pragmatism. As we finish our meal of goose liver and grilled fish, with Dayan explaining how peace might come because nothing is impossible in the Middle East ("twenty years ago nobody thought Israel was possible"), he grows restless. A man in an orange sport shirt who has been sitting inconspicuously nearby comes up and whispers something in Hebrew. Dayan smiles, autographs a menu for an admiring girl at the next table, gets up, shakes my hand, and is gone.

[1969]

Sweden

I N THE LANGUAGE OF CANADIANS OF A CERTAIN AGE and political persuasion (the middle generation of liberals), Sweden for the last twenty years or so has served as a kind of shorthand symbol for a functioning utopia. You know the kind of situation I mean: two socially aware, politically involved, deadly serious people are talking about a Canadian Problem and they end their summation of our absurdities by saying, "Now in Sweden, they solve this so sensibly by. . . ." Certainly, if most Canadians had to make a list of Worthy Nations, Sweden would probably come at the top. The Swedes seem to have abolished poverty, defeated unemployment, wiped out slums, banished ignorance, redistributed wealth, dispelled sexual repression, and confounded ideology by building the world's best living standard on capitalist production and socialist distribution. Their country (Europe's fourth largest which, if it could be rotated at its southernmost point, would stretch down to Naples) is a clean, well-lighted place. The industrial revolution came late to Sweden; only fifty years ago it was one of the most backward nations of Europe. There is little industrial ugliness. Superhighways glide by eighteenth-century castles; factories are set unobtrusively in forests. It is a country obsessed with orderliness. Nothing seems improvised. From the way farmers pile their firewood to the elegant folds in restaurant napkins, everything is painfully tidy. And silent. Eight million characters in search of an author, the Swedes are brooding individualists racked by introspection and it is the silence of Sweden that really sets it apart from other countries.

Sweden's silence is something more than the absence of sound. It is a kind of tumultuous stillness, deafening in its intensity – as if within

44

the silence negotiations of some primordial, unspoken sort were implacably proceeding. Trains, buses and streetcars full of speechless people rumble through the avenues of Stockholm like wheeled coffins. There are few street noises; there is little clatter of trade or cries of children. Clean walls cry out for desecration.

Russian friends bear-hug when they get excited; the French kiss. Swedes show emotion with a firm, mute handshake, and when they do speak the cadence of their language reduces the exchange to the tonelessness of a weather forecast. They are a nation of spectacle wipers. You ask them a question and, figuratively or literally, they pause to wipe their spectacles before they answer. Conversation thus becomes a series of pauses interrupted by words.

One reason for all this silence is that the Swedish character was formed by the nation's rural past, when nearly everyone lived in isolated hamlets, with only a weekly church service to interrupt their solitude. This legacy has imbued the Swedes with a spiritual loneliness they call *ensamhet* which is their most noticeable characteristic. In a typical Swedish anecdote, an emigrant to America returns home after thirty years and invites one of his boyhood friends to the local inn for a *schnapps*. After an hour of drinking they still have not spoken and the visitor finally asks: "Well, how's everything, anyway?" His friend groans: "Hell, I thought we were going to drink, not make a lot of conversation."

The crew-cut makes him look like the second-string coach of a midwestern football team, but the darting blue eyes and sensitive, rabbit nose mark him an intensely political animal. At 44, Olaf Palme, the prime minister of Sweden, is Western Europe's youngest, most radical, and least formal head of government. Deep in Swedish politics for the past twenty years, he was radicalized by the ten months he spent hitchhiking through thirty-four states of the u.s. during the late Forties. He says it was the poverty surrounded by affluence he saw on the journey that first inspired his deep commitment to socialism. Palme's ideology is real and much of Sweden's current unrest stems from his intention to turn the country into something close to a classless society. "I'm against wet-finger politics – testing public opinion before you do anything," he says. "Without an ideological consciousness and a real will behind practical politics, you only have accommodation from one day to another."

An ostentatious rebel in a country that still clings like an old maid to social niceties, Palme made a brief screen appearance in the sex documentary *I Am Curious (Yellow)* and in 1968, when he was minister of education, joined Hanoi's ambassador to Moscow in a march on the American embassy in Stockholm to protest the Viet Nam war. His great fear is fascism in all its forms. "Today's radicals just sit and wait for the revolution," he says. "They say: 'Everything has to collapse before we can begin to do anything.' But it is possible to get within the existing system and guide it. The longer you sit outside, the greater is the risk of fascism or at least reaction."

I meet Palme in the cafeteria of Stockholm's new parliament buildings, a sleek structure with aluminum ceilings, brown carpets, and birchwood walls. Discreetly chewing gum and swinging his leg over an armchair, he talks softly about the social equality he is trying to achieve. "I'm being attacked because of my utopian ideas, which are supposed to be forcing an atmosphere of confrontation. But I believe the opposite. The real confrontation comes from the economic gaps dividing members of the society. We can't do anything about happiness. But we can try to steer technology in a more humane way. We've been circling too much in the past, taking care only of society's victims. Now we have to give more power, real power, to the people involved in the production process. Power is very important and you don't need ownership to exercise it."

Essentially Palme's message is that a society can be fundamentally altered without a revolution and that the political leaders of democracies should be committed to such a transformation. "The Swedish example," he says, "is interesting for only one reason: It shows that social progress is possible through somewhat boring, bureaucratic action."

The Swedish attitude to sex approximates the observation once made by Mrs. Patrick Campbell, G. B. Shaw's actress-friend, to the effect that she didn't mind what people did so long as they didn't do it in the streets and scare the horses. Most Swedes see little connection between sex and morality, though they recognize love, however fleeting, as one way to deal with the Swedish curse of loneliness. Trial marriages are common and nearly half of the brides are pregnant on their wedding day – a hangover from Sweden's agrarian past, when marriages rarely took place until the girl was pregnant or had given birth to a son. Marriages can be dissolved by simple mutual agreement between husband and wife. Sexual equality has reached the bedrooms of the nation. A recent survey by Professor Nils Gustavsson of the Sociological Institute in Stockholm found that 57 per cent of the young men questioned first had sexual intercourse because the girl insisted on it, and 26 per cent of the men polled even claimed the girls forced them into it.

It is a statistic one tends to discount. Soft felt slouch hats and tendrils of blond hair framing elegant cheekbones, figures and faces put together with exquisite care, the girls of Sweden must be the loveliest in the world. Instead of having different characters, they seem, from a distance at least, to have various flavours. Cinnamon, maybe.

The most surprising sights to the visitor are the many shops selling every style of pornography from the disgusting to the philosophical, including a treatise about a man who undergoes an operation for the removal of his navel because its intricate structure fascinates him so much that it interferes with his meditative contemplations.

I watch the tourists trooping into one of the porno shops near Stockholm's main railway station. Germans, smoking cigars as thick as fire hydrants, march in purposefully. They have discovered sex and are determined to conquer it. Englishmen act curious but yellow, as if sex were a duty, a matter of keeping fit. Americans seem to be snickering to themselves. "Hey, Maw, here I am in a porno shop in Stockholm, doing my own thing." And then there are the Japanese. Who knows what goes on behind those closed faces? Inside the porno shop, a book whose careless typographer must have had the Asian export market in mind, proclaims on its lurid cover: 50 BLAND NEW PHOTOGRAPHS.

A country is defined by its images. I had never appreciated the cumulative impact of Ingmar Bergman's films on my imagination until, flying across the Baltic, I caught my first view of Sweden and was astonished to see it flash green and yellow and brown below, instead of the bleak, black-and-white shadows of the Bergman landscapes that I had been expecting. Bergman was too busy working on a film to see me, but his spirit followed me around Sweden like the devil in his *Seventh Seal*. "I want knowledge," one of the characters declares in that film. "Not faith, but knowledge. I want God to stretch His hand toward me, to uncover His face, to speak to me." Such themes – the hunt for God, love as a kind of agony without end, the idea that in order to achieve reality the psyche must first be stripped and humiliated – these are the preoccupations of Bergman's dark and violent masterpieces, and in their snorting, volcanic profundity they add up to a tour of the Swedish soul.

Bergman uses his films as a kind of personal wailing wall. Tense with existential agonies, they are peopled by characters whose derisive laughter originates in the darkest corners of his self-made Hell. God's in his heaven, he seems to be telling us, and all's wrong with the world. ("If God is not here," Bergman once wrote, "life is an outrageous terror, ruled by fate which has no answers, merely appointments.")

Bergman's obsession with loss of life's meaning and a lapse into the silence of God's betrayal dominates the Swedish psyche. Bergman's father was an evangelically inclined Lutheran parson who became chaplain to Sweden's royal family, and it is the moral rectitude of his upbringing that Bergman, and many of the Swedes of his generation, find so difficult to exorcise.

Bergman has been married five times and keeps moving to ever more remote retreats on ever smaller islands. The Swedes wouldn't be surprised if eventually he ends up perched on a rock, alone somewhere out in the Baltic Sea.

He sits in a large round room with carved ivory ceiling, once the home of Alfred Nobel, the inventor of dynamite, and he is the most powerful man in Sweden. As head of the *Landsorganizationen* (LO) Arne Geijer controls the destiny and votes of more than 1.6 million unionized Swedish workers – backbone of the governing Social Democratic Party. He smokes Kent cigarettes and there is an open copy of *U.S. News & World Report* on his desk. "In Sweden," he says, "we can't afford to have unemployment. The Canadian figure of 6 per cent wouldn't be acceptable here. Of course, the big change is that 80 per cent of the youngsters who go through higher education here can't be offered the kind of jobs they expect any more. Somebody has to do the menial work. The pay and living standards of the educated will have to stop rising until the others catch up."

Sweden is experiencing its first major labour troubles since 1934. In the past, wage agreements with management have quietly been negotiated through an elaborate system of annual meetings between LO and its industrial counterpart. But last spring the government took the unprecedented step of moving in to prevent a general strike. Even though Sweden is a socialist country, the state has traditionally concentrated on social policies, leaving business and labour to operate in relative freedom. Sweden has had a socialist government since 1932, but so little industry has been nationalized that only 6 per cent of the labour force is employed by the state. One example of Sweden's enlightened labour policies is the experiment at the Saab plant in Sodertalje, the first modern mass-production automobile factory to drop the conveyor belt system. Instead, cars are assembled by production groups that plan their own work schedules. Absenteeism has dropped while production quality has significantly increased.

Although official statistics rank Sweden's standard of living just behind that of the U.S. (and just ahead of Canada's), it is probably the world's highest on a per capita basis because income is much more evenly distributed. The cost of living went up 7 per cent last year and Stockholm is among the most costly cities in the world in which to live. Coca-Cola in restaurants costs the equivalent of 42 cents; liquor outlets charge ten dollars for a bottle of Scotch; the price of admission to a first-run movie is four dollars; it cost me a dollar to get a shirt laundered in my hotel; a pound of butter sells for 95 cents. It is a mystery how people can afford such prices, because even though wages are roughly equivalent to Canadian rates, income taxes are very much higher. The basic income tax is 60 per cent, and there is a 16-per-cent sales tax that applies to most goods.

But the Swedes also get a lot more back from their government in terms of free services, including free annual holidays for housewives; fat pensions amounting to 60 per cent of a man's average earnings during the ten highest-paid years of his life; free universal education up to the PhD level; state dowries for newlyweds, and subsidies for single-parent children. The Swedish state has become an essential structure for guaranteeing everyone's self-interest. "The Swedes have their medical expenses taken care of, all of their welfare costs paid for, their rent subsidized, and so much done for them, that if they lose their car keys they promptly commit suicide," Godfrey Cambridge, the U.S. comedian, once remarked.

I am enjoying dinner with a Swedish journalist in the Kallaren Aurora, a legendary cellar restaurant off the Stora Nygatan in Stockholm's old city. A place with great trestle tables of hewn planks, torches flaring on whitewashed walls and waiters who look like superannuated philosophy professors, it is named after Aurora, the mistress of some forgotten Swedish king, and its gastronomic traditions go back to 1565. An American tourist clumps ponderously down the stairs, the inevitable cameras bouncing off his stomach. Red socks tucked into two-tone shoes, pale-blue suit with huge side-vents, grey hairs curling out from under a peaked cap, his body seems slack, nearly devoid of tensile meaning. The wife, a man-eater called Mabel, tells him where they will sit. A long way from Marlboro Country, they remind me of the kind of ambassadors from Middle America who stand outside the cathedrals of Europe, saying: "Okay, Harry, you do the outside and I'll do the inside."

They both order snow grouse roasted on the spit. The diners hush as their waiter serves their meal and retires to his side table. The American tourists stare at the snow grouse, eyelessly gazing back at them. Then the husband turns to the wife and says: "Honey, I think with this beautiful bird one must have a Pouilly Fuissé, say, 1959." The diners look down at their plates; their relief is audible.

The untidy office on the nineteenth floor of the University of Stockholm's Institute of Economics is dominated by a sign DUE TO LACK OF INTEREST TOMORROW WILL BE CANCELLED. Its tenant is 72-year-old Gunnar Myrdal, the social scientist whose international reputation is based as much on the man's angry moral vision as on his brilliant scholarship. A generation ago he wrote *An American Dilemma,* which remains a basic text on U.S. racial problems; he has been a Swedish cabinet minister, an influential international civil servant and most recently has published an iconoclastic study of why poverty lingers in much of the third world. A chubby presence with sailor eyes and an unbounded capacity for joyous outrage, Myrdal is probably the least silent Swede in the world. He interrupts the blasts of his opinions by relighting his big pipe with special matches that go off like flamethrowers and are then tossed into a huge ashtray, where they keep blazing away, adding to the intensity of his views.

"Come in, brother," he yells. "You must review my book. Not one economist has read it, you know. They're all mad. Crazy. Everybody else writes gloriously about it. They think I'm a rebel. I'm so goddamn angry." The object of Myrdal's anger at the moment is inflation: "I used to say that the only thing the capitalist system can't stand is deflation, but now I have to add inflation. It really destroys society, but in a democracy it's goddamn difficult to stop it."

"Let's forget those poor Americans with their wars and moon flights for a moment and talk about small countries like Sweden and Canada. We Swedes are like you Canadians, we want better roads, better schools, better hospitals and all these things are capital intensive. Don't forget to put that in. And at the same time, we want higher incomes, more consumption and lower taxes. Well, it's impossible. You have to make a choice, brother. And so now we have inflation. All hell is loose."

Myrdal often visits Canada, has dined with Trudeau, and believes Sweden can become our model in many things. "We're both reasonable countries, with similar traditions of democracy. You Canadians don't have the horrible problems of the United States and I always say to my friends: 'Be careful, brother, that you don't let it drop down to that.' The first thing I'd do is nationalize all the American trade unions. Canadian unions must be independent. Let them cry how much they want. The other difference between us is this French-English business. Is it really so serious? I mean, I was in Quebec City recently, a marvellous, wonderful place. I saw some models of French sculpture, but my motel was as American as you can imagine; the food was completely American. The only difference was the language, for Lord's sake, plus a few intellectuals who make poetry and stuff. Hell, that's not French culture. They're as far away from France as the rest of the Canadians are from England. I mean, how in hell can they be independent? It's all nonsense."

By some mysterious inner arithmetic the Swedes use the ten weeks of summer to balance out the harsh winter, when the sun seldom appears for more than six hours a day. Virtually everybody flees the cities to their cottages or boats. The 800,000 Stockholmers own 80,000 boats and on Sunday nights the waterways are as jammed as Canadian highways on Labour Day weekend.

Ola Wettergren, of the Swedish Sailing Association, invites me to spend a weekend on his boat. The *Dione* lies heaving softly on her docklines, a sixteen-ton yawl, her mast sweeping the sky in the gesture of grave ambiguous urgency that marks championship boats. Along with his warmly hospitable family, we sail most of the day out to Sandhamn, an idyllic island in Sweden's outer archipelago. That evening, after much *schnapps* and singing sad Swedish songs like *The Glitter Is Not The Sea* (or was it *The Sea Is Not The Glitter?*), I sit in the stern of the *Dione* listening to the suckle of water under the hull, the clatter of loose halyards hitting the mast and the occasional splash of the tip of a gently cresting wave, brooding about my brief, intense experience of Sweden.

I remember a phrase from André Malraux, that "the mind gives the idea of a nation, but it is its community of dreams that creates its identity," and it strikes me that nobody in this elegant northern country is out searching for the Swedish identity. These silent, admirable people know exactly who they are. Unlike most Canadians, their convictions have not yielded to their convenience. Part of the explanation is that Sweden is a unitary state with few of our constitutional problems. But a more important consideration is that the character of the people has created an inbred conviction that Sweden's national destiny is theirs alone to control. It is the only country I can think of which has protected itself against Americanization without becoming anti-American in the process. At the turn of the century, a fifth of Sweden's population emigrated to America (and "American fever" is still a recognized entry in Swedish dictionaries), but the awful leverage of materialistic anticipation which has turned so much of Europe into an outpost of the American empire has made little headway here.

Any comparison of the Americanization of Canada with the immunity of Sweden adds to the realization that we have, in Canada, blindly been concerned with only one side of an equation. The conquest of any nation takes place not on battlefields, not in business boardrooms, but in the soul of its people and the minds of their leaders. Colonization is not an isolated act. Conquest requires surrender. (Without surrender, colonization is ultimately impossible, as it was in Viet Nam, for instance.) The choice between surrender and resistance is dictated not by material resourses or available manpower, but my a state of psychological abdication that Canadians have succumbed to and the Swedes have not. As Northrop Frye once noted: "Our country has shown a lack of will to resist its own disintegration. Canada is practically the only country left in the world which is a pure colony – colonial in psychological terms as well as in terms of mercantile economics."

If the American conquest is based on American strength, the Canadian surrender is based on Canadian weakness. Surrender is essentially the admission that something is lacking and a willingness to take the chance that the conqueror will be able to supply it. The Americans are in the process of taking us over not because they want to be our conquerors but because we want to surrender.

Sweden remains on this side of paradise, but the determined survival of the Swedes and their exhilarating willingness to experiment are lessons Canada might examine. Perhaps, even at this late date, we can fashion a future that will be distinctively our own.

[1971]

52

Laos

I F EVER A WORLD CRISIS LOOKED ABSURD and improbable seen at close range, it is the war in Laos, as viewed from Vientiane, this pathetic country's scruffy little capital city, squatting on the northern bank of the muddy Mekong River. Vientiane resembles nothing so much as a leftover set from a low-budget Tarzan movie. Mothers on the way to market publicly suckle their young, as they stroll among the chickens pecking aimlessly on main streets. The daily bulletin issued in French by the government's ministry of information carries news of the latest skirmish with the Pathet Lao rebels on the same page as the description of the *plats du jour* being served at local hotels.

It is only at night, when the siesta-wrapped afternoon has been exchanged for an ebony dusk and packs of half-wild dogs begin to roam closer to the open doorways, that the quiet war which is tearing this nation apart takes on even a measure of reality. A few miles out of Vientiane, where the dirt roads narrow into deep-rutted bullock cart tracks, the Pathet Lao scurry through the darkness to lay mines. The city itself has about it an air of musky impermanence, like a nest of cats about to erupt into violence.

This atmosphere of barely submerged chaos finds open expression in the conversations of western diplomats stationed here. To most of them, it seems all but inevitable that in this small, sleepy Buddhist kingdom, the Americans are faced with humiliating defeat. Laos is as militarily indefensible as Berlin, as ungovernable as the Congo. But, for the Americans it has always held a strange fascination. "Laos is far from American, but Laos' safety runs with the safety of us all," John F. Kennedy once declared.

53

Laos is one of the most backward lands on earth. Eight out of ten Laotians are so primitive that they spend their lives entirely outside the money economy. The commerce of their livelihood is conducted on the basis of rice barter. In a U.S. Bureau of Social Research public opinion poll involving sixteen villages near Vientiane, 80 per cent of those questioned believed that the world is flat, and peopled entirely by Laotians.

A former French colony, Laos is a landlocked, mountain-serrated nation about the size of Great Britain, covered almost entirely by monsoon forests that hide elephants, leopards, cobras, pythons and a relatively harmless variety of crocodile. Most of the country's three thousand miles of road are passable only by pack pony. Laos has no railways, although Savannakhet, the capital of the southern provinces, boasts an unexplained railway station. No accurate census has ever been taken, but United Nations estimates place the population at about two million. They are mostly border peoples, minorities of many races whose forefathers spent centuries or at least generations in China during their southward migration. The fourteen main racial groups speak sixty dialects of six mutually unintelligible languages.

The most important distinction is between the ruling elite, of about twenty historically important families, and the rest of the population. The international machinations that have gone on in Laos since World War II have involved various factions of the country's great families, nearly all of whom are allied to one side or another in the cold war. The majority of Laotians, if they know anything at all about what kind of government they have, view it in a passive sense, as something which may be affecting their lives but in which they themselves are not personally involved. The supreme concern of most Laotians is to win the daily contest against starvation and disease. Families shiver and starve through the winter months before harvest time, suffering from malaria, dysentery and body lice. Three per cent of the population has leprosy. The infant mortality rate is an unimaginable 65 per cent.

How can you hope to resolve a serious twentieth-century ideological conflict in a country where wounds are treated with soot-covered spider webs and the poisoned blowpipe remains the main indigenous weapon? One mountain tribe doesn't even bother to grow rice. Its members forage for snails, catch edible insects, and chew tree bark. The more civilized Laotians who live in the fertile valleys grow only as much rice as they can eat. When the Americans tried to introduce modern food production methods, they were adopted just to the extent

54

that they reduced the work involved in raising the same size of crop as before.

Laos comes close to having no economy at all. There are only three installations in the whole country remotely resembling large-scale modern industrial enterprise – a brickyard, a tobacco factory, and a small tin mine. Aside from a few elephants and some teak floated down to Thailand, the main export is an estimated annual seventy tons of crude opium, smuggled out illegally to Hong Kong. The chief dollar-earning export last year was words. The Laotian government collected $300,000 at its Vientiane cable office from foreign newsmen filing their coverage of the war. The country has a unique balance-of-trade problem: Last year, exports amounted to exactly one per cent of imports. The gap is met by American aid. A third of a billion dollars has been spent here since Washington decided in 1955 to transform the little kingdom into "a bulwark against Communism." Laos has received more American aid per capita than any country in the world. But this assistance has been so badly administered that one American congressional investigator commented that there was, about the whole program, "an almost fairy-tale implausibility." The primitive economy was flooded with goods that couldn't possibly be used, including imitation Laotian sarongs from Japan. Millions of dollars were spent on highways which disappeared with the first rainy season. In 1954, there were five cars in Vientiane. So many local businessmen have grown rich on the profiteering and corruption which has accompanied the U.S. aid that the city now has something like three hundred Mercedes-Benz.

Three-quarters of the American aid funds have gone into building up a pro-western army in Laos, and this has been the worst bargain of all. On paper, the Vientiane-based Royal Laotian Army looks impressive. It has a total of sixty thousand men under arms, compared with less than half that number fielded by the Pathet Lao. But, despite generous military aid which at $4,500 per man has made the price of maintaining one Laotian soldier twice as high as that of any other nation receiving American assistance, the Royal Laotian Army must be the world's least effective group of fighting men. A visiting British general recently offered this assessment: "The Royal Laotian Army is without a doubt the worst fighting force I have ever seen. It makes the South Vietnamese army look like the Wehrmacht." In nearly twenty years of retreating before the numerically inferior Pathet Lao, the Laotian army has inflicted few casualties and won no major battles. Until recently there was only sporadic fighting in Laos. Each time one side or another retired from a hill to shelter from the sun, the movement was reported as a "battle."

The Laotians specialize in loud and dramatic artillery barrages fired in the general direction of the enemy, use a lot of land mines, but shy away from hand-to-hand combat. When the Laotian army invaded the capital city of Vientiane during one *coup d'état* to restore the government's authority, there were three hundred civilian casualties but only seventy-five among the troops.

There are two main theories on why the Royal Laotian Army is so bad. One is that the Buddhist religion, to which most soldiers belong, prohibits killing. (In fact, the Laotians so dislike killing of any kind that all the butchers in Laos are imported Chinese.) The other, simpler explanation is the difference in morale between the Royal troops and the Communists. "This difference in morale," the military attache at the Australian embassy in Vientiane told me, "is that the rebels are fighting their way toward the fleshpots of Vientiane, while the Royal Laotian troops must leave them to go into battle." (This may or may not be a realistic theory, but the fleshpots certainly exist and Vientiane may be the only city in the world where you actually have to bribe a taxi driver *not* to take you to a brothel.)

One of the few tough military engagements fought by the Royal Laotian Army took place on August 8, 1960, when Kong Le, a paratroop corps commander, fed up with the corruption of the u.s.-backed Boun Oum government, captured Vientiane with his troops. This presented a considerable problem because Kong Le was only a captain at the time, and no *coup d'état* in Laotian history had previously been staged by anyone under the rank of colonel.

Kong Le tried to legitimize himself by tearing through the streets of Vientiane in a jeep bearing the emblem *Chef de Coup d'Etat*. But he was driven out by General Phoumi Nosavan (the strong man behind Boun Oum and a close ally of the U.S. Central Intelligence Agency) a few weeks later, joined his troops with the Pathet Lao and promptly promoted himself to lieutenant-general.

Probably the only fighting unit in the world less effective than the Laotian army is the Laotian navy. Commanded by Prince Sinthanarong (a cousin of the king), the seven-hundred-man force has, according to Jane's Fighting Ships, twenty-three ships in reserve and five vessels in commission. The reserve fleet consists of some rusting hulks on the banks of the Mekong River and the only activity aboard these relics comes from the chickens who provide the Laotian navy with its egg

56

supplies. The fleet-in-being boasts five wooden transport vessels, all lack engines and only one is armed. The navy's only capital ship is a thirty-foot iron-hulled monstrosity, built in 1904 and powered by a wood-burning furnace. It was this vessel that participated in the Laotian navy's most daring maritime engagement. During one military coup, it shelled Vientiane. Even though it scored no hits, the navy happened to be on the losing side of that particular revolt and the ship was promptly placed in "reserve." Not the least of the Laotian navy's problem is that what it lacks, apart from ships, is water. Laos is a solidly land-locked country and naval operations are limited to the Mekong River.

The most formidable anti-Communist fighting unit now operating in Laos is a CIA-backed force of mountain tribesmen known as the *Armée Clandestine,* commanded by General Vang Pao, a former sergeant in the French Foreign Legion. When one reporter recently interviewed Vang Pao, he asked him three questions: Are U.S. jets bombing Communist targets in Laos? Are his troops armed with U.S.-made M-16 rifles? Are U.S. helicopters giving him tactical support? The general unequivocally denied that there was any U.S. involvement in Laos, although part of his answer was drowned out by the noise of U.S. jets streaking overhead on a bombing run; he explained he had no American weapons, even though his personal bodyguard all had M-16 rifles, and no, he said, of course there were no American helicopters in Laos – then climbed into a U.S. Marine chopper and flew away.

The most important political influence in Laos remains Prince Souvanna Phouma, a pipe-puffing, Paris-educated patrician with an undiminished vision of himself as the only man who can successfully reunite Laos. He is the John Diefenbaker of Laos, tending to view his relationship to the Laotian people as a kind of holy bond. When things don't go well, he blames unnamed enemies who create evil illusions. He described his policy to me as "neutrality in neutralism" but found it difficult to elaborate beyond condemning both the communist and CIA influences on his country. In more leisurely times he used to enjoy censoring the dispatches of foreign correspondents during his evening bath.

The resentment most Laotians feel toward foreigners goes back to the fifty years the country was a colony of France. French policy was to maintain the country as a worthless buffer state between their wealthier colonies of Cambodia, Tonkin, Annam and Cochin-China on one side and the expansionist aspirations of the British in Burma on the other. During the half century of French rule, Laotian schools turned out just sixty-one high-school graduates; elementary education was provided for less than one per cent of the population. Since France granted Laos its independence in 1953, the country's history has revolved around the inability of the central government in Vientiane to defeat the Pathet Lao, led by Prince Souphanouvong, a half-brother of Souvanna Phouma. Souvanna Phouma became prime minister in Laos' first elections held in 1956 and a series of civil wars that claimed thirty thousand lives followed until President John Kennedy and Premier Nikita Khrushchov reached an agreement in Geneva that the super-powers would withdraw and allow a coalition government to be formed. It lasted less than a year and there has been fighting in Laos ever since.

The U.S. promptly launched an air war against communist installations in Laos and Washington had admitted that its aid program in that country is being used as a cover for CIA military operations. Now, the Americans and South Vietnamese are escalating their operations to recapture the Plain of Jars on the Laos-Vietnamese border, which affords North Viet Nam a protective buffer for the Ho Chi Minh Trail as well as a staging area for its troops. Despite all this activity, very little changes in Vientiane, the country's sleepy little capital. The city's main street, the Avenue Lang Xang, is vaguely modelled on Paris' *Champs Elysées* and ends in the *Place du Monument,* a rococo imitation of the *Arc de Triomphe,* built with U.S. aid funds, though exactly what triumphs it celebrates no one really knows. Like most other primitive societies the Laotians have reached into their folklore to describe their plight. They quote an ancient proverb sadly appropriate to the times: "When the elephants fight, it is the grass that suffers."

[1961]

Washington

I

A FTER A WEEK HERE, SPENT INTERVIEWING American politicians of the left, right and centre, the mood of despair they exhale becomes contagious. For the first time in memory, Americans seem muted and depressed, unable to project the self-confidence that's always been their dazzling trademark.

The Viet Nam war, which has turned from a crusade into an obscenity, hangs over Washington like a dense smog and no one has breath or determination enough to blow it away. The city eats, sleeps and drinks the war. Almost every conversation, no matter how casual, eventually ends on the same semi-hysterical note: How the hell do we get out of there?

The war, the endless war, has contorted the national conscience, left in tatters three decades of American foreign policy and turned the minds of thoughtful Americans to some dark and troubling questions about their way of life.

There is something oddly insubstantial about the speeches, press conferences and TV interviews, the stream of arguments, discussions, and declamations that flood out of here, all arousing old emotions instead of stirring new thoughts. The critics make their points and the administration spokesmen counter them, but neither side convinces the other and it seems as though the whole political process has somehow become unhinged from the realities it is supposed to represent.

At the centre of this uncertainty is the figure of the president himself. I saw Richard Nixon closely only once this week, at his press conference in the East Room of the White House. Impeccably dressed and made up, he resembled nothing so much as a headwaiter in a once-great restaurant that no longer has a first-class chef, nervously greeting diners with the hope that a patina of charm will hide his underlying insecurity. In the glare of the television lights and under the timid assault of the reporters' questions, he seemed to be constantly on his guard, patrolling himself, listening to his own voice, adjusting its cadence, putting the adjectives in their proper order. His aides, dressed in blazers and short hair, hovered, straining with him as he recited answers larded with memorized statistics. His responses, whether they dealt with the tax bill before the Congress or the My Lai atrocities, came from a man anxious to dispute definitions and shades of meaning when he should be arguing facts and convictions, a man hoping to mediate but unable to lead.

Even though he holds the most powerful office on earth, Richard Nixon gives the impression of still pursuing power, campaigning against himself, trying to allay the old fears and the old suspicions that have always haunted him. About fifteen minutes into the press conference, Nixon began to sweat and as I looked around the magnificent East Room, festooned with gilt chairs, crystal chandeliers hanging from the Adam ceiling, the portraits of George and Martha Washington flanking the temporary stage, I wondered how this great nation could have at its head in this agonizing time such a plastic parody of a leader.

I kept watching Nixon, searching for some glimmer of human response under the careful television mask he wore. His face somehow lacked dimension, a spongy invention of cardboard, like those gaudy cutouts carried aloft at carnival times in Rio. Then, our glances briefly locked, he noticed me looking at him and just for an instant – a frozen flutter of time – I caught the real Nixon. In that small stillness of insight, I recognized a man so terrified – his breath and muscles seemed as taut as a pole-vaulter's – that he could barely keep himself under control. Wild gooseberry eyes looked out at me with the plea of a man who had spent a lifetime being snubbed, begging for belief. Whenever he mentioned Viet Nam, Nixon acted as if his (and America's) virility were at stake, as if he could enlist us all in his quest for final absolution from his inner doubts that he wasn't being taken seriously enough. "It is not our power but our will and our character that are being tested," he said, as if to show the world that he (and America) had not lost their manhood.

I can think of easier and more pleasant ways for middle-aged men to prove their manhood, but it is the long-term implications of Nixon's consummate insecurity that really frighten me. Manhood should have something to do with the comprehension born of experience and a capacity for making moral judgments. Once it becomes a function of brute force, we are all doomed to eventual nuclear extinction. The trouble is that the Americans have never understood the nature of the Viet Nam war. They still regard it as a kind of white man's burden of bringing their brand of democracy to the benighted; they really believe that the dominos will topple all the way from Saigon to San Francisco.

Even though the Americans have now lost 50,000 men, suffered 278,000 casualties and spent $126 billion in Viet Nam, they cannot accept the fact that they have lost the war. For Americans, raised on John Wayne movies in which the tongue-tied hero rides off into the Technicolour sunset after treating the villains he has just vanquished with condescending generosity, the revelation of the massacre at My Lai was a traumatic shock. But as more Pentagon files become available, My Lai hardly emerges as an isolated incident. Take the 1968 bombing of Khe Sanh. In a period of six weeks, American jets dropped 100,000 tons of fire bombs and fired 700,000 rounds of machine-gun fire into a five-square-mile area around Khe Sanh, even though there were no more than twelve hundred enemy troops reported in the area. Destruction on this scale is unprecedented in the history of warfare. The fire bombs that thundered down on Khe Sanh are equivalent to five times the destructive potential of the nuclear device that devastated Hiroshima. During all of World War II twenty-two thousand tons of bombs were dropped on Hamburg, which was among the most heavily bombed of German cities. Yet five square miles of Viet Nam were subjected to nearly five times as much fire power. The raids prompted one U.S. Air Force general to boast that Khe Sanh was "probably the first ground action won entirely by air power."

When war becomes this irrational, the motives of the men who wage it and the society that produces them must be re-examined. Under Richard Nixon's leadership, the u.s. is going through some perilous changes. America is approaching a kind of metabolic flashpoint that could, at some distant time, bring about a total loss of contact with reality (through the establishment of military dictatorship) or an unprecedented social upheaval (through the kind of revolution that shook Russia in 1917).

In either case, Richard Nixon will be one of the men mainly responsible. It was I. F. Stone who best summed up the record of America's

37th president with this terrible indictment: "The Eichmann trial taught the world the banality of evil. Richard Nixon is teaching the world the evil of banality."

II

APART FROM VIET NAM, THE DOMINANT ISSUE troubling Washington these days is how to create a new alignment of political forces that somehow will make the United States governable again.

Until the 1968 election, the wide, tilted umbrellas of the Democratic and Republican parties always managed to cover enough of the widely divergent strains of American politics to make majority government possible. But now the party structures are disintegrating and traditional sources of political power are drying up. Massive shifts are altering the geographic and ideological make-up of both the major parties and no one can predict the final outcome.

At the moment there exists no functioning "government in exile," no rallying point for opponents of the administration, such as there was during the Johnson years under the leadership first of Eugene McCarthy and later Robert Kennedy. Teddy Kennedy, the natural inheritor of this role, forfeited his claim that terrible July night at Chappaquiddick. While the politicians are busy vying for the succession, the blacks, the young and the poor – who together make up at least half the U.S. population – feel themselves disenfranchised.

The Republicans are determined to mould a new kind of coalition that will steal the initiative away from the "eastern establishment" that has dominated American politics since the early days of Franklin Roosevelt.

In these efforts, Nixon is helped considerably by the fracturing of the old-line liberal alliances. Exhausted by the assassination of two Kennedys, the betrayal of Lyndon Johnson and the alienation of the new radicals (who view liberal preoccupation with economic instead of moral issues with mounting contempt), American liberals are finding themselves exiles in their own land – men with good intentions but no power base from which to reclaim political office.

One result of all this is that party banners are losing their importance. More and more, the American future will belong to politicians who can unite behind themselves loose coalitions on specific issues.

To test this theory on some of the men who are actually involved in shaping the political process, I spent a day wandering the halls of the U.S. Senate.

The first man I met was Strom Thurmond, the senator from South Carolina whose backing of Nixon during the crucial negotiations at the last Republican nominating convention made him one of Washington's most influential legislators. I had read a great deal about how Thurmond had opposed his state's anti-lynching laws, how he starts each day by throwing his feet over his head thirty times ("to keep the blood flowing to my head"), about how he abstains not only from liquor but from carbonated soft drinks as well – and expected to meet a kind of political neanderthal who walked around with knuckles rubbed raw from scraping the ground.

Instead, the senator turned out to be a southern gentleman whose voice, whether relishing the profane or intoning the sacred, never rose above an elegant whisper. Still, there was little doubt about where he stood. "The anti-Viet Nam demonstrations," he said, "merely encourage the Communists to continue the war. The quicker we can show the enemy we mean business, the quicker the war will end. But even when it does, these demonstrations will find other ways to promote trouble because they're opposed to the fundamental form of American government – the free enterprise system."

As Thurmond was being called back to the floor of the Senate for a vote, I asked about the sixty thousand or so American draft resisters and deserters who had crossed the border into Canada since the Viet Nam war began. "Why, you just send them back to us so we can prosecute them," he replied. "Our countries are so close together, why, we're just like one big country and we oughta help one another. You just send those boys back and we'll know what to do with them."

I left Thurmond behind and went to seek an old hero of mine, Eugene McCarthy – poet, political gypsy, destroyer of a president, party outcast. His anteroom is dominated by a large blue sign that proclaims, "The ABM Is An Edsel" and a framed photo of the 1960 Democratic convention, inscribed: "For Eugene McCarthy with affection, gratitude and everlasting memories of my 'finest hour' – Adlai Stevenson."

McCarthy slouched by and invited me into his office. Painted dark grey with mahogany bookshelves, it is a place to contemplate William Butler Yeats, not read the Congressional Record. McCarthy himself was so subdued he occasionally seemed to disappear inside himself. I have never met a politician who exudes less power, who cares so little for the small gestures that make up the politician's trade.

We sat there in the early winter twilight, talking about the American dream and the exhaustion of liberalism. "The trouble with American liberals," he mused, "is that they're like the Labour Party in the U.K. They've never been able to unite on anything except economic issues. That's why American liberalism has failed. We lost the labour movement when we moved into civil rights, for example. True liberalism has never really been tried in this country. Of course, it's not a certifiable faith or theological system. Liberalism is distinguished by only one thing – its approach to human problems. The liberal is an optimist who bears the mark of humility and demonstrates a deep concern for human freedoms. Up until Viet Nam, we Americans thought we could solve all the world's problems. But now everything is out of phase. There is basic disharmony between what we really believe and the kind of programs Congress puts forward. Everybody's against poverty but the reality would contradict what we believe about Americans, so we don't do very much about it." He spoke vaguely about his future, saying that "if concern over not being involved in the political process is as deep as I think it is, it should be possible to establish a new party in the next presidential campaign."

It was dark now and the senator seemed lost in thought, a man reporting from another world. And so I tiptoed out of there.

III

ON MY LAST DAY IN WASHINGTON, I hopped a cab for Arlington Cemetery to see the grave where John Kennedy is buried. I was seeking I am not sure what – some kind of uplift, some stirring of old emotions, some rekindling of the feeling that the U.S. is a great nation which has produced great men with great ideas and will do so again.

The graveside was bleak in the December rain, with a lone fat policeman waiting to direct the non-existent traffic. Two middle-aged Middle American ladies in plastic rain bonnets kneeling in the cold grass were the only visitors, and there was all the time in the world to pace the Kennedy monument and read the words engraved from JFK's 1961 inaugural address: "The energy, faith, the devotion which we bring to this endeavor (the defence of freedom) will light our country and all who serve it. And the glow from that fire can truly light the world. . . ."

Here, in this muted setting, chiselled in Massachusetts granite, was the epitaph of the American Dream. Kennedy's words harked back to the great American patriot Thomas Paine, who wrote in 1776 that "the cause of America is in great measure the cause of all mankind." It was this same faith which had prompted millions of the world's dispossessed to sail past the Statue of Liberty in pursuit of their share of its bounty. To be an American during the first six decades of this century was a kind of holy mission.

In the years since Kennedy stood in the Washington snow and "let the word go forth," the gap between his rhetoric and the realities of American life has grown so wide that it is difficult to believe this is the same country. The Americans have tried every possible kind of leader – a young prince with his shimmering retinue; a back-forty buccaneer with the crude qualifications of a Texas sheriff; and now this pathetic, hollow Horatio Alger figure. Yet none of these leaders have been able – even with the help of all the president's horses and all the president's men – to put the broken American Dream back together again.

Three assassinations – the two Kennedys and Martin Luther King – have stilled the voices of reconciliation. The massacre at My Lai has debased the image of Americans as global good Samaritans. Poverty and its relentless insensibilities, the racial demonstrations and their growing ugliness, have permanently altered the Americans' opinion of their achievements at home. (If New York's welfare recipients, most of whom are black, left to set up their own city, they would found the nation's eighth largest community.) The gross national product, which always measured American achievement, is now recognized to include the polluted wastes belching out of factories, the special locks and guns needed by city dwellers to keep out intruders, and the napalm used to incinerate innocent villagers in Viet Nam.

A country which has always prided itself on the openness of its society and the settlement of disputes through the due process of law now boasts nearly a million soldiers trained for domestic riot duty. A special Civil Disturbances Planning and Operations Office is run out of secret bunkers under the Pentagon's parking lots, manned by computers with files on potential troublemakers and records of sites that could be used as detention centres when conventional jails have been filled.

Out of all this turmoil has emerged a political mood of counter-insurgency. Since the overthrow of the government lies beyond the capacity of the loosely-allied groups of the young, the blacks, the poor

65

and the otherwise alienated, they are determined to undermine the moral authority of those in power. This new radicalism is very different from the ordinary kind of protest that grows up in a democracy and eventually emerges as an alternative government. These outsiders do not seek a change of government, but a change in the way people live. Their aim is to invest authority in the people, as opposed to the old liberal idea of allowing an elite to exercise power benignly on the people's behalf. In the process, the radicals are establishing a counter-culture which is bringing about profound changes in the values and life styles on which American society has traditionally been based. This is the real meaning of the drug culture, the rock festivals, the new sexual freedom, the idea that being spontaneous – doing your own thing – is the best way to protest the dehumanization of a materialistic culture.

What response established authority will make to these pressures – whether it will reach out to accommodate the rebels within the accepted structures or suppress their demands by force – is not yet clear.

Certainly, no one can live on this planet without being aware of the saturating force of American civilization – the economic compulsions of u.s. society that are washing away national cultures and values everywhere, turning the globe into giant extensions of Wall Street and Madison Avenue. The u.s. economic empire is so huge that American companies abroad now account for a gross national product equivalent to that of the third largest country in the world – only the u.s. itself and Russia exceed their output. About a third of u.s. foreign assets are based in Canada and as we become ever more essential suppliers of raw materials and energy for the American industrial machine, an even greater share of our economy is coming under u.s. domination. Chances are that Canada will be the last outpost of the American empire.

[1969]

PART TWO   *Pierre Trudeau*

Moving Up

EVERYWHERE YOU GO AT THIS LIBERAL CONVENTION, you catch the professional politicians clustered in small groups, trying to size up the political magic of Pierre Elliott Trudeau. They follow him about as though they suspect he has some trick they might master. They ogle him, talk at him, touch him. But they come away still puzzled, telling each other tentatively that it must be his looks or maybe his age, his "radicalism," his money, or his reputation as an intellectual.

Yet Robert Winters is handsomer, John Turner is younger, Paul Hellyer is richer, Eric Kierans is more radical, and Paul Martin has as many degrees. But the other candidates, seasoned men pursuing understandable political ambitions, are no match for Trudeau. Nobody can draw the crowds, get the laughs, fire the enthusiasm. All the jockeying at the convention is for second or third place. Trudeau is the man to beat.

Three months ago this would have been not just remarkable, it would have been unthinkable. Yet there he is, and when he comes into a room, the room is somehow different. He has that incandescent glow that thousands of photographers' flash bulbs impart to the flesh. He looks remote and austere, his very presence generates an undercurrent of the unexpected. In one of the workshops he was addressing, the solid cadre of photographers and television men who follow his every move was blocking the view of the delegates. Finally, an exasperated member of the audience stood up and yelled: "Down in front." Trudeau instantaneously barked back: "How far in front?" – quizzically implying that they wanted him to sit down. It was a small joke, but it relaxed the audience, persuaded the photographers to move back, and won him a round of applause.

Any political convention develops into a circus for the candidates, with enough pressure to break the composure of even the normally reserved. Yet Trudeau refuses to dissolve his real personality, maintaining a sense of inner repose, and the more he holds himself back, the more the crowds want a piece of him.

"I was for him right from the start," says an elderly delegate from British Columbia.

"I made him get his hair cut today," says one of his handlers.

A woman turns to her husband just before Trudeau enters his Chateau Laurier hospitality suite and says: "What if I faint when he comes in?" He gives her a look of sheer disgust. But when Trudeau shakes his hand, his eyes are moist.

All through such encounters, Trudeau remains himself, a cool man in a hot world doing his grainy thing. His style consists of being totally self-contained, of remaining the custodian of his own potentials.

He brings with him into the Liberal contest a sense of reawakening. In Trudeau, many Canadians see a hope of ceasing to be an old nation which clings to the status quo, fearful of change. When he says: "What we need are new guys and new ideas," they see in him the new guy and the new ideas. Few delegates worry about or even consider the direction in which Trudeau is proposing to lead Canada; it is enough for them to realize that he represents something new. They see in his style the promise that the process of discovering Canada has not come to an end, that we are, after all, a young nation with unexploited possibilities.

Unlike all of the other candidates – except Eric Kierans – he answers questions not in terms of our feelings about the past, but in terms of an unknown, exciting future. He seems to be saying that there is space for intelligence in public life, that politics is not just the business of trading power in backrooms, but a way to share in the passions of our age.

The delegates sense that in Pierre Trudeau there is an unusual meeting of a man and his time. In spite of his casual, dispassionate manner, what he says carries conviction because his words appear moored deep in his conscience. Yet he is so self-contained, so detached that it is not easy to discern what moves inside him, what inner forces sustain him. This is the ultimate mystery that makes him the source of such fascination. This is the trick that the professionals cannot uncover.

[1968]

70

Consolidating Power

THE TWELVE MONTHS SINCE PIERRE ELLIOTT TRUDEAU'S election victory have provided a fascinating study in the interaction between a leader and a nation during a period of intense development for both. Canada has changed since June 25, 1968, but not nearly as much as her fifteenth prime minister. The carefree swinger of the hustings has become an earnest technocrat, a sort of Buddhist monk in mufti.

The change in the nation has been subtler, but what it amounts to is that Ottawa has rejoined the mainstream of Canadian life. During most of the Pearson and Diefenbaker years, the capital appeared to the country-at-large like the scene of some inane puppet show, with the two chief puppeteers continually getting their wires crossed and puppet-ministers stumbling over each other in a series of unintentionally hilarious blackouts.

Now at least, Canada feels as though it's being governed again. By using the first year of his mandate to restructure and revitalize Ottawa's decision-making apparatus, Trudeau has gained the most precious commodity any new prime minister can have: time to brief himself on the nation's problems so that he need not attempt their solution until he has tested the limits of his power.

In the interval, Trudeau has been broadening the reach of that official power and the stretch of his personal authority. Though he won his party's leadership with only a fourth-ballot count of 51.1 per cent of the voting delegates, he has since captured the loyalty (if not yet the affection) of his party's many factions. Inside the cabinet chamber, Trudeau's ministers have been transformed into a league of awed men,

71

not so much afraid to challenge the PM's views as uncertain of their own in the face of his strength.

Politics is a harsh trade that normally requires half a lifetime's apprenticeship, but Trudeau seems to have mastered its vital elements in one hectic year. His political style, a hang-loose version of Gaullism, combines his conviction that a man's prestige grows in direct proportion to his aloofness from the herd with the offhand carelessness which has produced such political bloopers as: "Where's Biafra?" and "Why should I sell your wheat?"

There have been other mistakes (the incident with Eva Rittinghausen in London, the two-per-cent ceiling on the social development tax, the curious forelock-tugging attitude he adopted on his first visit to Washington) and there is no doubt that he has severely disillusioned the reformers who were the first to support him last year. You could not get the intellectuals and artists this spring to lose their heads for Trudeau; you could not get them organizing committees or writing pedantic love letters in the *Canadian Forum,* or holding quilting bees in artists' lofts in his honour. But then you probably could not get Trudeau himself to go swimming in a motel pool and invite a girl to join him in the nude or to bugaloo on a campaign bus. He has managed to turn himself from a pop hero into a stodgy statesman without appearing to be anything but passive in the process.

Yet in the most important situations, such as federal-provincial conferences, the confrontation with the St. Jean Baptiste Society, the passage of the Official Languages Bill, Trudeau has demonstrated a tough, disciplined application of personal power. The remarkable thing is that in any crisis he becomes as much a stage director as an actor, so that he is able to project not only himself but to impose on the public mind the entire scenario of an event. Paul Hellyer's resignation, for example, which might have shaken any other administration, was fobbed off as being based on the former transport minister's misreading of the constitution, and thus reduced to a two-day sensation.

The one major decision Trudeau has taken which altered government policy in a fundamental way was his NATO statement of April 3, 1969. Previously, any policy jointly underwritten by the departments of national defence and external affairs was almost automatically approved by the cabinet. Although he had the eventual support of eight ministers, Trudeau's new defence policy represented his first (and only) significant clash with the Ottawa establishment.

Political management of a diverse economy rather than any distinctive political ideology sets the priorities and guides the actions of the Trudeau government. "Process," Marshall McLuhan said recently, "is Trudeau's forte. He is corporate. He refuses to reveal a point of view but fascinates everyone with process."

Trudeau's ideal is derived from the Jesuit principle of not imposing your views on others but of letting people find their own way to your beliefs. In this, he has failed. Not only is genuine mass participation in the democratic process just about impossible to achieve, but Trudeau's objectives have undergone an important shift which has made them less acceptable. By concentrating so much on the Ottawa side of politics, he has gradually become more preoccupied with government than with society, less interested in social change than in stability and continuity, more committed to the legal concepts of Confederation than any adventurous attempt to fashion independent nationhood.

His conceptual approach to his job has tended to bury the perceptual view of the country he radiated during the last election campaign. "What we'll be trying hard to accomplish during Year Two," says one of the prime minister's aides, "is to bring him back to what he was before Year One, to make him once again part of the crowds. That's where Pierre gets his Brownie points."

One potential difficulty in maintaining Trudeau's political popularity may be the fact that his most impressive breakthroughs in the last election were in British Columbia, Alberta, Winnipeg, urban Ontario, and the English-speaking seats of Montreal. It is largely to the voters in these areas that he owes his power, and certainly part of his appeal to them was based on what they interpreted as his willingness "to stand up to Quebec." Now, he must reverse the process and convince French Canada's nationalists that the rest of the country, notably the areas where he received his most ardent support, will back him in the kind of constitutional concession that will be required on a national scale to keep Quebec within Confederation.

This will be a dangerous manoeuvre, because it will threaten Trudeau's existing power base without guaranteeing him a new one. His only choice may be to challenge Quebec separatism directly, demanding that Canadians, both French and English, back him in joining battle with René Lévesque and his followers.

Trudeau has not done so many of the things we thought he would last spring. He has not made great speeches in the House, he has not

73

entertained glowingly at 24 Sussex Drive, he has not invited the best brains to Ottawa, he has not revolutionized our society and made it into a bicultural participatory democracy. And yet, he is still somehow a man of whom one expects greatness. A year ago everyone wanted to know what Pierre Trudeau was really like. We still do.

[1969]

Brief Encounter

WHEN YOU COME TO OTTAWA FROM OUTER CANADA (which is anywhere beyond a six-block radius of Parliament Hill) the capital has a curiously remote quality, especially in high summer when it lies hot, green, somehow antique under the shimmering sun, its political fervor stifled since the MPS abandoned it to the tourists. But then you are conducted into the bowels of this political fortress (in the East Block offices of Pierre Trudeau and his immediate retinue) and you suddenly realize that as far as they are concerned, the city is all vitality and action and change.

Probably more than ever before, the government of Canada is being run by one man, and the East Block office Trudeau uses between parliamentary sessions turns out to be an exciting place to be. This is not, God knows, because of its furnishings – upper-echelon civil service standard far less pretentious in their total effect than the office of any small-time university president. What creates the excitement, what gives the office a sense of aliveness, is its occupant who, no matter how often he is observed in public, watched on television, caught open-mouthed and flower-buttoned by press cameras, is still something of a surprise when viewed in person.

Trudeau appears smaller, more fragile and yet more commanding than you expect; and while in public he is a man constantly in motion, jumping bannisters, dodging (or slugging) picketers, swimming, hopping onto platforms, in person he is incredibly still. If it was true that John Diefenbaker often "thought with his heart," it is equally true that Pierre Trudeau frequently "feels with his mind." Except for his bimonthly public outbursts, such as his slugfest with a heckler in Van-

75

couver last weekend, his emotions remain remote and inaccessible. But his mind is an open city, unfettered by political dogma, committed only to a kind of functionalism that measures policies strictly by how well they might work.

It was this kind of non-ideological response that he gave to my opening question about his use of closure to impose the guillotine rule (75-C) on future parliamentary debates. Democracy in the past, he claimed, has failed for one simple reason: It wasn't efficient enough. "Why did Fascism arise in Italy, Naziism in Germany and Gaullism in France? Not because some political party exaggerated its powers and used Parliament to squash the Opposition, but because in these countries the judgment was made that Parliament couldn't settle the issues fast enough. In other words, Naziism, Fascism and Gaullism arose exactly for the reasons we're trying to correct by making Parliament more efficient."

Trudeau claims he would like somehow to draw out of the country a true picture of what it really wants, by presenting the electorate with the facts, then challenging them to make the relevant choices. "We need to tell people," he said, "Okay – if we want to have portable fridges on the beaches and portable television sets and so on, that's fine, but maybe, we can't swim in the water because it's polluted. But if we want clean water, we'll have to pay higher taxes which means we don't have our portable television sets. Now what will people choose? Perhaps they'll choose television sets. But at least they won't say then that the government can't do anything about pollution. They'll say we don't want it to do anything about pollution. I'm suggesting we have to explain this to people. Explain that they must have choices. . . . It's a sense of helplessness which destroys society. It's the feeling that everything is out of control. But government can't really solve the problems by itself. . . . What preserves free societies is the facing of difficulties by all its citizens."

Did the prime minister think the kind of excitement and competition involved in the space race, particularly the recent moon walk, might eventually transform it into a substitute for war? "Well," he mused, "it's a feat that has to stand and fall on its own merits. It's something which doesn't preclude other things. I had an argument yesterday with a person who was telling me, my gosh why should they go to the moon when there are so many poor people. Well, why should we have museums and why should we have writers and artists and painters and dancers when there are so many poor people? Shouldn't

76

we use all our resources to eradicate poverty rather than to teach people how to play the flute? The answer is of course that the spin-offs from technological innovation like the spin-offs from symphony concerts are extremely valuable. But there's a danger if people begin saying if we can go to the moon we can do anything. This will create expectations which we won't easily be able to fulfil. Going to the moon proves that men's minds working together can build pretty perfect mechanisms, but it doesn't prove that we've made one inch more progress into the exploration of man's mind itself. So to go back to your question, the way to eradicate war is not going to the moon. It's understanding what happens inside man's brain which makes him aggressive and makes him want to fight."

Could he tell me what was going on inside his own brain since his elevation to power? "Yeah, well I'm still myself," he said, "I enjoy reading these (official papers on his desk) and I enjoy answering hecklers and I enjoy sitting down in a farmer's kitchen and asking him what he does with the other six months in the year, but I am still myself and I urge you to believe me. I'm not being forced to do anything by the people around me. . . . It's not true that I'm becoming an automaton just working sixteen hours a day. As a statement of fact, I feel just as human and sometimes a little more tired, but that is easily corrected by a long weekend. I'm getting a hell of a lot of fun out of it and I hope you're having a lot of fun in Toronto too."

[1969]

Journey to London

I

PIERRE TRUDEAU'S SUNDAY AFTERNOON TEACH-IN at London's Westminster Theatre proved once again that for Canada's fifteenth prime minister the method is the message and style is the substance.

He was completely at ease with himself and with his audience. He did again what he had done for many years as a university lecturer, combining theoretical musings with leaps of intuition, classical references with colloquial quips. To his familiar posture as a seasoned academic were added the embellishments of the professional performer that he has learned during the past twelve months. This involved calculated movements (as well as run-on jokes) — putting his hand in his watchpocket, taking sips of water whenever he wanted a moment to think, raising his eyebrows to indicate that he and the questioner both realized the complexities of human existence without adding to them by creating new ones, and always the exaggerated shrugs.

These and other tricks of stagecraft, all beautifully exploited, lifted the audience to such a level of rapport that no one would have been very surprised if he had suddenly assumed a yoga position on the platform. All through the questioning, which was often penetrating but never very tough, Trudeau was supremely comfortable and in a state of being *chez lui,* so that when he got a really fresh question, such as one posed about whether an intellectual can remain an intellectual after he becomes a politician, he spontaneously spun out an interesting answer: "Not in the true sense of the word, no. The intellectual is one who looks for absolute truths, . . . who states his belief as to the best answer on moral grounds, on philosophical grounds, and who doesn't inject a sense of politics into his answer. A politician's answer is only second-best in that sense. He takes the best ideas that come from intellectuals and very often from the common man and he says 'what can I do with this absolute truth and how can I apply it to reality as I see it?' His assessment is of the possible and not of the ideal, which means that one is looking very often for second- and third-best solutions. I make no apologies for that. I just hope that those who are intellectuals will continue to think it their duty to look for the best solution. . . . The politician will water it down. He will say, 'I can't get away with it,' or 'I must compromise or it won't pass Parliament.' So. [Shrug, shrug]."

This diversion, which revealed something of Trudeau's personal feelings on having to compromise principles to position, was handled in the acceptable manner of the academic. As was another question about whether he was a socialist and whether he thought theoretical socialism ("from each according to his abilities, to each according to his needs") was a workable ideology. "Do you know of any society apart from a few religious orders which has achieved this ideal?" he countered. "If we could only all be saints we could have this perfect society. But we ain't."

The deliberate vulgarism gave variety to the cadence of his sentence structure and provided the audience with the release of laughter. One of the reasons the meeting never threatened to overwhelm Trudeau was the nature of those who made up that audience of seven hundred. They were open-faced, docile, well-kempt students, laughing in a low-key mood at the end of their Christmas holidays, the girls with the glistening hair and white shiny teeth that indicated a happy lifetime of good nutrition, regular dental appointments and solicitous parents. An astonishing number of the boys had short hair, glasses and blazers – the students of the fifties, still alive and well in swinging London. They had been summoned to the meeting through Canada House (not exactly your average radical's hangout) and were mostly graduate students enrolled in British universities. This meant they were either the children of parents rich enough to send them abroad in this new version of the grand tour, or on scholarship. They were Rhodes Scholars, Athlone Fellows, Commonwealth Scholars, Beaverbrook Scholars and kids from Westmount and Rosedale, not a separatist or wild-eyed New Leftist in the lot. And just in case some Danny-the-Red of the Frozen North had managed to sneak in to pose an uncomfortable question, the chairman during his warm-up speech warned that anyone causing any trouble would have his mike cut off. Even the press was tightly controlled, confined to a special section at the front of the theatre. A few British reporters had come along, glumly intent on picking up new gossip about Trudeau and his unorthodox ways. ("I say, all the questions will be in English, won't they? I speak French, you understand, but it's French-French, not that bloody awful dialect.")

The exchange that probably best summed up the Trudeau method of government was his answer to a question from a student at the London School of Economics, about how he intends to improve the status of Canada's Indians. "I think," Trudeau said, "that all of us feel a sense of guilt, not so much toward the Indian as toward the fact that we haven't really addressed our minds to his problem." He then outlined how two of his ministers are consulting the Indian population, trying to discover whether any consensus exists among the Indians themselves. He mentioned that a band of Indian chiefs had come to see him a few weeks ago and reconstructed their conversation: "They came to Ottawa on the occasion of the twentieth anniversary of the Declaration of Human Rights and they asked to see me. They all made speeches, many of them saying things like, you know, 'I'm sixty-five years old and I've been an Indian all my life (shrug and laughter) and this is the first time I've talked to the Big Chief,' and so on, and then they sat down and sort of said, 'Now give it to us.' And I said, 'Forget it. This is pure symbolism. You thought that the day you saw the Big Chief he would have the answer. But I don't have any answers. I want to get them from you'."

It was a good show, but Trudeau revealed no new commitments, made no news and held on to his urbanity like a carnival mask. Watching him, one had the uncomfortable feeling that he was at about six removes from the hall, that he was able to watch the image of himself as prime minister in a Caesar haircut parrying questions under the television lights without really being part of the scene. Trudeau has said often that he despises sentimental maunderings, flights of rhetoric and public displays of emotion. Still, without losing his detachment he might easily have said something stirring or at least stimulating in response even to the pedestrian questions he was asked. He might, for instance, have made clear the intellectual French Canadian's indifference to the British monarchy and its irrelevance to the nation he is governing; or he might have made an appeal to the French- and English-speaking African nations and described Canada's unique, if imperfect, qualifications for bringing them closer together. He could have said the Commonwealth conferences would serve some useful purpose if only they reminded fat nations like Canada of the troubles of lean nations in Asia and Africa. He might have said that he is unequivocally opposed to war but instead he only meekly affirmed that, "as a matter of principle I always put the militaristic solution last." He might have said – well, something, anything, that was not a repetition of statements made often before or coy re-workings of old epigrams about the joys of bachelorhood. ("One always likes to see pretty smiling faces.")

Trudeau's accompanying retinue of advisers alternately looked proud (as though he had sprung full-blown from their furrowed brows) and nervous about getting him back to his private suite at Claridge's Hotel. At the end of the performance, they climbed gratefully back into black limousines, shutting out the curious, delighted with their leader's success, but glad to have him once again safe, where they alone had access to his thoughts.

[1969]

II

THE COMMONWEALTH CONFERENCE FINALLY GOT UNDER WAY with most of the participants acting about as interested as a road company preparing to give HMS Pinafore for the hundredth time, with everybody properly costumed but no one prepared to put much heart into the performance. I saw the action close-up when, by some wild chance of wilder inefficiency, I was herded into the delegates' lounge with the prime ministers and their advisers. I had edged up the steps of Marlborough House to escape the crush of demonstrators and the frenzy that accompanied the arriving prime ministers. The doorway to the historic building was ringed by policemen and guardsmen in ceremonial uniform, all bent on checking credentials. But somehow I was shoved through the doors without any check. I stood uncertainly for a moment in the main hall and was promptly approached by a man in a morning coat who asked me with intense courtesy whether he might "take my coat and then direct me to the delegates' lounge, sir?"

Since the press was being treated here with bare tolerance and was strictly forbidden any actual contact with delegates, the enormity of the guide's mistake very nearly unnerved me but I followed his decorous figure across the marble hall and found myself standing beside Harold Wilson. Wilson stared at me sourly for five seconds, then turned back, irritably issuing an order to Michael Stewart, his foreign secretary,

81

while glowering about the room at the assembled statesmen, apparently disenchanted with his role as the villain of the conference at a time when he is plagued with so many domestic issues.

Everywhere prime ministers and their advisors were whispering to each other, sounding like a group of professors forming up an academic procession just before a university prize-giving. They all seemed to be discussing British failures or omissions. The British ought to have taken a firm stand on Rhodesia; the British had no business supplying arms to Nigeria; the sanctions against Rhodesia have been disappointingly ineffective, etc.

The most colourful delegates were the African prime ministers in long gray, blue, and red gowns, earnestly reading documents stamped "Secret" produced by their assistants out of leather dispatch cases. Makarios of Cyprus gloomed by, wearing his familiar four-cornered archbishop's hat and a long jewelled medallion under his beard. Most of the prime ministers looked at me in puzzlement, as though they suspected I might be part of a recent *coup d'état* in some distant corner of the Commonwealth, but they left me alone, secure in the knowledge that, with all that pass-checking outside, I couldn't be there unless as an official delegate. The prime minister of Ceylon came up grandly and expressed the hope that Rhodesia would not be at the top of the agenda and I said I hoped it wouldn't and the president of Zambia gave us both a dirty look.

Then Pierre Trudeau spotted me, registered incredulity, and demanded: "How the hell did you get in here?" We shrugged at each other eloquently, exchanged three or four inane pleasantries ("What will you do here this morning?" "Oh, I don't know," [shrug], "What would you do?") that were one part Marx brothers, one part Peter Ustinov. Then Trudeau went off shaking his head, to seek the company of his peers. He must have reported my presence, because shortly afterwards I was abruptly ushered back out on to the street.

But by then I had seen what I had always suspected from the outside: that while all of the underdeveloped countries happily acclaimed their transition from Empire to Commonwealth (and the change in their status from colonial satellites to membership in a council of equals) they still lean heavily on British leadership and generosity, like spoiled children full of demands and ingratitudes. But the British under Harold Wilson do not have adequate political leadership themselves, or the money, to give the Commonwealth ideal any concrete meaning.

At the same time, the more mature members of the Commonwealth have either been drifting into other spheres of influence (such as Australia's close participation with the Americans in Viet Nam) or have become preoccupied with their own domestic difficulties.

And so it is becoming increasingly difficult to take the Commonwealth seriously, except as a kind of ceremonial safety valve. No one attending these meetings really expects any solution to the Rhodesian or Nigerian problems will be put forward, and it is almost as though the entire proceedings will be counted a wild triumph if only the Commonwealth survives to meet again in a year or two for yet another "civilized dialogue" without concrete result.

What emotion was evident at yesterday's opening session came not from the delegates but from the mobs of pickets, most of them black, who lined the street outside Marlborough House. It was cold and wet and the sidewalk was jammed with eccentrics, peaceniks and angry Africans straining against an impregnable line of London Bobbies. A group of South African freedom fighters, carrying lighted torches, were badgering a woman in a green feather hat who was stolidly holding up a sign that read: "Britain stands by our kinsmen in Rhodesia."

Many of the pickets were Biafrans protesting the Nigerian war, but there was at least one peacemaker in the crowd whose sign mildly proclaimed: "To keep Nigeria one is a task that must be done." The loneliest picket, who looked across the line of policemen out of great wet dark eyes, his dignity unimpaired by a deerstalker cap, was holding up a piece of cardboard on which was lettered the urgent message, "We Yorubas demand an independent Oduduwaland."

[1969]

III

WHEN A MAN BECOMES THE POLITICAL LEADER of a democratic nation the intense public scrutiny he must endure magnifies both his strengths and his weaknesses of character so that eventually an image is created which becomes his historical stereotype. For Pierre Elliott Trudeau the fourteen days he has just spent in London and Rome on his first journey abroad as prime minister speeded up this process and he stands momentarily revealed as self-willed, cautious, cold, self-protective, mysterious and autocratic.

Last year at this time, just as he was being catapulted into the Liberal leadership race, his behaviour was almost exactly the opposite – he was, or seemed to be, relaxed, radical, warm, carefree, open, and modest. (Question: "How much do you want to be prime minister, Mr. Trudeau?" Answer: "Oh, not very much.")

In the way he handled himself at the Commonwealth conference sessions, in the Westminster Theatre student teach-in, during his brief visit to Rome, and in his tirade against the press in London, Trudeau demonstrated that he regards the job of being prime minister as something quite separate from his inner sense of self. It is almost as though he gets up each morning and casts himself in the role of prime minister, putting on the various masks appropriate to the occasion. Now he is the young tweed-jacketed colonial prime minister fresh from a weekend at Chequers, discreetly charming the British press; now the dashing post-adolescent bachelor swinging into Annabel's with some pretty girl, any pretty girl, at his elbow. Now he is the professional politician slouching on stage in baggy grey pants telling the young how hard it is to be a rational man and true in the temples of power; now the disdainful disciplinarian who is going to sic the police on the vulgar press; and then the luminous statesman in morning coat, consecrated to world peace after a hushed audience with His Holiness, the Pope.

His attitude to his job is thus fragmented and almost entirely cerebral and these images, all of them, are tricks of a brilliant performer's craft. He uses power technocratically and seems to believe that he can learn to be the best prime minister that brains alone can buy. This absence of gut feeling or passion in his approach to leadership has been apparent since his election, but in London, for the first time, it let him down. It may, for example, be sound theory for a new prime minister to say little and learn much at his first Commonwealth conference. But surely a man who has been widely hailed as an exciting new kind of politician should *feel* that he has to contribute more during his debut as an international figure than his mere presence and his external affairs department's platitudes.

During these critical two weeks in London Trudeau's reputation was diminished, not only in the British press (which he handily described as "lousy," although among the papers that criticized him were the *Times,* the *Guardian* and the *Daily Telegraph,* which rank among the best in the world) but in the delegates' lounges as well. By the conference's end he was being described, as one Pakistani put it, as "the firecracker that never went off." The world stage is too crowded and events move too quickly for Trudeau's off-hand "don't-call-us, we'll-call-you" attitude toward the Commonwealth to be interpreted as anything but bored disdain.

This tactic of figuring out what the consequence of his actions ought to be and then being incapable of adjusting to what they actually are is what triggered Trudeau's feud with the press. It is inconceivable that so perceptive a man cannot realize that his unorthodox mode of personal behaviour makes him interesting to the public (and therefore the press), that at least part of the reason for his selection as Liberal leader and his victory at the polls on June 25, 1968, was the curiosity he aroused as a romantic figure devoted to women, cars and clothes. Now he wants to pretend that these things are entirely peripheral, and that he never deliberately made them elements of his public life. But what about the campaign buttons trilling "It's spring"? What about the Trudeau bunnies or whatever they were called (and their den mother with the transmitter in her bra)? What about Trudeau himself? Was he forced to display his torso in bathing trunks and obligingly do backflips into an Oakville swimming pool? Did he have to do a quick bugaloo by the roadside near Montreal while they were repairing his campaign bus? Was all that kissing inflicted on him? Or, what is more pertinent to the current disagreement: did he really have to spend his first lunch in London, only two hours before his initial meeting with Harold Wilson, with a blond adventuress who had been boasting for months that she intended to marry him?

If he really feels suddenly so inverted and shy, then why does he continue to display himself in the kind of situations he pretends to despise? If he displays himself, why is he so shocked when the press reacts and reports his activities? "Dating" in Canada and in most western societies is a phenomenon usually confined to the age group from fifteen to twenty-five, so when there appears a forty-nine-year-old prime minister who "dates" (and talks constantly about his "young ladies") it's news.

Any politician who uses personal exhibitionism for effect (as Trudeau certainly does –why else did he slide down the bannister in full evening dress at Lancaster House?) must be prepared to risk the consequences. Publicity is not a controllable commodity that can be turned off at the whim of its creator. One of the difficulties in his press feud – and he has some reason to be furious with its excesses – is the well-known fact that he has long harbored a very nearly uncontrollable disdain for most journalists. His staff treats reporters like snarling dogs to be propitiated with large bones, or if that doesn't work, as it didn't in London, large kicks. "You chaps must learn," one of his press secretaries remarked one night at Claridge's Hotel, "that Pierre's public popularity is such that he's virtually invulnerable."

That may be true, and perhaps his invulnerability will survive into the next election campaign and beyond. Trudeau is well aware that his mandate has at least four years to run, that domestic problems, particularly Ottawa-Quebec relations, must be his first priority, and that there will be other occasions for international initiatives. But what this journey demonstrated is that he has yet to learn two lessons about power: the private man must always be secondary to the public man though the electors judge both; and the public man must have some feelings, not just thoughts, about his job.

[1969]

Becoming Isolated

A S PARLIAMENT BEGINS ITS THIRD SESSION under Pierre Elliott Trudeau's leadership the enormous difference between Trudeau and his fourteen predecessors comes more sharply into focus. In the two and a half years that he has been in office, Trudeau has deliberately upset the apple carts of all those partisan interest groups who have shared for generations the political power that counts, rendering the formerly smug impotent with one cold gaze or one colder action.

In his treatment of his cabinet, his caucus, his party organization and even his own office staff, he has remained within the mould he has cast for himself – and outside the traditional behaviour patterns of prime ministers. He governs the country like the headmaster of a rigorously administered private school, ruling by fear and keeping all those nearest him – not excluding the electorate – permanently insecure.

The effect on Ottawa has been to cool the noisy crisis atmosphere of the past decade. All of the great confrontations between provincial governments, with the parliamentary Opposition and among party leadership challengers now seem outdated and irrelevant. Cabinet authority has been dispersed into so many committees and the decision-making process so fragmented that no minister except Trudeau himself has much influence on over-all government policy. With the possible exceptions of John Turner, all of Trudeau's ministers could disappear as quickly as Paul Hellyer did last year, leaving behind them hardly a ripple to show they had ever existed.

The power of the backroom boys within the Liberal party has evaporated, simply because Trudeau chooses to ignore them. He refuses to attend most party functions, or to dip deeply into the porkbarrel to find rewards for the faithful. This week's only slightly partisan Senate appointments must have shattered a thousand veteran Grits' happy dreams. By undercutting the influence of most of the traditional party power brokers, Trudeau has retained only one indispensable man: himself.

When Keith Davey was the Liberals' chief organizer during the Pearson years, the whole country knew of his exploits. But who has ever even heard the name of Torrance Wylie, the man who now has Davey's job? Trudeau's relationship with John Nichol, the bright young senator from British Columbia who managed his 1968 election campaign, is now described by a close acquaintance as "non-existent."

Another source of Trudeau's strength is that unlike most prime ministers, who gather around themselves a kitchen cabinet of political cronies, he functions as his own brain trust. It is a cliche in Ottawa these days that he relies exclusively for advice on what insiders call his "French chapel": Regional Development Minister Jean Marchand, Secretary of State Gerard Pelletier and principal secretary Marc Lalonde. But the fact is (and these three men admit it) that nobody, but nobody, tells Trudeau what to do.

Compassion is a quality which has not cast much of a shadow on the interior landscape of Canada's fifteenth prime minister. Trudeau in office has behaved like some abstracted actor whose cool eyes detach themselves from whatever is happening around him, never allowing it to ravage his emotions.

There are moments in every political career when mind is not enough, when passion must clamour up and make a leader more than a guest of his time. Trudeau seems constantly to be creating his own reality, retreating ever deeper into the mantle of enigma which he wraps like some dark burnous around his actions.

The prime minister has a shimmering intellect; he is one of the most resolute political leaders this country has ever had. But in his tendency to stifle dissent there is a deep fallacy that may yet prove tragic for Canada. Tolerating dissent is an essential means by which a society comes to terms with change. The prime minister and his inner court seem to believe that they can impose logic on events; that they can govern the country through legalism and reshape events to fit those legalisms. But the events themselves – history, in other words – are not logical; they are born out of harsh realities and even harder emotions which cannot be cut to fit a leader's wishes.

Politics in Canada has always been the art of making the necessary possible. This process depends for its success on a leader's ability to mix a genuine infection of the spirit with negotiating skill and a creative urge to heal. But Trudeau has projected a kind of personal impertinence, a feeling that he cares more for what he *is* than what he represents. In effect, Trudeau is perpetuating the good old Liberal ethic which holds that the chief function of government is to defend and refine a set of bureaucratic routines. He seems to view social problems in terms of efficient management rather than as the inevitable outcome of unequal wealth. This creates what Charles Abrams, the American housing expert, has described as "socialism for the rich and capitalism for the poor" – a system that doesn't satisfy either group.

Too often, Trudeau and his inner circle have equated the slightest sign of dissent with disloyalty or stupidity or worse. The prime minister gives the impression of believing that he and his inner court of advisors (who gaze upon the world as if they were inhabitants of the walled-off Chinese city of Cathay before Marco Polo came) have a monopoly on truth. But in a democracy, the minority's dissent is no less important than the majority's consent.

Perhaps the prime minister is suffering from the conflict that faces every intellectual who enters the world of politics, for it is a world oriented toward different ultimate values than the one he was used to: the intellectual seeks truth; the politician, power. Yet, truth distilled from many viewpoints has a message that can never become irrelevant to the exercise of power. Before he became prime minister, Trudeau traveled the country on the slogan that he was seeking "new guys with new ideas." Now he behaves as though he wanted "the same guys with the same ideas" – the same as his own.

[1971]

Reflections on a Fall from Grace

I CAN REMEMBER A JULY EVENING IN 1968, *sitting around a polished pine table in a refurbished farmhouse near Ottawa with a little knot of people from the capital – a couple of journalists, a civil servant, a television producer, and a scientist of vaguely radical leanings – eating curry, drinking sangria, and talking politics. To talk politics 'that summer meant you talked about Pierre Trudeau and, as the conversation buzzed excitedly on, somebody mentioned a French book he had just been reading called* The Morning Of The Magicians *and then put forward, not entirely tentatively, the theory that Trudeau was a kind of magician. We were all pretty deep into the Spanish red and the clover-laden nightfall, but all the same we weren't that far gone, and what seems astonishing now is that nobody hooted with derision, nobody laughed the man out of the room. In fact, his suggestion was considered with respect and one or two people even resolved to buy the book next day and try to fit Trudeau's perfections into its tortured theory about the kind of political sorcerer needed to transcend the complexities of the twentieth century.*

I haven't thought about that scene for years – it seems in a way to belong to another lifetime – but flying home from the west on the morning after this fall's extraordinary election it kept flashing into my mind. And in its wake came a number of questions that must have been troubling a lot of Canadians that day: "What happened to the magic? Or more important, what happened to the man? Did he ever possess the qualities we endowed him with? Had he been altered by power? Why didn't he turn into the leader we had been yearning for and so many of us were sure he really was?"

90

These questions were answered during the post-election confusion in a variety of ways. The sour naysayers and hindsight seers were quick to point out that they had never been so foolish as to be taken in by Trudeau in the first place and he delivered what they expected, which was not much. The blind loyalists maintained either that the election results indicated an ugly bigotry against French power in Ottawa or that the failure had been not Trudeau's at all but a simpler one of communication lag; his achievements had not been put across to the dingbats in the heartland.

But to those who didn't belong to either camp, myself among them, who were simply trying to figure out what had really happened, it was plain that the campaign had been a referendum on Pierre Trudeau. A referendum that he lost.

The more that loss was discussed by Trudeau's friends, opponents, intimates and critics, the more apparent it became that the election result was due to one central fact: Trudeau had committed the cardinal sin for a politician, he had lost touch with his constituency. He functioned during his first fifty-four months in office as the head of a government and not the leader of a nation. He didn't understand Canadians and their concerns. And what was worse, he did not appear to care.

His fall from grace is all the sadder – and all the more demeaning to him and the people who believed in him – because he once seemed to possess in ample measure the attributes necessary for greatness. He had the intellect, the nationwide mandate for his crusade to unite the country, the charisma to attract the best minds to his cause, the wit to leaven the burdens of office. But as prime minister he displayed one fatal flaw. He was guilty of what the ancient Greeks called *hubris* or overweening pride. It was a flaw that rendered him incapable of responding to any sensibility but his own. He would not listen to his critics in the Commons. He paid no heed to the MPs in his own caucus. He stifled the dissenters in his cabinet. He scorned the professionals in his party. He ignored the spoken and written pleas of citizens who sought to focus his attention on their concerns. So that in the end he could only be forced to listen by the voice that really counts in a democracy: the verdict of the ballot box.

When you look back, his four and a half years in office unfold like a drama with Trudeau as the willful hero trapped in a vacuum of his own making. As the circles of isolation grew around him it was almost as though he was alienated even from himself and from the very purpose that had catapulted him into power. He moved through his first term in office like a Sun King in a latter-day Versailles, surrounded by courtiers whose chatter he mistook for the sound of reality.

The minority situation Trudeau found himself in at the end of October, 1972, had its origins in a theory of government he formulated nearly seven years before. When he was a freshman MP from Mount Royal during the last blundering phase of the Pearson government, a group of men would meet in his office every Thursday for what might have been called a bull session if the company had been less rarefied. They were all intellectuals like himself, the "new guys with new ideas" he spoke of so admiringly when he sought the Liberal leadership later. Most of them had observed the machinations of power from the sidelines for years as assistant deputies or young lawyers working on constitutional reform or executive assistants covering up ministerial mistakes. They were convinced Pearson's embarrassments proved that the old politics was dead, that the bureaucratic mandarins were obsolete and that a government should be run with the modern administrative techniques originated by the Harvard Business School. Nobody had yet labelled them technocrats but the essence of their approach was emotional cool, implacable momentum, and dedication to abstract principle. They saw public service as the reduction of issues to manageable proportions and unconsciously modeled themselves on McGeorge Bundy, a White House adviser, who once explained that "man's real motivating force is the simple, natural, almost unexaminable human desire to do something really well."

When Trudeau swept into office in the spring of 1968, he kept these highly theoretical conversations in mind and determined that he was going to replace all the inept, old-fashioned, fumbling, politicking human beings who traditionally surrounded the seat of power with a new breed of perfectionist – and replace them he did, in many cases with members of the old Thursday Club. In doing so, he set up what his critics soon started to call a parallel government in the East Block. (By 1972, he employed on his personal staff and in the Privy Council Office four hundred and fifteen people for an annual budget of $11 million, three times as much as Pearson spent on his advisers and fifteen times as much as Diefenbaker.) Trudeau got himself so entangled in the process of government that he spent fifty hours a week at meetings of one kind or another. In trying to bypass one bureaucracy, he created another and unwittingly became its victim.

It is important to assess the group of people who surrounded him in terms of those it excluded as well as those it included. "Within six

92

months of coming to office," said an old friend later, "Trudeau had truncated all of his outside sources of intelligence. There wasn't one guy in his entourage you could call an agitator, nobody who really had political moxie or was willing to remind Trudeau that he was human and therefore fallible. It was a court without a jester."

Two of the men who were quickly excluded from the prime ministerial presence happened to have the shrewdest political minds he had been in contact with; both of them were open, funny, responsive, and sufficiently realistic to understand that listening to other people's opinions did not mean that you had abandoned your own. They were Eddie Rubin, Trudeau's twenty-seven-year-old former special assistant in the justice department and a key strategist in his leadership drive, and Senator John Nichol, president of the Liberal Federation of Canada and organizer of the victorious 1968 election. It was Rubin who put down a thousand dollars of his own money as rent on Trudeau's leadership campaign office, and it was Rubin that Trudeau turned to and hugged in that first emotional moment at the Liberal convention after John Nichol announced his victory. Rubin and Nichol were frozen out by the PM's indifference before the end of his first summer in office, and by the beginning of 1969 he had cut off a score of other friends, in essence anyone who still felt close enough to him to commit the transgression of probing his infallibility.

Most of the men who did fit the Trudeau style of technocratic government were alike. They were highly educated, nearly all of them at great universities abroad. (There were six Oxford men in Trudeau's closest circle, three of them Rhodes Scholars.) Most belonged to the monied strata of the urban east, several had spent their working lives outside the country in embassies or international agencies, and, with rare exceptions, they were all bent on ridding themselves of any taint of provincialism. "They treated people who existed outside the Ottawa-Montreal axis as though they belonged in colonial outposts and were always afraid somebody was going to dump the tea into Vancouver harbour," said one of the few powerful people in Ottawa with a genuine feel for the country.

Trudeau's chief of staff was Marc Lalonde, an Oxford graduate and former law professor at the University of Montreal. Lalonde stood out in the entourage as a man who fully subscribed to the PM's technocratic principles but who managed at the same time to keep himself rooted to certain basic realities. His family had farmed land on Île Perrot off the southern tip of Montreal Island for three hundred years and Lalonde

93

never lost his peasant shrewdness. ("I'm a Norman farmer," he was heard to say more than once. "It's like being from Missouri.") Lalonde was tough, undazzled by social fripperies or intellectual pyrotechnics, and he had an understanding of Quebec politics that was visceral as well as cerebral. But he never pretended to know what made the rest of Canada tick and it was to Trudeau's great disadvantage that his staff didn't include an English equivalent of Lalonde.

Next to Lalonde, probably the most influential men in the PMO were Jim Davey and Ivan Head. An Oxford graduate in physics, Davey is an introvert, pale, compulsively hardworking, given to talking about such things as "reality consciousness" and to believing there are few human needs that cannot be reduced to one of his colored graphs or "critical path flows." Davey's charts were locked in a war room to which only people whose names were inscribed on a secret list were admitted. Both he and Ivan Head wrote speeches for Trudeau that were, as one disgruntled Liberal complained, "not speeches at all but monographs for papers to be published in *Foreign Affairs.*" Head is a Harvard graduate and former law professor, who became a kind of non-swinging sub-Arctic Henry Kissinger, flying the world on behalf of the prime minister, and bypassing apoplectic officials from the Department of External Affairs while he was at it.

Other key staff members were L. D. Hudon, a Quebec City economist, who functioned as deputy secretary (operations) of cabinet and had spent most of the previous twenty years on various economic assignments at Canadian embassies abroad and with the International Bank for Reconstruction and Development in Washington; Gordon Gibson, a millionaire's son from Vancouver whose imaginative policy ideas were muted by the sound of louder voices and who finally decided he might be more influential as a member of the House of Commons; and Tim Porteous, a graduate of the University of Paris and member of a distinguished old family from English Montreal. Porteous worked as a writer of policy papers and speeches and once inspired a journalist to say, after interviewing him, "My God, JAMM is running the country." (JAMM is the Junior Associates of the Museum of Montreal, a group of social devotees of art and dowdy chic which gives an annual fundraising party called Strawberries and Champagne that turns Westmount pink with pleasure.)

The regime's most influential public servants were Gordon Robertson, the clerk of the Privy Council, and Michael Pitfield, deputy secretary (plans) of the cabinet. Robertson arrived in Ottawa from Montreal in 1941, served as Mackenzie King's secretary, and became the lord high mandarin in 1963. Although he epitomized the passion-drained competence of the old bureaucracy, Robertson was sufficiently adaptable, compatible (he too was an Oxford man) and knowledgeable to become part of the magic circle. ("The thing I like best about Robertson," Trudeau told a friend, "is that when I come in first thing in the morning he presents me with a series of answers to questions I didn't even know had been raised.") Pitfield, the son of a Montreal financier, was a different matter. Young, rich, brilliant (he was probably Trudeau's only intellectual peer in the whole operation), he had a social conscience that sat oddly on his elegant frame. He went on holidays with Trudeau to Spain, Mexico, and Yugoslavia and because of this, and his disdain for people he felt weren't "gentlemen," he was thought in Ottawa to have a Machiavellian influence with the PM which he himself disclaimed.

Every morning at 9:30 the prime minister conferred with Robertson, Lalonde, Hudon, and Peter Roberts, his press secretary. Roberts was also a Rhodes Scholar who came to Trudeau's office after fifteen years abroad as an officer with external affairs, years that had wiped out all trace of his Alberta origins. Apparently chosen because of his compatibility with the PM rather than with the press, he treated all but the most sycophantic reporters as "a crummy lot" (as Trudeau publicly described them) and made enemies for his boss with effortless grace. Roberts' predecessor, Romeo LeBlanc, now a Liberal MP from New Brunswick, was better at the job but he was hampered too by the PM's disdain for the press. LeBlanc once confessed to a friend, "I go in there every morning shaking and if I try in any way to put forward a reporter's point of view, Trudeau cuts me down. I sometimes feel as though I ought to walk in bowing and back out in deference as soon as I'm dismissed." The only person in the Trudeau press operation with a genuine sympathy for reporters was Vic Chapman, a former pass receiver and kicker with the B.C. Lions and Edmonton Eskimos, a man with a husky voice, a boxer's face and a warm heart. Relegated to functioning as a kind of baggagemaster and cattle prodder on the PM's press tours, Chapman was sealed off from real influence with the Trudeau inner circle. Flying back from the official tour of Russia in 1971, he answered a reporter's complaint about Trudeau's inaccessibility with the feeling remark, "Listen, I can't do a damn thing about it. Those guys don't have any respect for my intellect. They think I'm a bull."

Inside Trudeau's Ottawa knowledge was power, and most of his aides acted as though the very time of day were a state secret to be entrusted only to certain high-minded and certifiably serious officials. The East Block bought a heavy-duty paper shredder which could handle up to a ton an hour of what was called "classified waste." The blanket of secrecy even smothered departmental studies that had always been in the public domain, such as the background papers for Edgar Benson's white paper on taxation and J. J. Greene's studies on Canadian oil reserves. "Goddamit, my tax money paid for those studies," a Toronto businessman wrote in a fury to the PM's office, "and I'd like to know by what divine right you can keep them from being published."

Fortified by de Gaulle's famous dictum that "nothing enhances authority more than silence," Trudeau's men saw themselves as belonging to an elite with little obligation to spend time on or with lesser people. Most of them were not exactly born snobs, but once they got into power they were overwhelmed by what is known in India as *darshan* – a blessing Hindus believe is bestowed on them through being near a great person, a kind of drugless high that comes only in the presence of an exalted maharaja or guru. To them, Trudeau was both.

The source of their own power was access. Access not only to the most inaccessible of prime ministers but, equally important, to control over which policy proposals would or would not be presented to full cabinet. Each minister's legislative ideas had to be submitted to the East Block contingent who would then decide which cabinet committee to send them to and when to bring them forward for cabinet consideration. Since all the cabinet committees were staffed by the East Block managers, they could easily pigeonhole some legislation (for example, many of John Turner's initiatives in justice; Trudeau's people didn't want him to top their man's record in the portfolio) and push the issues they thought really mattered to the PM. That usually meant policies on federal-provincial relations or some bill dealing with the process of government.

Theoretically, the cabinet should have been a counterweight to all this introspection. Most ministers were as much under the spell of Trudeau's assumption of superiority as his advisers since they owed their presence around the Privy Council table to his popularity. In any case, they were what A. R. M. Lower, the Queen's University historian, once described when he was writing about another Liberal cabinet, "Whigs: people who in general were on the side of righteousness, took a benevolent attitude towards it but felt no urge to advance interests other than their own or those with which they identified themselves." Cabinet undertook to run the affairs of the nation as inevitably and unquestionably as though it were its ordained role and natural task.

Trudeau allowed his ministers a fairly free hand in the running of their departments, but cabinet authority was dispersed into so many committees that only the PM and his immediate entourage could exercise any real influence on over-all government policy. He conducted cabinet meetings like Jesuit seminars, encouraging ministers to criticize each others' proposals, not imposing his views on others but allowing them instead to find their own way to his convictions.

These mental gymnastics muffled the effectiveness of progressive politicians in the room, notably Robert Andras and Eric Kierans, and rendered totally silent other ministers unsure of their dialectic ability. "You were always listened to with great respect, but nothing would ever happen," Kierans complained after he resigned in the spring of 1971. "You know, when the Pope gets down off the altar at St. Peter's and walks down the aisle, the one thing you're sure of is that he's going to get to the other end. You can argue and argue, but the procession always goes on its way."

The only ministers who were part of Trudeau's inner circle were Otto Lang, yet another Rhodes Scholar and former dean of law at the University of Saskatchewan, and Charles Mills "Bud" Drury. A man with a stiff code of ethics and an Ottawa background dating back to World War II, when he was the youngest brigadier in the Canadian army, Drury's politics were so rigidly conservative that he considered anyone to the left of Pope John a dangerous radical. It was Drury who kept rationalizing away the country's spiraling unemployment statistics, telling anyone who would listen that the numbers did not mean what they used to mean because they merely reflected the decline of the work ethic. According to Drury, anybody who wanted employment could find a job.

Even stranger than his treatment of cabinet was Trudeau's response to his caucus of Liberal MPs. Normally, even the most self-assured of prime ministers realizes that his loyal troops in the Commons are a source of personal support and of hard information. Trudeau didn't seem to want either from his backbenchers. He imposed new regulations on the weekly caucus that effectively cut off the free interchange of ideas. MPs were limited to discussing items on a prearranged agenda and even then they could not talk for more than three minutes and only if they had their names on the caucus chairman's list. At one point, when there was a severe economic crisis in the country, the topic under discussion was recognition of the Vatican and nobody had the nerve to suggest that this nicety be put aside for a calmer time. "The average MP is useless as teats on a bull," said Phil Givens, a former mayor of Toronto, when he became one of six Liberal MPs who quit the federal party in disgust.

Trudeau believed he could bypass the unaesthetic ramblings of the caucus and get at the heart of the country by setting up regional desks in the East Block. He seemed blissfully unaware that people don't talk to "desks." After the original organizer, Pierre Levasseur, left in 1969, the scheme turned into a feed-out of praise and rationalization for the PM's programs: little hard data came in.

What was more damaging than any of this to the prime minister's public image was his open arrogance in the Commons. Whenever Robert Stanfield got up to ask a question, they would sit there, row upon row of Liberal ministers, hooting with derisive laughter, looking not like sober men conducting the nation's business but like a clutch of obnoxious prefects from the upper forms of some expensive private school, sneering at a drudge. And in their midst sat their leader, the existential hero, clad in a dark suit from London, a yellow rose from the Governor-General's greenhouse and an air of elegant boredom, turning his attackers off with quips, *non sequiturs,* and historical allusions. He complained about "the whiny demands of the Opposition" and put everybody down, making fun of their pretension in questioning his wisdom. He acted as if he really believed (as he said in the Commons on July 24, 1969) that Opposition MPs were "nobodies," a fairly risky assumption since even after the 1968 election the opposition side of the House represented 54 per cent of Canadian voters. Trudeau was just as rude to MPs outside the House. After his son was born on Christmas Day, 1971, one of the most popular MPs in the House, a Conservative from the Maritimes, decided to send Trudeau a congratulatory wire. He went down to his local telegraph office only to find that the operator, a staunch Tory, was prepared to give him a hot fight about transmitting the message. The MP finally persuaded her to send it anyway and filed the episode away in his mind as a wryly amusing, if apt, reflection of his riding's political style. A few weeks later, back in Ottawa, he saw Trudeau at a cocktail party, and thinking the PM might be amused as well he went over to tell him what happened. Trudeau stared back at

98

him, bored beyond endurance, and said offhandedly, "Oh, I never saw any of the wires. There were so many hundreds, we decided not to be bothered."

Still, none of this would have mattered very much if Trudeau had not allowed himself the most dangerous alienation of all – that from his own party apparatus. His 1968 victory which he more or less won on his own, confirming his long-standing suspicion that party organization played a vastly overrated role in the political life of the country. Because he had never experienced the chastening apprenticeship of a period in opposition, he could not understand that a party's organizational apparatus is an essential part of the fabric of any prime minister's power. From June 1968 to early 1972 he deliberately ignored the party regulars, refused to attend most party functions and failed to recognize the need for powerful proconsuls of the breed that had kept Mackenzie King in office for such a long time by bringing back to Ottawa word of what was really happening in their domains of influence. There was no one in his orbit like Jimmy Gardiner, Jack Pickersgill, James Ilsley, or Chubby Power, except perhaps Paul Martin, and he was consulted only rarely. (In the mid-Twenties Chubby Power used to spend his weekends touring the taverns of the poor sections of Quebec City, drinking five-cent glasses of beer and listening to people's beefs. When King once objected that cabinet ministers shouldn't be seen in taverns, Power replied, "Listen, if you want my resignation, I'll write it. But I won't give up the taverns and I bet I'll win my seat in the next election and you won't win yours." Which was exactly what happened.) In brief, Trudeau did not have, either in his office, his cabinet, or out in the country, a single political crony other than those from Quebec who functioned on their own. In English Canada, he was left with a party structure that had only one all-powerful presence. Himself.

At the beginning of 1972, when he realized that it was soon going to be constitutionally necessary to hold an election to settle what he described as "all the little piddling questions," he assumed that the party machine could be kicked into high gear by the simple act of offering himself for re-election. What he didn't know was that the machine was rusty from neglect.

For four years he had nurtured a basic misapprehension of the Canadian party system. The two old-line parties especially are loose aggregations of like-minded people who commit themselves to working in a campaign with little reward except the promise of some fun and the vicarious thrill of being close to power. These people are held together, ready to commit their all, by what John Nichol once called "psychic patronage": they know a guy who knows a guy who can talk to the PM.

When Nichol was running the Liberal party in the mid-Sixties, he would continually take soundings across the country, listening to constituency complaints before they were magnified into rebellious indifference. He was endlessly willing to sympathize with the self-important bores who infest any political organization and, like his predecessor, Keith Davey, he made politics fun. Nichol and Davey both had a network of workers across the country they would call for daily or weekly gossip sessions, dropping Ottawa rumours here and there, making everyone feel he was an insider and getting back a fairly accurate accounting of just what was going on in the country. This is what a party machine is in a democracy: a network of guys who talk to each other. And this is what Trudeau destroyed with his notion that politics ought to be intellectually satisfying or morally important at all times. He and his staff considered talking to all those cats out there meowing their little songs of complaint as a boring waste of time.

Liberal loyalty (i.e., appetite for power) being what it is, the party regulars rallied to the first soundings of the election horn last spring, but they rallied halfheartedly and functioned throughout the campaign as one of them said, "at about 40 per cent capacity." Whatever enthusiasm they could mount was dampened by the PM's indifference. At one campaign communications committee meeting held in Ottawa on April 25, several party regulars gave voice to their misapprehensions about Trudeau's methods. The consensus of the gathering, chaired by Toronto advertising executive George Elliott, was that Trudeau had to dispel the notion that his government constituted a "smug majority," that he was not really very interested in the country's problems or his job. One suggestion made was that on the day the election writ was issued, a telegram be sent out under Trudeau's name to the party's fifty thousand key workers, simply saying "I NEED YOU." (The idea, which was too emotional to appeal to Trudeau, was never followed up.) The committee's most important recommendation was that the party fashion a dozen specific "hard-edged" policy pronouncements that would clearly set out the directions of the Liberal government during the next four years. This was to become a kind of electoral version of a speech from the Throne, stressing the importance of a national debate on the bread-and-butter issues.

But when Trudeau finally called the election, on September 1, he

100

ignored their advice entirely. During one of his first forays outside Ottawa, to address Ontario party workers, he described the campaign as not a fight with the opposition but "a dialogue between ourselves and the people." He seemed to forget that a democratic election is not a royal procession or a teach-in, but a struggle for power, a clash of ideas, personalities, and perceptions of the future. He projected no notion of where his ideas might lead. Instead of taking the public into his confidence and discussing the many real issues facing the country, he acted like some bored sophisticate distractedly telling the masses that everything was fine because he was in charge and they could all go back to sleep again.

Trudeau went into the campaign believing that his popularity was undiminished. (Months before when an old friend suggested to him that there were signs of discontent in the electorate, he strode over to his office window and pointed to the autograph seekers waiting at the East Block door and said, "See that? It happens every day, people wait for hours just to watch me get into my car.") He was sustained in this illusion by the polls (which could not show how many of the "undecided" were really undeclared anti-Trudeau voters), as well as the crowds of cheering children and party workers who were turned out everywhere he went.

As the Liberal campaign unfolded in September and October, it soon became apparent that it lacked both strategy and content. In most previous elections, the party had taken positions on issues that set it off from its rivals. Out of this basic strategy flowed all tactics, policies, itineraries and advertising. Trudeau decided simply to ask the voters to trust him. During a pre-election dinner at 24 Sussex Drive, which the PM was persuaded to hold for his provincial campaign chairmen, most of whom he hadn't seen for four years, Senator George van Roggen of British Columbia was particularly adamant in urging him to prepare some answers to the unemployment issue and to establish a prices and incomes policy. But Trudeau put him down with a stern lecture on the kind of high-minded campaign he intended to run.

Instead of strategy and issues, the Liberals had a slogan, THE LAND IS STRONG, coined by George Elliott. It reflected perfectly the lulling effect Trudeau's campaign was intended to have. Probably no Canadian party has ever fought an election on a less meaningful slogan – though that might have been the case if Elliott's first version, A DIRECTION FOR CANADA, had been adopted. When he presented that gem to the campaign committee one of its right-wing members passed a scribbled note

101

to a friend suggesting an alternative: FROM THOSE WONDERFUL FOLKS WHO GAVE YOU BENSON, BASFORD, AND MACKASEY. Although few Liberals took THE LAND IS STRONG theme seriously (Alberta campaign chairman Blair Williams even refused to use it in his advertising campaigns), only John Turner had the courage to question it in public. "I've used it once in the whole campaign," he told a group of students at the University of Winnipeg on October 20, "and that was to see if I could get it out without breaking up." The only cabinet minister who effectively dealt with the bread-and-butter issues on the hustings was Bryce Mackasey.

It was Trudeau's program secretary, Jim Davey, who thought up the complementary "national integrity" approach, though the wispy references to it in Trudeau's speeches were written by Ivan Head. "When Davey and Head concoct a speech," said one Liberal organizer, "they aren't thinking about an audience in an arena, they're thinking about a seminar full of their peers. The fact that there aren't, thank God, any more than a couple of thousand such people across the whole country has never occurred to them." At times, the Davey-Head sense of audience verged on the bizarre. When local Liberals mounted a rally in Edmonton and broke their backs trucking in busloads of people from local old-age homes, the ancients sat in their wheelchairs with uncomprehending stares as the PM launched into a discourse about the importance of physical fitness. In Hamilton, Trudeau delivered a lecture on the social implications of the decline in the work ethic before a lunchpail audience of steelworkers.

And everywhere that Trudeau went, he would add to his lengthening list of insults, so that by the end of the campaign the semaphore of his smile transmitted not reassurance but the assumption of superiority. In Winnipeg, when a heckler, fed up with Trudeau's easy dismissal of unemployment, shouted: "Don't insult our intelligence!" Trudeau replied: "I'll speak at a lower level, perhaps you'll understand me then." When he was on an open-line radio show at Wingham, Ontario, and made a donnish joke about his relations with God ("I can talk to Him in a familiar tone and He hasn't objected so far") it was uncomfortably reminiscent of another comment Trudeau had made as far back as the spring of 1968. A reporter asked him when he intended to call an election, and he had replied: "In God's good time, whenever *I* feel it is best."

Probably the most cynical phase of the Liberal campaign was the series of announcements that Trudeau himself referred to as "election

102

goodies," including the $30 million plan to develop the Toronto waterfront and the $5 million scheme to establish a wood products industry at Cabano, Quebec. This was the very kind of electoral opportunism, practiced crudely in the Fifties by Maurice Duplessis in Quebec, that Trudeau was supposed to have gone into politics to reform.

But the single factor that hurt Trudeau's campaign the most was his failure to comprehend how much the high level of prices and unemployment was really hurting voters. In his proud tower he had psyched himself into believing that the economic state of the country was nothing to worry about. Trudeau's advisers had been relying all along on the old "trade-off" approach which holds that there is a direct relationship between unemployment and inflation. According to this theory, if government fiscal and monetary policies create enough unemployment, eventually this will take the pressure off wage demands (because of the availability of alternate labour) and this in turn will reduce the over-all demand for goods so that businesses will hold down their price increases and break the inflation psychology. Despite some solid advice to the contrary from the Economic Council of Canada (which repeatedly documented that unemployment and inflation are not necessarily at opposite ends of a seesaw) and the warnings of such independent economists as Senator Maurice Lamontagne and Dr. O. J. Firestone, the government persisted in deliberately fostering a shortage of jobs to hold down rising prices. On June 28, 1970, when Trudeau was questioned about his policy on the CTV program W-5, he replied: "I'm not really trying to govern in order to be re-elected. . . . If the Canadian people don't like it, you know, they can lump it."

Despite this tough attitude and the staggering loss of jobs and industrial output that resulted from it, inflation was, in fact, never conquered. Between September, 1971 and September, 1972 food prices, for example, increased by 9.7 per cent. At the same time, the unemployment rate continued to hover over 6 per cent and mid-way through the campaign it reached 7.1 per cent. This meant that the number of Canadians reporting themselves either out of work or in manpower retraining programs totaled about 627,640 – an army of jobless that nearly equaled the full-strength complement of men and women enrolled in Canada's World War II active-service forces. Still, Trudeau went on believing that economic conditions did not constitute an important issue; his advisers kept at bay anyone who tried to tell him otherwise.

During the four-day break from campaigning Trudeau took in early

October, Jim Davey met in Ottawa with a subcommittee of the Liberal party's campaign organization for a progress report. He was astounded to find himself the target of a barrage of discontent about the lack of substance in the PM's speeches, about his offhand insults, and the fact that no new policies to deal with unemployment had emerged from the campaign. Davey cut off the complaints with a twenty-minute harangue. "I don't want to hear any more of this negative talk," a Liberal strategist remembers him saying. "We're not going to allow the prime minister to descend to the grubby level of discussing unemployment. He's having a dialogue with the people about the Canadian identity." Marie Gibeault, president of the Women's Liberal Federation of Canada, was on the verge of tears after Davey's lecture. "Who do you think you are?" she asked. "We're all loyal Liberals. Why do you question our motives?"

After the meeting broke up, Bob Andras, the Thunder Bay cabinet minister who was co-chairman of the campaign, went to the PM and complained about the inept advice Trudeau had been getting from those around him. Trudeau became intensely angry and said, "Stop attacking my staff." From that moment on there was a definite split between the mood of the party regulars and the attitude of the PM's entourage. The old hands figured the game was over, though they went doggedly on with their tasks, all the while making weak jokes about this being the only non-campaign in history that had peaked too soon. (David Greenspan, a former vice-president of the Ontario Liberal Party, came astonishingly close in his predictions of the outcome, while B.C.'s John Nichol and Mel Hurtig in Alberta were deeply uneasy about their regions and felt in their bones what would happen and why.)

But the PM's men marched happily forward. Jim Davey was betting his colleagues that Trudeau would win 172 seats and Dave Thomson, head of the western regional desk in the East Block, sat in an Edmonton living room ten days before the election and forecast a majority of 170 seats, including five from Alberta. They continued to act as though Trudeau were some kind of prince; they cosseted him, encouraging him to take time out from the campaign for afternoon sleeps (which were called "government business" on his official itinerary). They protected him from all the rude intruders with their unpalatable messages, continuing to believe that his mystic bond with the voters would hold.

What they didn't know was that the morning of the magicians was over. [1972]

104

PART THREE *Survivors*

Eric Kierans

HIS EYES HAVE THAT POACHED-EGG LOOK of permanent fatigue, he holds the lowest cabinet rank in Ottawa and has yet to create for himself a permanent foothold within the federal Liberal hierarchy. But in a cabinet advertised as being dominated by young swingers, Eric Kierans, at 54, is the only minister who has taken Pierre Trudeau at his word, demonstrating that he is not afraid to challenge the established order of things, to articulate ideas calculated to stimulate national debate on vital issues.

"Pierre has denied that each time he makes a remark he does so with the infallibility of a pope," says Kierans. "Since he's rejected the purple, that puts me down somewhere among the assistant curates. But even an assistant curate can think and that's what I propose to do."

Eric William Kierans is a deceptive quantity on first encounter. His open face, stocky build and plain manner make the uninitiated observer wonder what the excitement is all about. It is only when he begins to expound some pet theory or to talk about Quebec's or Canada's future that the real man emerges. His forehead creases with excitement and his words tumble out, a mixture of fatalism and utopian fervor. He is possessed by a strong streak of existentialism, rare in Catholics. He feels that when a challenge of any major proportions exists, he destroys a part of himself if he runs away from it.

All this adds up to a barely subdued tension that draws other men to him, especially when it is felt in small groups. His political style is to discard the protocol in any given circumstance for an examination of the fundamentals involved. This was true in 1965 when, as Quebec's acting minister of national revenue, he wrote to the United States

107

secretary of the treasury, Henry Fowler, to protest Washington's guidelines on foreign investments, and it is true now.

Over the past few weeks he has publicly set out a strong anti-NATO position and plans to speak out on other issues as they arise. Kierans' outspoken views have angered some of his wary colleagues. "The boys have become distrustful of Eric," says one of his fellow ministers. "No member of the cabinet likes to have some guy play with the angels at his expense. It's a delicate enough job running a department without having a devil's advocate in your own cabinet." Kierans flatly rejects the idea that he is only stirring up political trouble. "Hell," he says, "foreign policy and defence are wide-open issues that affect everybody in Canada. If a particular view like mine doesn't prevail it would simply mean that I haven't been able to sell it and therefore that it's a lack on my part or that Canadians aren't really interested in the issue. The trouble is that in foreign policy for the greater part of Confederation we've followed a line that hasn't been particularly Canadian. First it was British and since World War II, it's been American." As an alternative to NATO Kierans advocates the rechanneling of Canada's defence expenditures into the establishment of a permanent United Nations peacekeeping force and a generally increased foreign aid effort: "Expo demonstrated just how rich was the array of talent we can find among ourselves. The question, the choice to be made, is how we can best exploit such areas of expertise for ourselves, but far more important, for others."

Kierans is also the only Trudeau minister who still publicly supports the objectives of the Watkins report on foreign investment but he admits economic nationalism has become a difficult issue on which to arouse public opinion. Inside cabinet he is a firm advocate of the Canada Development Corporation as "an instrument for helping to rationalize Canadian industry."

Always a moderate, Kierans admits that the Trudeau administration is temporarily at least following a conservative line. "It's like a business," he says. "For four or five years you expand like mad and get the banks pretty edgy about the way your overdrafts and loans are mounting up and then when you decide you're going to retrench and make yourself more liquid, the banks begin wondering why you're not using their facilities." Kierans is part of a government pledged to the creation of a "just society" and attempting to do so by the methods of business administration, but he recognizes the conflict between the measurable impact of efficiency and the idea of justice, which is only a

108

concept, an idea, a wish even. He predicts that the protection of humanism will require the acceptance of a certain amount of inefficiency and is fond of quoting David Hume, the eighteenth-century philosopher, who wrote: "Men cannot change their natures. All they can do is change their situations."

"Our problem may be," he says, "that the challenges we face are of such magnitude that we will have to change not only our situation but, to some degree, our natures."

[1968]

J. Watson MacNaught

IT IS A GOOD INDICATION OF HOW DISILLUSIONED Ottawa has become
with the Liberals' so-called "new politics" that no one here was very
upset or surprised when Lester Pearson last week once again used
loyalty to the Liberal party as his criterion in appointing the latest batch
of senators.

What did anger Ottawa insiders was the appointment of J. Watson
MacNaught as chairman of the Dominion Coal Board. This resentment
was based on the feeling that naming partisans to the Senate, where they
can do little harm to the governmental process, may be commonplace,
but it becomes a matter of concern when a failed politician is placed in
a responsible position within the public service, where competence and
knowledge, not party affiliation, should be the decisive factors.

J. Watson MacNaught has seldom demonstrated either quality. He
is a gentle nonentity from Summerside, Prince Edward Island, who
richly earned a reputation as the Liberal government's least effective
minister and was known by the irreverent in his party as "J. Watson
MacZero."

Pearson's appointment of MacNaught demonstrates a strange approach to the public service from a man who was, for twenty years, one
of its most distinguished members. Even John Diefenbaker, who
strongly believed in rewarding his faithful followers, was much more
circumspect about making appointments of this nature. He did name a
former MP (A. D. McPhillips) to be a member, though not chairman of
the Tariff Board. But in 1961 when the Conservatives had to pick a new
chairman for the Dominion Coal Board, Diefenbaker chose Colin
Lewis O'Brien, a forty-year veteran of the public service, and author of
many technical papers on coal and energy.

While chairmanship of the Dominion Coal Board is hardly one of Ottawa's more important positions, it is not a trivial appointment either. The chairman (paid $20,500 annually, which is $5,500 more than a senator) is responsible for a $22-million-a-year budget. It is essentially a technical department of government, concerned with administering coal subventions and recommending policies to the government on the production, import and distribution of coal. The Coal Board chairman, along with seven colleagues, recommends (through the minister of mines and technical surveys) what the government's policies should be. O'Brien is now succeeded in this responsible post by the Hon. J. Watson MacNaught.

An active Liberal since he was a law student at Dalhousie University in the late twenties, MacNaught practiced criminal law on the island and became law clerk of the Prince Edward Island legislature. He won a Liberal seat in the 1945 election, lost it in 1957, and won it back in 1963. When he picked his first cabinet, Pearson put MacNaught in the solicitor-general's office, then the most junior of portfolios.

During the next three years the Island lawyer established himself in Ottawa as a man very nearly innocent of the arts of statesmanship. At a private dinner shortly after the government was sworn in, MacNaught interrupted two Quebec ministers deep in animated conversation and repeatedly asked them to speak English. The government used him for routine assignments, such as representing Canada at the inauguration of a new president of Mexico.

Official Ottawa was baffled when in the summer of 1965, Mac-Naught was suddenly promoted to the mines and technical surveys portfolio. This seemed particularly illogical since Prince Edward Island happens to be the only province of Canada which has no known mineral resources. "I'm going into the department with a very open mind," MacNaught stated firmly at the time.

In the 1965 election MacNaught probably had more going for him than any other cabinet minister, since shortly before the campaign started, the government had pledged $148 million toward the construction of the long-promised Prince Edward Island causeway. But he lost his seat anyway. He managed this feat by deliberately neglecting to invite Walter Shaw, the Island's premier (and a Conservative) to the sod-turning ceremonies for the causeway, which MacNaught had thoughtfully arranged for just three days before the November 8 vote.

Now MacNaught has been assured a sinecure as chairman of the coal board. One reason he was not appointed to P.E.I.'s existing vacancy in the Senate was that a delegation of progressive Prince Edward Island Liberals descended on Ottawa a few weeks ago imploring the prime minister not to name MacNaught. By choosing instead to place him in a responsible position within the public service, Lester Pearson appears to be bidding a final farewell to the "new politics" which he described in the hopeful springtime of his stewardship as the abandonment of "narrow and nasty, short-sighted and selfish partisanship."

[1966]

Walter Gordon

IT WAS A CURIOUS SETTING FOR COMBAT. The big ballroom of the Chateau Laurier Hotel, all gilt and creamy elegance, was lit by tiers of television lights and crowded to the doors with Liberal delegates who were hoping to see a knockout fight between Mitchell Sharp, in the right corner, and Walter Gordon, in the left.

Most of the delegates were young, as politicians go, under forty, well-dressed, still tanned from the summer sun. They looked as fresh as the people you see in the new car ads, but they sounded about as sympathetic as a heavyweight bout audience at Madison Square Gardens.

They rushed up to each other, eyes darting through the crowd, repeating eagerly the wisdom of the moment. ("Gordon will be clobbered. . . . It's going to be a real bloodletting. . . . It's a Greek tragedy. . . . Walter has a death wish.")

But the bloodletting never came, for this was, after all, a Liberal crowd, and the drama was badly-staged and not tragic after all but merely sad. Under the glare of the kleig lights, delegates lined up at microphones, waiting to have their say on the compromise resolution dealing with economic nationalism. Mitchell Sharp was sixth in line behind the first microphone and he stood there patiently, democratically, the good man who was no doubt the model boy, waiting to say his rational piece and the lights glanced off his fading red hair and the strong planes of his face. "One of the really great faces," murmured an entranced would-be power broker. "One of your really great television faces. Even McLuhan says so."

And Mitchell Sharp stood there, moved by popular request to the head of his microphone line, and he made a Mitchell Sharp speech.

113

("Let me suggest to this workshop that our approach should be Canadian and Liberal. . . . It should be positive, outward-looking. . . .") He was for American investment and for Canadian enterprise at the same time. We must, he warned, not allow our brain power to be drained, but we cannot, on the other hand, take a narrow, nationalistic approach, for everything would be lost and nothing would be gained in a world growing increasingly interdependent. And the delegates loved him. They stood up and cheered, because he sounded as though he knew what he meant. It was not a brilliant speech, but there was just enough chauvinism, enough partisanship, and above all enough strength in it, to make it rousing.

Walter Gordon was then called, and he was his shambling self, polite, self-effacing, a little apologetic, a little sad. He was not, he said, of the extreme, and he was not really so far from Mitchell Sharp. But he was farther than he knew or could admit, for he was a marked loser and Sharp was now the winner and farther apart than that in politics you cannot get.

Gordon sat down to small applause, his speech an anticlimax – a man who was once a power and is now a fading force. What he stood for in the green springtimes of 1962 and 1963 was not what he said now in the sadder fall of 1966. In those brave early days, he was the Leader's confidante, the moulder of great victories, the maker of political miracles, but now he is dispossessed and the umbrella of Liberalism is no longer broad enough to cover this man and his passionate ideas.

[1966]

Quentin Durgens

I KEEP SITTING IN FRONT OF A TELEVISION SET from nine to ten these Tuesday nights, thinking how exciting it would be to live in the keyed-up Ottawa that Quentin Durgens, MP, inhabits.

It's not that this CBC-land capital doesn't like Ottawa. There they are, the same long grey corridors, the same box-like elevators, the same private dining rooms off the Parliamentary restaurant, even the same overweight tourists on the Hill. And it's not that it isn't good television. There are even moments when it's superb, and this week's episode, *Hold High the Mirror,* was particularly admirable.

The trouble is, alas, that the real Ottawa doesn't operate the way the television Ottawa does. It is not inhabited by teams of hard-nosed self-seekers who accomplish their objectives in an afternoon of tough confrontations; it is instead an amorphous grey mass, an obsolescent machine that wheezes, lurches, belches and occasionally throws off a decision.

Gordon Pinsent, who plays Quentin Durgens, has authority and carries himself with the feline dignity of a crusading loner. He is the kind of man Canadians ought to be electing to Parliament – and on rare occasions do. But he has this unfortunate tendency to act like a passionate human, to shout and pound desks when he is making even minor points of principle.

Hardly any important people shout in Ottawa.

John Diefenbaker used to shout and look what happened to him. Decisions are taken here in a series of inconclusive word matches which wind up as an in-group consensus.

115

In Durgens' country protagonists snap at each other, level with each other, insult each other and generally display a directness seldom encountered in Ottawa's political landscape. Each of the Durgens' shows has at least one yelling match, with Durgens and some flinty minister, or special assistant, or national organizer facing each other, and the maverick MP finally having his way because he is on the side of right and fair play. But this is not the way power works in Ottawa. It oozes from man to man in an unaccountable series of inconclusive encounters based on temporary, mutually beneficial alliances.

Then there is the dialogue which to the well-tempered ear has more Toronto ad agency pizzazz than Rideau Club control. Nobody here ever refers to a failed parliamentary manoeuvre as "winding up on the cutting room floor." Despite these complaints, the series often achieves stunning authenticity, right down to the night noises in the parliamentary corridors and the fat old-fashioned brief cases carried by Ottawa men.

There are some great touches, like the quick shot of Durgens meeting a reporter on an elevator and, neither quite sure how much the other knows, testing reactions with the phrase, "I hear that . . ." Probably the program's greatest value is its illustration of the continuing importance of the backbench MP as a sort of ombudsman not just to his own constituents but to his fellow Canadians. Most of the character portrayals hold up. The ministers are appropriately unctuous, and the Opposition MPs suitably rambunctious. But there are some mistakes in casting and the occasional caricature. The Iron Curtain commissars in a recent episode were straight out of the Bob Hope school of anti-Communist spoofs. Red diplomats in Ottawa are amazingly *soigné* and unfailingly affable. The really serious flaw in the program's authenticity is the absence of a prime minister. He never appears in the series – presumably because the writers were afraid of being accused of caricaturing one of the recent incumbents. Yet everything that happens in political Ottawa swirls around that single powerful figure. The status of MPs is judged by the number of times the PM stops to whisper something to them on his way in or out of the Commons. His rumoured displeasure can drive a man to a nervous breakdown. He is the centre of the Ottawa universe and without his presence no portrayal can seem entirely real.

Still the series is getting at them in political circles here. During a recent show there were more MPs watching Durgens in the lobbies behind the green curtains of the Commons than there were sitting through the droning deliberations in the House itself. And every Wednesday morning, there is a noticeable quickening of pace on the Hill, as MPs stride purposefully along, imaginations fired. Men of Destiny in rumpled suits.

[1966]

Bryce Mackasey

HERE HE IS, A GENUINE LEFT-WINGER, one of the last of the breed, talking his way through the Ottawa day, his big Irish heart on his sleeve, a unique apparition among the dauphins and the deacons of the Trudeau government.

It's Bryce Mackasey, the minister of labour and he is a little out of place in this eclectic administration that combines the cool intelligence of the new technocrats (long since bored by the conditioned reflexes of small-l liberalism) with the hard cynicism of veteran ministers whose political steepings have grown dark and bitter, like tea bags left in the pot too long.

Mackasey has never for a moment in a hard lifetime been either cool or cynical. He charges into each day, his enthusiasm tempered by an inner awareness of his own vulnerability, a craggy character with calloused hands and uncalloused instincts. The labour portfolio he occupies has for years been a throw-away job held by a succession of misfits, time-serving tokens to Ottawa's reluctant recognition that labour too has a legitimate claim on the benefits of our evolving society.

Mackasey lobbied with both Pearson and Trudeau to get the labour job and he is already turning what was a minor portfolio into the main source of policy-making in a government publicly dedicated to the Just Society. His department, which has suffered from poor morale since its staff was reduced by two-thirds in 1965 when most of its newsworthy functions were transferred to the then-new manpower ministry, is being revitalized with a new deputy, new ideas and Mackasey's own inexhaustible zeal.

The minister loves his title, his department and his responsibilities.

118

He is proudest of what he calls "my war room" – an office on the thirteenth floor of his departmental headquarters building, manned by busy assistants putting little plastic markers into a wall-sized pegboard. It is a giant critical-path flow chart which keeps track of Mackasey's daily timetable and tries to correlate it with twenty-three new programs under study in his department.

It also lists some of the main events in Mackasey's future and the biggest, brightest marker of them all is reserved for December 19, 1968 – the day he hopes Canada's railways will reach an agreement with their operating unions. Mackasey's intervention in the rail wage dispute at this early stage in the negotiations is unusual. Contracts are normally allowed to run out without action being taken until a crisis stage is reached, usually at midsummer, and steps to recall Parliament have to be made (or threatened) to impose some form of compulsory arbitration. Instead, Mackasey has, with the consent of both management and the unions, injected the services of a mediator to attempt a settlement now even before the current contract runs out – while there is still what Mackasey calls "a residue of goodwill on both sides."

Mackasey had his first personal triumph in labour relations when he had been in his department less than three months. This was his last-minute settlement of the grainhandlers' strike on September 13, 1968, when he went over the heads of the negotiators and hammered out an agreement directly with management at 5:30 in the morning of the day Parliament opened. (It was probably the only strike in Canadian history settled by a minister of labour wearing a tuxedo. Mackasey went to the negotiations straight from the Governor-General's ball inaugurating the new session.) Earlier in the year he visited the Montreal waterfront to make sure that management had put in new washrooms for dockworkers as promised in a conciliation report. When he found they were inadequate he put pressure on the companies for new facilities and attended their unveiling.

Mackasey's union feelings are in the bone. The son of a CNR machinist, he served for twelve years as a shop steward for the Brotherhood of Electrical Workers, made two attempts to take university courses but had to quit each time to help support his family. He earned part of his tuition by playing hockey and fighting sixty welterweight bouts (he won fifty-nine) and later by operating a small printing firm.

In the House of Commons, Mackasey is one of the few ministers able to rouse the ire of Robert Stanfield who once called him "the Liberal party's hatchetman," a label Mackasey boasts about whenever he gets the chance. The real test of Mackasey's political skill will come when he introduces legislation incorporating the recommendations of the Freedman report, which will limit management's right in layoffs resulting from technological changes.

Despite the heart attack he suffered while rallying Trudeau's supporters on the day of the Liberal leadership convention, Mackasey puts in a fourteen-hour day and seems to thrive on his exhausting schedule.

He has his war room and his critical-path flows, but he is not really at home with the technocratic aspects of this administration and no one would be surprised to see him resign on a question of principle. Meanwhile, he goes on attacking accepted beliefs, laughing a lot, crying a little, and taking risks where other ministers scurry for the safe options.

[1968]

Willy Brandt

F OR ME, OR INDEED FOR ANYONE who has lived or fought in Europe and holds in his mind a firm preconception of the German charac-ter, the most startling thing about Willy Brandt is the way he arrives for our interview. He has turned himself into a major world figure during his first four hectic months in office, yet the German chancellor comes softly and simply through the streets of Bonn, slouched in the back of a black Mercedes, with no helmeted outriders, no uni-formed security guards, none of the para-military apparatus one ex-pects to see surrounding the leader of what was, not so very long ago, the world's most militaristic nation.

In conversation Willy Brandt makes it clear that he does not intend to run with history. He intends to change it. He will be to the Europe of the 1970s what Charles de Gaulle was to the Europe of the 1960s – a statesman reaching out beyond his country's domestic issues to break the East-West impasse that has paralyzed European politics since 1945.

My talk with the German chancellor takes place in a small, modern guest room at the Bonn headquarters of the Social Democrat party. Brandt walks in, accompanied only by one harried male assistant, look-ing like a man confident in his power even though it rests on an uneasy minority coalition within the *Bundestag*. He seems relaxed despite a killing schedule that includes his visit next week to London where he will be paid the singular honour of being asked to address a joint session of both Houses of Parliament. Later in March he will go to Berlin to open negotiations between East and West Germany, and in early April he will be making his first visit to the United States.

121

Up close, Brandt is a bigger, more impressive man than his photographs suggest. Standing, he holds himself at attention and, when making a quip, lifts his heels from the ground as though to launch his wit with extra bounce. His Scandinavian face seems to alter shape according to his mood, ranging from passionate intensity when he talks about his impending negotiations with East Germany to bemused sophistication when he reminisces about his early days as a socialist.

The only sign of tension he displays is his idle toying with a match box from which he occasionally extracts a matchstick and then resolutely snaps it in two to emphasize a point. After we have exchanged half a dozen stately sentences in German, he slips courteously into careful English, speaking in a raspy voice that makes him sound like a highly cultivated Louis Armstrong. "What I'm aiming at," he says, "is much more than a *modus vivendi* with Eastern Europe, though this would be a considerable advance from the situation as it is now. But I'm in favor of entering these talks with East Germany in a pragmatic way to see how far we can get without concentrating on strictly judicial problems."

Brandt is a realistic politician aware that in his pursuit of an East-West detente he is caught between two worlds: the old Europe in which nations act and react according to the narrow dictates of their sovereignties and a new Europe of the future in which political diversity might become possible. But Brandt knows that before such a new Europe can be born, the old one first has to be transformed and this is his present preoccupation.

He views the Russian invasion of Czechoslovakia in August of 1968 as a major setback to such hopes. "The problems raised by the Czech crisis will reappear," he says, "because they result from two main sources, each of which is bound to get stronger in the future. One is that any modern society, whether it is governed by democratic or communist principles, produces a need and desire for exchanges of ideas, goods and people. At the same time, in this period when the world is getting smaller, national identities still want to find an expression of their own and these two forces are bound to collide.

"Deplorable as it was, I don't think the invasion of Czechoslovakia has reduced the basic interest in greater East-West co-operation," he says. "There's no doubt that among the leaders of East Germany there is a strong feeling against talks with us. They think our approach is too early and includes too many risks. But if a general trend toward the reduction of tensions should be confirmed then I'm convinced East

Germany will not be in a position to exclude itself."

The formula that Brandt proposes as a solution to the German problem sounds familiar to Canadian ears. It is the creation of "two German states in one nation." Exactly the opposite of the Quebec separatist demands for "two nations in one state."

"What I mean by nation," Brandt says, "is something that is the result of history and culture and a will of the people who are formed by that history and culture to live together. In our case, for example, even if we stuck to the principle of national unity, this wouldn't necessarily take the form of Germany as it was before. It could also become possible, during the next generations, to live together as one nation, especially in a cultural sense, within the larger framework of European federation." The idea that both East and West Germany might come to acknowledge the existence of some form of single nationhood is a bold challenge to conventional wisdom on both sides of the Iron Curtain. Before Brandt, the United States and Russia had become heavily committed to the existing divisions of the continent. Unlike his predecessors, Brandt is less concerned with large legal issues than small human problems and he would be quite happy to wrest from the East Germans some minor concessions such as visiting privileges across the Berlin wall in return for some modified form of recognition for the German Democratic Republic.

"In foreign policy," Brandt says, "a realist without imagination is a simpleton. But anyone who is not a realist is a dreamer. Not a day goes by that doesn't give rise to new realities and anyone who believes that present-day realities can be frozen for eternity is a reactionary fool. . . . The final third of the twentieth century will decide whether the nations of the world are so caught up in the past that they will forfeit the future, or whether they have the vision necessary to master that future."

As Willy Brandt pursues his new domestic and foreign policies, it is increasingly apparent that his election late last year signalled an irrevocable change in the nation's political climate. None of West Germany's postwar Christian Democrat governments were sympathetic to the Nazi legacy but Brandt's Social Democrat regime is the first to be aggressively anti-Nazi and this is a shift in emphasis with spectacular implications. Brandt has formed the first postwar administration which includes not a single ex-Nazi in its ranks. He is constantly reminding Germans that World War II "was undertaken for the perpetration of criminal actions for which there are no parallels in the modern age." It is as though he means to use the psychotherapist's technique on a

123

national scale, purging the German conscience by open admission and then driving the country onward.

When I ask him what he had meant by declaring shortly after taking office that he intended to be the chancellor not of a defeated but of a liberated Germany, he replies: "Well, that was a remark strictly for domestic consumption. But what I meant was that Germany in 1945 was liberated from the Nazis. It was defeated, too, of course, but for me it was chiefly a liberation. During the process of the last twenty-five years we have left behind many burdens, so that by now we can say that the past is really behind us." When Brandt says, "twenty-five years is enough," it is not so much a cry of absolution as a realistic reminder that a new generation has moved into power in Germany and they must not be condemned for the crimes of their fathers. (Nearly two-thirds of West Germans were born after 1930 and were too young to be part of Hitler's insanity.) This new generation has altered the character of the country because it has little interest in the once glorious concepts of German fatherland patriotism. West Germany is no longer being run by cliques of barons steeped in the misty Bismarck legends of the Weimar days. The new power elite is the money aristocracy which clogs the inner lanes of the autobahns, impatiently blinking the headlights of their yellow Mercedes at the Volkswagens blocking their routes to winter chalets and luxury ski resorts.

The combination of the country's economic prosperity and the purge of its Nazi roots has earned West Germany, for the first time since World War II, the right to bargain with other nations on an equal footing. Brandt is attempting to justify this new sense of equality by pushing his country into the forefront of the efforts to ease the tensions between communist and free Europe. "What West Germany needs above all," he says, "is a sure eye for proportion. To know where we stand and where we want to go, that's part of the self-consciousness of a mature people. And that can be the source of healing for the inferiority complex that keeps telling us that we are a misunderstood nation."

There is no better illustration of the dramatic change that has occurred in the German character than Brandt's own election to the chancellorship last fall. He defies, both in his personality and background, nearly every tradition of successful German politicians.

He was born out of wedlock in 1913, the son of a Lubeck shopgirl, in a country which until last year legally discriminated against illegitimate children. (Once, while he was mayor of West Berlin, his eastern counterpart taunted him about his birth and Brandt shot back: "At

124

least I was born a bastard. You've made yourself into one.") In 1933, Brandt fled Germany because of his disgust with Nazism and went to Norway where he joined the army and was briefly interned in a German prisoner-of-war camp. He returned to Germany after the war as a Norwegian major attached to Oslo's military mission to Berlin and only resumed his German citizenship in 1947. After joining the socialist party he eventually was appointed Berlin representative on its executive committee. He became mayor of West Berlin in 1957, gradually moved into federal politics and in 1966 was named foreign minister in the Kiesinger coalition.

Worse than having neither of the prerequisites of the country's political leaders (being a "good German" and coming from a "good family"), Brandt belonged to the wrong party. He was a member of the same Social Democrats whom Bismarck had denounced as being "enemies of the Reich" and is the first socialist chancellor to hold office since Hermann Muller, whose party was forced out of office in 1930. Brandt's domestic reform program includes many tax revisions and welfare schemes designed to foster a more democratic West German society, but his brand of socialism is highly diluted by such Mackenzie King-like phrases as: "Competition as far as possible. Planning as far as necessary."

When he makes this kind of pronouncement, Brandt is the very epitome of the cool, contemporary liberal political leader – and the very antithesis of the shouting glory of a frenzied German gauleiter of old. Germany has digested its history at last.

[1970]

John Kenneth Galbraith

D OWN IN THIS SOUTHEASTERN CORNER OF VERMONT, intruding hard into the dark pine hills of New Hampshire, lies the venerable, time-passed village of Newfane. This is Johnny Cash country, with American flags planted proudly in front of once-prosperous farms, bingo at the local firehall every Saturday night at eight, and men in suspenders rocking on porches as they taste the peppermint autumn haze. It is an odd hiding place for one of the most influential thinkers of our time, a man whose writings have become textbooks for Western civilization. Yet it is here, on an abandoned farm at the dead end of a dirt-track road, that John Kenneth Galbraith goes to relax and to write. As I drive my car into the farmyard, I am greeted by Macduff, the Galbraith collie, and then from his study – a small, white, red-roofed building set above and apart from the main farmhouse – emerges the man himself. John Kenneth Galbraith is an imposing sight. A monument of a man, with a liturgical face bisected by a great, double-angled nose that marches on before him, a beacon to his avowed intention of altering the world to his own specifications.

Galbraith, whose books, *The Affluent Society* and *The New Industrial State,* have transformed him from economist to oracle, has come far since his birth sixty-one years ago at Iona Station, in Ontario's Elgin County. During World War II, he served in Washington as assistant head of the Office of Price Administration; he helped write John F. Kennedy's inaugural address; distinguished himself as United States ambassador to India; seconded Eugene McCarthy's nomination at Chicago in 1968. One of the most influential critics of American society, he has, at the same time, been responsible for reshaping some basic attitudes in his adopted country. Although he is a certified member of the American establishment, big business tends to regard his very existence with suspicion. Paul Samuelson, a fellow economist, once wrote that "an unguarded remark by Galbraith can send the Dow Jones average down two dollars; his guarded utterances can send it down five dollars."

Galbraith, who regards himself as "an independent operator at the guerrilla level of American politics," is a man who understands power, is drawn to it, and tends to project a certain sense of detachment from lesser men. "Galbraith," says William F. Buckley, the conservative critic, "always gives the impression that he is on very temporary leave from Olympus, where he holds classes on the maintenance of divine standards." I keep the definition in mind as we settle down for our talk.

QUESTION: As far as I know, you are the first important Democrat in the United States to suggest that your party will win the 1972 presidential campaign only if it turns toward socialism. Are you, in effect, referring to the kind of welfarism which has passed for liberalism in Canadian politics?

GALBRAITH: No. I was thinking of socialism in the sense of public ownership of the means of production. I am persuaded there are substantial areas of modern business enterprise, notably the railroads and the weapons firms, as well as sectors of the housing industry, which do not function effectively or efficiently under private ownership. What we have had in the past twenty-five years is a kind of disguised form of socialism in which we closed our eyes to the fact that these industries are very largely under public sponsorship – through subsidies and regulations. In the case of the munitions industries, for example, it's been a device for paying larger salaries and getting some degree of private support for the Pentagon from what amounts to a public bureaucracy. My own feeling is that as long as liberals in the United States are elaborately explaining they are not socialists as they have in the past, they won't take hold of these industries and have pride in some areas of public activity, notably the Tennessee Valley Authority.

There is a parallel here with Canada. There has never been in Canada quite the ideological resistance to public ownership that there is in the United States. The political right in Canada has never campaigned with quite the fervor against public ownership and socialism as the American right has. Therefore, the position on public ownership of the railroads, public ownership of electric power production, public ownership in the grain trade and so forth has always been pragmatically acceptable.

127

QUESTION: Are you abandoning the small-l liberalism which has always been the dominant ideology of the American Democrats? Would it not be more realistic to expect a new political party to take up your ideas?

GALBRAITH: No. The Democrats will always move to the left. You can always accomplish more in the Democratic party than you can outside it, and since the Democratic party is not ideologically exclusive it will always embrace such positions. In this respect I suppose, it has some parallel with the Liberal party under Mackenzie King. It was King's genius, among other things, to make sure that he had no serious opposition to the left of him. Well, the Democratic party functions in somewhat the same way.

QUESTION: But is not even the enlightened element of the Democratic party trapped in its liberalism? Can they take the kind of radical steps you suggest?

GALBRAITH: The old guard can't. There's no question about that. But a younger and mentally much more flexible group is coming along. The people that marched with McCarthy and Bob Kennedy have no trouble in accepting my ideas. In fact, many go beyond them.

QUESTION: Who would lead such a party?

GALBRAITH: We need somebody who will hold together the young, the blacks and the poor and give them confidence that the Democratic party will act on their behalf, and who will not repel the unions. There are people who can do this. George McGovern could do it. George would have his major trouble on the union side. But he could do it.

QUESTION: Do you think it is possible, then, that Nixon will be a one-term president?

GALBRAITH: Yes. It's possible. But Nixon has one thing going for him which in some ways, however, is a wasting asset. He has going for him the fact that people do not compare his Viet Nam policy with a perfect one. They compare it with Lyndon Johnson's. People compare imperfect de-escalation under Nixon with all the anxieties associated with escalation under Johnson. People worried that they were going to wake up one morning under Johnson, and find that we were bombing the supply routes out of China, that we were bombing Haiphong harbour. Now under Nixon, other than the Cambodian insanity, one has had a record of inadequate, inefficient withdrawal. The Cambodian invasion cost Nixon very heavily in this regard. It caused him to adopt the war. As the Vietnamization process continues, and is shown to be phony, he's going to be subject to pressures to forestall the retreats of the Viet

128

Nam army. More and more, this is going to look like Nixon's war. This is particularly true now that the Democrats are out of power, and the initiative is passed to people like Fulbright, Kennedy, McGovern and so forth, who are attacking on the war. Nixon's other great disadvantage is the fact that he has no formula for taking care of domestic, economic and social problems. He is inert on those issues and he's in an ideological tangle – an economic policy which is accumulating against him. The Democrats have had a handicap these past couple of years with the impatience of the black community and the fact that the violence in the ghettos has been used against them. The impatience of the youngsters and the fact that violence on the campus has been used against them. But I have the feeling that both in the ghettos and on the campus violence has run its course.

QUESTION: You believe the kids will be able to enlist themselves back into the political process?

GALBRAITH: Yes. What is happening is their discovery that operating outside the political process isn't a real alternative. It involves some very great disadvantages, including the disadvantage associated with the kind of insane rhetoric of the Weathermen – that sort of thing.

QUESTION: Despite your dissatisfactions with American society as it exists, you seem remarkably optimistic about the American future. How do you reconcile these points of view?

GALBRAITH: I was going to say that American society is a functioning anarchy, but that's not quite true. Its capacity to survive doesn't depend on Washington, doesn't depend on the state governments, it depends on a certain inherent capacity of people to organize and to come around to views that are consistent with survival. These lessons have to be relearned every once in a while. Every once in a while we have to relearn that non-violence is wanted, not as a concession to goodness, but because it's good in itself. The tendency is to respond with a certain measure of sobriety and wisdom to the stimuli of the situation, which is the thing that enables the United States to survive, and so I'm optimistic in the sense that I think these stimuli continue to work, and probably are working a little bit more rapidly as one gets a progressively more educated community. On the other hand there are offsetting influences from the fact that some of the old coadjutors of society, some of the old stabilizing roles of tradition, are weakening.

QUESTION: What do you think of Pierre Elliott Trudeau?

GALBRAITH: I suppose he is in the best tradition of Canadian liberalism, which consists in having an open mind on the whole range of legislative possibilities and on a variety of things having to do with personality and individual behaviour, but that he is a good deal less stuffy than his predecessors. I've always thought that the basic tradition of Canadian liberalism was to be open-minded on economic matters and somewhat limited on the questions of public morals. That Trudeau has, for the first time, opened the window on questions of personal behaviour, is most encouraging. I suppose it was inevitable that these issues, having to do with civil rights, drugs and so forth, should be brought out into the open by a French-Canadian politician, rather than one steeped more in the conservative Scots-Presbyterian tradition.

QUESTION: I have always thought of the Canadian political tradition as a mixture of pragmatism and Manchester liberalism.

GALBRAITH: Yes. Pragmatism, Manchester liberalism, plus some of the inhibitions of old-fashioned Protestantism.

QUESTION: You have written that ownership is no longer the dominant factor in big business, but can this thesis be maintained in Canada's case, where the fact that most of our big business is American has meant that our whole society has developed as a kind of adjunct to American society? I guess I am really asking whether you believe there is a cultural dimension to economic affairs.

GALBRAITH: I suppose there is. But it seems to me one has to distinguish here between the inevitable and the negotiable. There are at least three factors in this situation which are inevitable, yet Canadians associate them not with inevitability but with the United States. First of all, there is an inevitable uniformity in large economic organizations which imposes its cultural pattern on the country no matter where the ultimate ownership is. General Motors, which is American; International Nickel, which is nominally Canadian; Massey-Ferguson, which is Canadian; will all impose a somewhat similar production organization, similar labour discipline, a similar ethos of efficiency, a similar subordination to the goals of the common organization. Much of this is attributed to the United States, but it really belongs to the larger pattern of industrialism. Second, there is much that is associated with American cultural imperialism which is merely a part of a common preoccupation of advanced industrial societies with goods. This tends to be as true of Canada as it is of the United States. And then, of course, the third inevitability is that Canada is close to the United States. There is the inescapable fact of proximity. I have always thought that, given all these constraints, rather than worrying about the additional influence from General Motors in Oshawa being owned by General Motors in

130

New York and Ford in Windsor being owned in Detroit, this influence is relatively tiny and much more is to be gained by the strongest possible development of autonomy in television programs, autonomy in book publishing and that healthy support should be given to the Canadian publishing industry to make sure that the educational system is strongly supported. That's where real cultural autonomy lies.

QUESTION: Do you think we can establish a cultural identification strong enough to resist an economic takeover by the United States?

GALBRAITH: Oh, certainly. Canada seems to overemphasize the question of ownership. For the average Canadian the practical distinction whether he works for General Motors in Oshawa, the Canadian Pacific or the Canadian National, to take three cases, amounts to a hill of beans. One shouldn't try to create a distinction where it doesn't exist. On the other hand, I suppose there is a certain distinction between Canadian television, which strikes me as very good, and CBS, which strikes me as being, on the whole, rather lousy.

QUESTION: Do you still feel Canadian at all?

GALBRAITH: Well, sure. I don't have any very strong nationalistic instincts. I was brought up in southwestern Ontario where we were taught that Canadian patriotism should not withstand anything more than a five-dollar-a-month wage differential. Anything more than that, and you went to Detroit. I've always said that one could have a moral and emotional affiliation with any number of countries. I consider myself as much a Canadian as an American.

[1970]

131

Josef Skvorecky

THE CZECH CHARACTER IS ELUSIVE but it has its own warmth, sub-
tlety and wit, and it is beautifully caught in Josef Skvorecky's
novel *The Cowards,* recently published by Grove Press in New
York.

Skvorecky, a compact sparrow of a man who views the world with
a perpetual look of sad surprise, is spending a year as writer in residence
at the University of Toronto. Unknown on this side of the Atlantic, he
has become a major literary figure in postwar Europe, with Graham
Greene and the *Times Literary Supplement* hailing his achievements.
The Cowards, written in 1948, was suppressed by state censors, but
once it was circulated during the Dubcek Spring of 1968, quickly became the literary manifesto for the young generation of Czech liberals.
Translated since into German, French, Polish as well as English, *The
Cowards* qualifies as one of those rare books – like *Moby Dick* – which
can be read at two levels: both for the story it tells and the message it
conveys.

The Cowards describes eight days (May 4-11, 1945) in the adven-
tures of six young jazz musicians, living in a northeastern Bohemian
border town, as seen through the eyes of twenty-year-old Danny
Smiricky, a raunchy tenor saxophone player, with little taste for heroism. The boys in the band are caught up in the mad manoeuvrings of
the town fathers who, having made certain the Nazis are going down to
defeat, decide to stage an orderly, last-minute anti-German uprising to
impress their next invaders. Although they reach an understanding with
the retreating *Wehrmacht* and anxiously wait around to welcome the
advancing Americans, everything goes wrong. Fleeing ss troops arrive

and arrest everybody in sight. They are followed by hordes of humourless Russians. Communists emerge within the local underground to take charge of the revolution, which suddenly becomes real and bloody.

At one level, the book is an amusing Holden Caulfield tale of the student-musicians who somehow manage to float above the turmoil, the only rational presences in a Kafkaesque landscape. The "cowards" scoff at the self-appointed civil government; they find the military posings of each set of invaders equally ridiculous; their thoughts are mainly of the girls they want (or have had) and the music they play. They destroy a German tank, then refuse to claim the credit, even though one of them is shot in the encounter. The young musicians are only fleetingly touched by the ideological mania of the elders. They insist on measuring abstractions in human terms. History trespasses on their lives, but it cannot displace their marvellous, nose-thumbing gaiety. Or their music.

In the end, it is the music that survives. Jazz is their reality, and when the Communists finally reveal themselves, young Danny Smiricky (who can imitate Coleman Hawkins' tenor solo on *Sweet Lorraine*) confesses: "I didn't have anything against communism. I didn't have anything against anything, just as long as I could play jazz on my saxophone, because that was something I loved to do and I couldn't be for anything that was against that."

Since the essence of jazz is improvisation, it is a music hopelessly incompatible with political ideology in all its shadings, and Danny is left blowing his "fancy little flourishes" in "rough, sobbing tones that sounded like they came from heaven." *The Cowards* reflects both the philosophy ("a writer's job is to tell the truth") and the style of an early, still sober Ernest Hemingway. ("With blind eyes, I started down toward the town lying in darkness, a town that had turned all its lights out because everybody was afraid, and inside me all sorts of memories tumbled around in my head, memories of all those years I'd lived here, of Irena, of high school, of Mr. Katz my German teacher, of all the good old familiar things, of the music we played, of student carnivals and girls in bathing suits at the pool, and then I knew it was all over now, over and done with forever, as far as yesterday's wind, as those Russian tanks on the other side of the hill, as the gunfire and grenades at the customs house, as everything else in the world, and that I could never go back to it again, no matter how much I wanted to, and it seemed to me that nothing ahead could ever be as wonderful, that nothing could be that tremendous or glamorous again, and that all that was left were these memories framed in gold.")

Josef Skvorecky's style has matured since he wrote *The Cowards* twenty-two years ago. He has published five other novels, eight collections of essays and short stories, a half dozen screen and television plays, as well as translating into Czech the works of Ray Bradbury, Henry James, Ernest Hemingway, Sinclair Lewis, Dashiel Hammett and William Styron. Skvorecky lived much of his book, playing tenor saxophone in a high-school jazz band and later being drafted into the Czech tank corps. ("They tried to teach me to drive a tank," he says, "but in this they were not successful. So they immediately promoted me to be a tank commander. It's the usual way. That's how armies operate.") During the Dubcek liberation, Skvorecky became an editor in the English-language department of the state publishing house in Prague. He left for the United States in 1969 to accept a lectureship at Cornell University, and now lives in Toronto. He likes it here, but finds many of our concerns trivial. "I can't force myself to think about nudity in the movies, or about drugs or pollution," he says. "Such things are a luxury. Sure it's nice to see a naked girl on the screen, but the issues that really interest me are justice and the right of innocent people to a fair trial."

The Cowards is an evocative, indispensable book. Wars and invasions always kill men in the name of ideology, destroying their bodies for the sake of their souls. Through his saxophone-blowing anti-hero, Josef Skvorecky proclaims an important truth, which seems relevant to Canada in this autumn of the FLQ-War Measures Act crisis: in a mad world, only through acts of individual affirmation can men feed their souls and protect themselves from the winds of outrage.

[1970]

134

PART FOUR   *Quebec*

Marcel Chaput

I T IS SOMEHOW TYPICALLY CANADIAN that the leader of a movement whose aim it is to destroy the unity of this nation should be, not a hollow-eyed revolutionary in a back-street basement, but a middle-class civil servant in a dark blue suit. Dr. Marcel Chaput, president of *Le Rassemblement pour l'Indépendance Nationale,* currently the strongest faction in Quebec's separatist movement, sees himself as a firebrand leading his people into a bright new tomorrow free of the sinister Anglo-Saxons who hog all the good jobs. Paradoxically, Chaput's own career demonstrates that a French-Canadian can make out in an English-speaking preserve. One of seven children of a Hull printer, Chaput got his first taste of science as a laboratory assistant at the National Research Council in Ottawa. In the army he spent forty-four months in chemical warfare research, then studied biochemistry for six years at McGill University, earning a PhD. Chaput joined the Defence Research Board immediately after graduation and was assigned to chemical warfare studies. He was later switched to classified work with the Emergency Measures Organization. His fellow scientists never really got to know him, because he rarely attended their social functions.

His recurring altercations with the Defence Research Board eventually led to his resignation following a two-week suspension, ostensibly based on his defiance of the board's refusal to grant him leave of absence for a speaking engagement in Quebec City. He has become the first martyr to the cause of Quebec separatism. He will shortly move his wife and four children to Montreal. His book, *Why I Am a Separatist,* is in its fourth French edition; it was published recently in English.

A few days after he had resigned from the Defence Research Board, I called on Chaput at his home in Hull. He is a chunky, punctilious man who looks younger than his forty-three years. He received me in a book-lined study and proceeded to discuss his proposed insurrection. He talked with unemotional competence. Although I had heard him speak excellent English on previous occasions, he refused to use the language and our entire interview was conducted in French. Unlike most revolutionaries, Chaput has a lively sense of humour. In the small talk that preceded our interview, he hugely enjoyed demonstrating the insensibility of Ottawa's officialdom to French-Canadian aspirations, by telling me that the letter of suspension he had received from the Defence Research Board, had been written in English. Then we talked at length about the sort of Quebec his movement eventually hopes to establish:

QUESTION: What concrete steps do you plan to take in obtaining independence for Quebec?

CHAPUT: It's not the autonomy of a province we're after, but the full rights of a sovereign nation. This can be accomplished without violence. I consider Quebec independence to be a legitimate goal; it's unthinkable that we should be opposed with violence.

QUESTION: How long do you imagine this entire process will take?

CHAPUT: Probably ten years, although it could happen even sooner. Even if Quebec is not independent by 1972, by then we will certainly know whether independence is possible.

QUESTION: Once Quebec is independent, what sort of government would you like to see adopted?

CHAPUT: The majority of people in Quebec would like to see the establishment of a democratic republic, headed by a president.

QUESTION: Would you establish a state religion, like Catholicism in Spain and the Church of England in England?

CHAPUT: Definitely not.

QUESTION: How would you treat the English minority in Quebec?

CHAPUT: All nations have minorities. The English would be welcome to stay, providing they obey our laws, and recognize that they would be living in a country whose only official language would be French.

QUESTION: Would you allow the English minorities to secede?

CHAPUT: No. Westmount is not a nation.

QUESTION: Would you have your own foreign policy?

CHAPUT: Of course. We'd continue to have good relations with other countries – as masters of our own affairs. We would be represented, with our own embassies, in all the important cities of the world, and speak for ourselves in the United Nations. We would withdraw from the Commonwealth (if it still exists) but whether or not we would stay in NATO and NORAD would depend on the circumstances at the time. We would stay in any associations which serve Quebec's enlightened self-interest.

QUESTION: Would you establish your own armed forces?

CHAPUT: We probably would have to have our own army, navy and air force, and certainly we would need our own merchant marine.

QUESTION: Would you allow free use of the St. Lawrence Seaway?

CHAPUT: The Seaway would become international, like the Suez Canal, with all ships having the right of passage, but we might establish a system of tolls that would benefit Quebec more directly.

QUESTION: How would you handle commerce with the rest of Canada?

CHAPUT: We would probably establish a common market with Canada's nine provinces, but Quebec would charge duty on some imports. Business would be carried out in dollars, but instead of Canadian dollars, they'd be Quebec dollars, with new designs and only French printing.

QUESTION: What would you do about American investment in Quebec?

CHAPUT: We want political independence so that we can achieve economic independence. The one is essential to the other. There would still be American investment and other foreign money but we would like to recapture a significant share of our own industries – the riches that are now being exploited by foreigners. This would involve some nationalization, and we'd set up enterprises with government and private French-Canadian capital to run some of the industries. What would be left would have to conform to legislation that would guarantee access to top jobs by Quebec nationals and a certain share of domestic stock ownership. Businesses would have to conduct all their dealings in French.

QUESTION: How would you change Quebec's educational system?

CHAPUT: We would try to make it as modern as possible and accessible – I say accessible, not free – to everyone up to and including the university level, to give us the specialists we'd need. Also, we'd place great emphasis on purifying the French language in Quebec.

QUESTION: What if Canada's other provinces object to giving Quebec independence on legal grounds?

CHAPUT: Name me one country which became free entirely legally.

[1962]

139

Gilles Gregoire

MOST MEMBERS OF PARLIAMENT TAKE ADVANTAGE of the Easter recess for a quiet interlude among their constituents, but Gilles Gregoire is restlessly criss-crossing rural Quebec on an exacting mission: a hunt for strong candidates to carry the banner of Social Credit into the next federal election campaign. "If we get the right men," he says, "we'll elect at least fifty deputies. There's an aching political vacuum in Quebec right now that only our party can fill."

The temptation persists among the strategists of all other parties to dismiss such claims because they have been made too often before and all the expert opinion (including the public opinion polls) indicates that Social Credit is a declining force in Quebec politics. But Social Credit has always been an unpredictable element and with single-minded disciples like Gregoire devoting their considerable energies to its revival, anything is possible.

As deputy leader to the ailing Real Caouette of the breakaway *Ralliement Creditiste,* Gregoire has become a not unimportant influence in the House of Commons. In contrast to Caouette's cougar incoherence, Gregoire's manner is that of an articulate fox. A small man with cactus eyes and a toy moustache, he is a professional who listens to the warnings of his senses. His conversation is a counterplay between the sophistication of his academic background and the primitiveness of his position as theoretician-in-chief for a kooky political movement.

Gregoire's background includes degrees in civil law, literature and philosophy from Laval University, as well as nearly two years as a student in a Jesuit order in Montreal. He can quote Greek dramatists (in Greek) and reads French poetry between House sittings. But he is also the author of a comically unrealistic booklet on Social Credit's inflation cures and will debate for hours on the merits of "nationalizing money", whatever that means. His methods of relaxation reflect the dichotomy in the man's nature: he enjoys either playing Mozart on the piano or juggling a trio of tennis balls he keeps at the ready in his office.

In contrast to Caouette, who ignores the discipline of Commons' procedure, Gregoire has learned to exploit the rules of the chamber, and has become one of the most feared MPs on the Opposition benches. During the first sixty days after he assumed his seat in 1962, he was on his feet 134 times and in one exchange Speaker Marcel Lambert called him to order twelve times. His most successful inquisition was his questioning of Donald Gordon in the parliamentary committee which probed the CNR's hiring practices of French-speaking Canadians. His most humiliating defeat was at the hands of the committee which recently probed his alleged roughing up by the RCMP during the shenanigans (including a comic-opera arrest) that resulted from his refusal to pay a parking ticket because it wasn't translated into French. Although he has committed himself to such trifling crusades as correcting the spelling of "French fried potatoes" on the French-language menu of the parliamentary cafeteria, Gregoire is dedicated to the remaking of Confederation along lines that dramatically transcend the kind of compromise visualized by more moderate politicians. "A country cannot be developed by basing its system of growth on compromise," he insists. "Bold and daring solutions must be found, solutions based, not on compromise, but on realistic and logical principles which can give satisfaction to both groups making up the country."

The danger to Canadian nationhood represented by Gregoire springs from these "realistic and logical principles." They add up to the end of Canada as a political, economic and social unit. He is demanding exclusive Quebec jurisdiction over such fields as monetary policy, immigration, trade, direct and indirect taxation, as well as complete "legislative, executive and judicial powers." He would leave Ottawa with joint control over external affairs and national defence and "certain other fields," financing such operations by handouts from the provinces. "If the other provinces don't want their economic liberation," he says, "that's up to them. But we want ours."

Gregoire's high estimate of his electoral chances in Quebec is based on his assessment of his opponents. He attacks the Liberals for being "linked to international banditry" and describes John Diefenbaker as behaving "like a prophet wandering on the surface of the moon in another century." [1965]

141

Claude Ryan

THE MAN AND HIS SETTING ARE SOMEHOW REMINISCENT of one of those World War II propaganda films glorifying the French resistance movement – all grey shadow and noble enunciations. You wind your way past Montreal's financial district to the cobblestone end of Notre Dame, enter through a yawning door that leads into a bare cell of an office and there broods Claude Ryan, editor and publisher of *Le Devoir*.

He is a tough man. His face has the ascetic strength of wisdom born through suffering, with hooded eyes and a nose sharpened to probe a visitor's intentions. His speech is slow, elaborate phrases casting an incandescent light on any subject under discussion.

Because his has been the rational voice rising above the staccato din of Quebec's social upheaval, Ryan has become one of French Canada's most influential figures, and certainly its most articulate exponent. Not since J. W. Dafoe occupied the editor's chair at the *Winnipeg Free Press* has a Canadian newspaper possessed so much power in forming opinion or attained such a regional resonance with its readers. A continual procession of provincial and federal politicians call on Ryan for late-night chats, to seek his advice and approbation.

It is in his role as the great enunciator of the moderate approach in the settlement of political issues that Ryan has attained his reputation. He adhered fiercely to the moderate line and opted for "the Canadian solution" to Quebec's problems when it was unpopular to do so. "I realize," he says, "that on both sides people are looking for objective voices. They know that solutions to the difficult problem facing Canada can hardly come from the extremist elements." In the pursuit of his ideals, Ryan has turned *Le Devoir,* which in the Duplessis period was a voice of radical dissent, into a journal of reasoned opinion, dedicated to the formulation of policies which will allow both Quebec and Canada to flourish. Ryan has been the leading advocate in French Canada of "the spirit" of dualism – a sentiment without which Canada would have no more meaning.

"When I address an English-speaking audience," he says, "I tend to be a little more nationalistic than I really feel because I want them to understand there's a real problem. And when I'm speaking to my French compatriots, I tend to be a little more Canadian than I'm thought to be in Toronto or Winnipeg. This is part of my duty at the moment."

Obedience to his own rigid concept of duty has shaped Ryan's life. A former general secretary of the militant *Action Catholique,* he has spent most of his professional life in youth work and adult education. He joined *Le Devoir* in June, 1962, but for the first two years wrote mostly on religious subjects, advocating a more progressive approach. Appointed publisher in May, 1964, at the age of thirty-nine, he now also acts as editor-in-chief, filling in for André Laurendeau who is co-chairman of the Royal Commission on Bilingualism and Biculturalism. Ryan has no leisure and cares not at all for the luxuries of life. His home is a $110-a-month flat in a working-class district of Montreal's east end; he drives a stripped-down 1962 Chevrolet. His working day often stretches to fifteen hours and he is one of the most prolific writers in the country. (In 1965 he wrote 144 leading editorials, sixty-six shorter "bloc notes" and eighteen lengthy features in his paper.) Before he commits himself to any editorial position, he attempts to formulate a consensus on an issue by consulting a disparate array of friends and contacts.

In his daily outpouring of editorial opinions, Ryan is often angry, particularly with mishandling of the nation's business in Ottawa. But his basic purpose is to preserve the Canadian federation, while at the same time perpetuating the separate identity of Quebec. "Canada offers a chance to build a new type of society," he says, "a society suited to the development of different cultures without being rigidly or exclusively influenced by one. In time we will develop a new cultural type here that we can't even visualize at the moment."

Claude Ryan may well be the first of that brave new breed.

[1966]

143

Daniel Johnson

I

THE DOMINANT IMPRESSION DANIEL JOHNSON GIVES is that of a man pursuing political power in a world he considers barely civilized. Instead of passion there is an undercurrent of melancholy in this unusual politician as he prepares himself for the burdens of office.

When we met in his downtown Montreal law office, just hours before he left for Quebec City to assume the twenty-fourth premiership of his province, Johnson was exhausted. His voice, grated by weeks of speech making, was reduced to a low growl as he talked about his plans and prospects. Yet he remained fully in control of himself, occasionally leafing through an advance copy of *Time* magazine which had his picture on the cover. "When you've been proclaimed politically dead so many times by the same magazine, this is a remarkable resurrection," he said without surprise.

Throughout the interview he displayed a disarming, if deceptive, candour. Beneath the glad-handing, debonair exterior there is always a quicksilver elusiveness. ("I'm not backing out of anything that was said before. I just want to explain to you what should have been explained during the campaign.")

This is a remarkably complex individual, and it will take years, not months, before any kind of verdict can be reached about his impact on Quebec and Canada. He already possesses a sense of occasion, but he has yet to be touched by that aura of power which creates a feeling of distance around victorious politicians.

When I asked how he interprets the legislative majority he received from the voters, Johnson replied: "I have a mandate for the redistribution of taxes. The Liberals taxed the people to their vital maximum; most workers now have seven columns of deductions on their pay cheques. Everything in my campaign was planned to the last dotted 'i'. I predicted in January that the election would be called for June 5, and we worked back from there. The toughest grind I went through was preparing for my weekly television show. I worked seven or eight hours on each of my five-minute opening remarks. Every word I said was written by me, but I had the advice of the best people in the business."

Did he expect to beat Jean Lesage? "My friends kept telling me for two years, 'don't budge, power is going to spring right into your face.' Any government that loses whole sectors of the population is bound to go down. The school commissions were worried, the municipalities were worried, and so were the farmers, the doctors, the nurses, the police-men, the teachers and the newspapers. The trouble with Jean Lesage is that he had ambitions to go all the way. He's been in Ottawa and even Quebec looks like the bush leagues to him. He was trying to play on both jobs – his own re-election and Pearson's succession."

Since the prevailing wisdom in Ottawa at the moment is that John-son is a pragmatic politician who can be bargained with, I asked whether pragmatism was indeed his political faith. "Very much so," he said, "but never on basic principles. In politics you must project *les lignes de force* as we say in French. You must decide beforehand where the guidelines of your policy will lead and the basic objective must be the favorable evolution of French Canada."

But what about his campaign pronouncements on turning Canada into "two equal and brother nations" – the associate states idea that has roused so much apprehension in English Canada – "Oh, don't link me with that," he objected. "It might amount to something equivalent, but I don't want to use the term 'associate states,' because nobody knows exactly what it means. To me, it's the concept of two nations in the sociological sense, not in geographical terms. It's a question of semantics."

When I asked him whether he considered himself a Quebecker or a Canadian first, he hesitated not a moment. "If I have to choose, I would choose Quebec first, because that's my duty. With a name like Johnson I could have educated my children in English but I'm thinking of the guy in my county whose name is Laframboise." Johnson believes that the French fact in Canada is now in its most critical period, not because of any fears of Ottawa and the other provinces, but because of the influence of the American way of life. "Most of our population is

145

directly under the sway of television from the States," he complains. "The CBC is nine-tenths American content and in French they dub many American programs. That's why we want to link Quebec with other countries culturally. We have to make up our minds whether we're going to become Americans, if Quebec will emerge as the Scotland of Canada, or if we try to live with the rest of Canada but as French. This is the hardest of the three. In the next two years we're going to spend roughly a billion dollars on schools in Quebec. Are we going to be throwing this money away? I'm afraid that less than thirty years from now people will say we were fools to take this stand unless we find the means of preserving the French fact on this continent."

I brought up Johnson's election-night statement, blaming his lack of a decisive majority on "the English and the Jews," and he said: "I just meant that we didn't have any of the English or the Jewish votes, period. The *Union Nationale* hasn't elected an English member from Montreal since 1936. We're going after the English vote from now on; it's easier when you're in power."

One of Johnson's doctrines which is bound to raise controversy in the near future is his preference for presidential over parliamentary government. "I'm still very keen about the presidential system," he said, "and this is the moment when I would appreciate it most. As it is, I have to choose my cabinet within my ranks." He maintains this could be done within the British North America Act except for the role of the lieutenant-governor. "But," he says, "you can even play around with his powers and this is being studied. Then I could go and get Marcel Faribault and my McCutcheons and McNamaras for the cabinet."

"Some Quebec politicians in the past have been ready to save Confederation even at the expense of Quebec," he concluded. "We want not only to save but develop Quebec, even at the expense of Confederation. But we're not fanatics. There can be no compromise on the essentials, but there's lots of room for negotiation. I guess I'm really paraphrasing Mackenzie King's stand on conscription: separatism if necessary, but not necessarily separatism."

[1966]

II

THE FATE OF CANADA DEPENDS TO AN ALARMING EXTENT on the attitudes of a complicated Irish-French-Canadian named Daniel Francis Johnson, whose many contradictory pronouncements during the seven months since he became prime minister of Quebec have puzzled his

146

supporters and baffled his critics. Johnson is the *agent provocateur* of Canadian politics. He goes to meet bond dealers in Toronto and New York, and tells them: "Quebec won't separate, if we can live in Canada as a group." Then he comes home to declare: "Unless Quebec can live in Canada as a group, we'll separate." So the journalists subtract one statement from the other, end up with zero, and then Johnson attacks the press for misinterpreting his position.

My own memories of Daniel Johnson stem from the early sixties when I used to fly to Quebec City once or twice a year to interview Jean Lesage, René Lévesque, Eric Kierans and other activists then in the forefront of French Canada's quiet revolution. After the day's interviews were over, I would go back to the Chateau Frontenac Hotel and there at a restaurant bar, known as *La Place de la Fontaine,* looking impeccable but a little out of time and place, would be Daniel Johnson, then leader of the *Union Nationale* Opposition in the Quebec legislature.

After listening all day to Liberal ministers talking expansively about the brave new world they were creating, it was jolting to share a drink with Johnson, who seemed old-fashioned in those heady years. He was unfailingly courteous but always projected amusement at, and maybe even a little contempt for, the great goings on, asking pointed questions such as whether Jean Lesage had explained to me exactly how he intended to pay for his grandiose dreams.

I remember particularly an evening in 1962 when Johnson invited me to dinner and I asked him to define his political ideology: "You know," he said, "in politics it's very dangerous to have any philosophy. In a democracy you should have men to settle the problems that exist, not politicians who set out to prove philosophical ideals."

He would tell me how he was spending at least three days a week travelling alone around the province, organizing ridings, and how he had discovered that the technocrat politicians in Quebec City had lost touch with the people and that he was certain he could win the next election. I confess I never took his claims very seriously. (Hardly anyone else took them very seriously either; young Liberals would catch a glimpse of him in his sombre suit and say, laughingly: "There goes Danny boy.")

The dominant impression of this man, who is now so important to the Canadian future, is that he is very much a part of the Canadian past. His courtly manner, his correct form of dress, his tight grip over his followers, even his car (he is driven around the province in a tug-size

Cadillac with provincial flags fluttering on its fenders) are all part of a vanishing tradition in Canadian politics. Johnson's view of the political process is rooted almost entirely in the long, dark-Duplessis era of Quebec history. Like Duplessis who was his mentor, he believes that the essence of politics must be power, not law, and that Quebec can advance her case best by straining against the reality, not the legality of each new situation.

While his opponents argue about the shadings of meaning in the various clauses of the British North America Act, Johnson dismisses the whole constitution as only one of five arrangements which have governed relations between English and French Canadians. (The others being those of 1763, 1774, 1791 and 1840.) "Too many people," he says "treat the BNA Act like a sacred cow, even though it's been violated many times in closed committee sessions and even in hotel rooms. So why not get rid of it and draft a sixth constitution?"

This may sound like a flippant way to dismiss the document on which the existence of the country is based, but it is entirely consistent with the whole thrust of Johnson's policies. For nearly thirty years, he has been preaching exactly the same thing: that Quebec must be able to create and control the economic and social institutions which are the true reflections of French Canada's soul. He believes that the place of Quebec within the federal system inevitably inhibits English Canada from realizing its legitimate objectives, so that separation by mutual agreement into a loose alliance is the best way out for both groups. This was the theme of his book, *Egalité ou Indépendance,* best expressed in its concluding paragraph: "Where the French Canadian nation finds its freedom, there too will be its homeland." Around Quebec City, Johnson's book is referred to by civil servants as "the Gospel according to St. Daniel."

His concept of "two nations" is foreign to nearly everyone outside Quebec, because it is not an idea that can be accommodated inside the Canada we know. It jeopardizes the basic integrity of the country, substituting a hybrid arrangement which has no modern precedent except the madcap constitution of the Austro-Hungarian empire. But none of this weakens Johnson's resolve. He is dead serious about his intentions, and as far as he is concerned, it is only the timing and the details that remain to be worked out.

Unlike Jean Lesage, he has few lingering regrets and no sentimental attachments to Ottawa or the Confederation we have been evolving for the past hundred years. Yet there is nothing vindictive about Johnson's stand, just a bloodless assessment of the political realities as they strike him. "The trouble," he says, "is that too many people equate Canada with Confederation as it is – that is, a confederation of ten provinces. I'm not advocating the disappearance of any province. But what is the formal element of Confederation? At the present time, it is the geographical dimension. I would like to see a grouping under another dimension, which is the cultural one."

"We must have a new constitution," he insists. "We cannot leave the rights of any group to the whims of political struggle." One of the first steps he suggests is a reformed Senate which would contain two committees: a judiciary group (which would really sit as a constitutional tribunal) and an equalization committee (which would handle the transfer of fiscal revenues between the various Canadian regions). According to Johnson, the membership of such a Senate would be partially elected, and would "represent the two nations in the sense I use the word." He continues to stress that Quebec must have 100 per cent of all the present major tax yields from Ottawa, though he would consider a federal counter-offer transferring an equivalent amount of indirect taxation under provincial jurisdiction.

"Ottawa is dreaming these days," he complains. "For instance, they tried to fight inflation by establishing a five-per-cent temporary refundable tax on corporation profits. That postponed about $200 million of investment in the whole country. At the same time, the heads of Hydro Quebec, two or three of the large provincial road departments, and some other corporations and provincial governments could have cut that much from their budgets between breakfast and lunch. Ottawa just doesn't want to recognize that 80 per cent of public investment is now carried out by the provinces and municipalities. If this group had delayed some projects, they would really have taken the heat out of the economy. But Ottawa refuses to consult. It's all hopelessly inefficient."

The *Union Nationale's* slim majority in the legislature was built of the discontent that much of rural Quebec felt about the Liberals' quiet revolution. If discontent grows as a result of the economic slowdown that seems to be overtaking many of the provinces' industries, the Quebec leader may wish to divert the thoughts of his people to less mundane objectives, such as wars on Ottawa.

When that moment comes, it will be worthwhile remembering that despite his pleasant manner and soft tone, Daniel Johnson is not a premier like the others, but a man working out his own dark vision of the kind of Canada he wants.   [1968]

Marc Lalonde

THE YOUNG MONTREAL LAWYER who became Lester Pearson's chief policy adviser today brings with him a set of skills and attitudes refreshingly different from those of the bureaucrats and politicians who now set the style and outlook of official Ottawa. Marc Lalonde, a thirty-seven-year-old graduate of Oxford and former professor of law at the University of Montreal, is the first of a new breed of technocrats to move into positions of influence within Ottawa's inner circle of power.

He replaces Tom Kent, who left the PM's office on December 30, 1965, to become deputy minister of manpower and immigration, and like Kent, Lalonde will be one of only three men in Ottawa to have a private briefing with the prime minister every weekday morning. Lalonde's assignment is to become chief of staff for the prime minister, acting as his interlocutor on important policy and political developments.

Although his new job moves Lalonde very near the top of the Liberal party's internal power structure, he has not, in the past, been associated with partisan politics. Instead, he has been one of the youngest and one of the most influential members of that small group of French-Canadian intellectuals dedicated to the proposition that Quebec's best interests lie within Confederation, and that the only way to beat this country's Anglo-Saxon establishment, is on the grounds of competitive excellence. "We represent a new generation of French-Canadians who are aware of modern technology and not at all afraid of it," he says. "I have hope and enthusiasm for all the new techniques in communications, management, administration and politics. In that

150

sense, I suppose you could call me an enlightened technocrat."

He intends to introduce new techniques to the prime minister's office, including wall charts that depict "critical-path patterns" for policy problems and communications practices "more closely connected with the realities of society today."

Lalonde believes in Canada as a political entity within which the French-Canadian community can flourish, providing it earns its place. "If French-Canadians can't make their abilities recognized by competing with English-Canadians, we'd better forget about the whole thing," he says. "I'm interested in trying to help build a government that will have as wide responsibilities for as many people as possible. Whether they are French- or English-speaking Canadians is comparatively irrelevant." He feels that Ottawa has been too frightened of Quebec's initiatives, and presumably will advise the prime minister to that effect.

Unlike most Quebec intellectuals, Lalonde is more committed to existence than essence – a modern, problem-oriented man, whose ideological considerations are very much secondary. "I started, like many young people, being pretty socialistic," he says, "but today I'm radical only in the sense of being a reformer. Experience with governments and looking at the evolution of socialist states has taught me that you need to develop techniques much more adjusted to particular problems than ideologies provide. There will always be some ideology, in the sense that you need a basic morality in public life. But apart from saying that behind social action there should be the individual as a man, I get very suspicious when people try to trumpet appeals and slogans."

This position also makes Lalonde an opponent of the Walter Gordon variety of Canadian nationalism. In May, 1964, he joined (with Pierre Elliott Trudeau among others) a Montreal group known as the Committee for Political Realism, which issued a manifesto condemning nationalism of all varieties. ("To use nationalism as a yard-stick deciding policies and priorities is both sterile and retrograde. Overflowing nationalism distorts one's vision of reality, prevents one from seeing problems in their true perspective, falsifies solutions and constitutes a classic diversionary tactic for politicians caught by facts. . . . Our comments in this regard apply equally to Canadian nationalism or French-Canadian nationalism. . . .")

Lalonde is a tall, balding young man with a smile of singular sweetness. There is little pomposity in his nature but one senses a toughness in his resolve. He comes from a family which for nine generations has farmed on Ile Perrot, near Montreal. His father was forced to leave

151

school after grade four and Marc is the youngest of his five children and the only one for whom he was able to provide a university education. After attending St. Laurent classical college and spending two years in the Catholic Action Movement (which also served as a training ground for Claude Ryan and Gerard Pelletier), he took law at the University of Montreal and won three scholarships to study political science at Oxford for two years.

When he returned to Canada in 1957, he became a professor of law at the University of Montreal, and served briefly as a research assistant to then justice minister Davie Fulton. He later returned to private law practice in Montreal, though he continued to teach and began to involve himself in federal royal commissions. He served as assistant counsel to the Norris commission on Hal Banks, was an early member of the Carter taxation commission staff and a commissioner with the Fowler committee on broadcasting.

Early in 1966, Lester Pearson asked him to Ottawa on a part-time basis to head a task force instructed to co-ordinate national securities regulations. He was later retained as an adviser on federal-provincial relations, and now moves into the top job in the prime minister's secretariat. Lalonde's influence during this last year of Pearson's stewardship will probably be considerable, partly because he is outspoken by nature, but also because he does not regard his appointment as a career position. "I have eight generations of Norman farmers behind me," he says, "and a natural bent toward scepticism and practicality. I've seen how governments let people down and avoid tackling real problems by delivering political sermons. This is my big concern and my big worry: to give the country a feeling of identity through direct action by the federal government."

[1967]

Jean-Jacques Bertrand

I T IS ALL THERE, BEHIND THE IMPLACABLE DEMOGRAPHY of his face, the insight that comes from serious illness, the tensions that have killed three of his predecessors, the weight of the knowledge that his decisions could settle the fate of a province and a country he loves.

Jean-Jacques Bertrand, the twenty-fifth premier of Quebec, is desperately trying to fill the political vacuum that has existed in French Canada for the past nine months. In the process he is becoming a man whose moods and methods, whose ideology and sense of personal priorities, must be understood and respected if the endless round of constitutional bargaining is to produce a new country with Quebec still within its borders.

When I talked to Bertrand in his office on the first floor of Quebec's legislative buildings, he was fresh from having decided to contest the leadership of the *Union Nationale* party at its convention next summer. Even in repose there is an unexpected toughness to his features and the Ottawa mandarins who like to think that his affirmation in office will solve many of their problems, had better look again. "If separatism grows in this province," he said, "it will be due to Pierre Trudeau and his actions. The federal government is promoting the cause of René Lévesque as nothing else. Before he came to Ottawa, Trudeau made himself known as an advocate of true federalism. But he's not practising it. He now thinks he can further the unity of this country by insisting that Ottawa must be everywhere to stop, look, listen and decide. I hope that there won't be a confrontation between us, because politics should be fought on principles not personalities. But if a confrontation comes, I'll be ready."

Bertrand's strategy is to give the constitutional talks another year or so, then if nothing has been decided he may hold a referendum on Quebec's future. The terms of such a plebiscite will be set as much by Ottawa as by Quebec, because so far, according to Bertrand, Trudeau has been only interested in expanding federal powers: "If the other provinces want to stand for what Ottawa is doing, that's their business. But it's not according to the realities of Canadian life. I'm not inventing history. I'm a man of action writing history, whether others like it or not. Our compatriots in the rest of Canada, being in the majority, don't always reason the same way as we do. But they should put themselves in our boots and see our problems. Who wouldn't be a nationalist in my position? We'll never surrender what political powers we have in Quebec. Our future is based not on any inferiority complex but on the complex of self-preservation."

Quebec is at least two years ahead of all other governments in formulating its constitutional future and Bertrand is becoming increasingly impatient both with the pace of federal-provincial constitutional talks and what he considers to be Ottawa's repeated attempts to invade fields of provincial jurisdiction. "The Quebec of the future," he said, "will be a different Quebec with a dynamic economy and French as its working language. This is a nationalist, not a separatist, position and I hope Ottawa will participate in our future instead of trying to destroy the autonomy of Quebec by such programs as medicare." He will demand Quebec jurisdiction over welfare programs and urban development, as well as provincial control over financial institutions. The kind of federalism he visualizes would grant Quebec special status (he prefers to call it "a special arrangement") by giving the province full legislative and administrative powers in a number of fields now belonging to Ottawa, even if the other, English-speaking provinces agree to yield these fields to the federal government.

His conversation reveals Jean-Jacques Bertrand to be very different from his predecessors. A man without grandeur or guile, he is a reformer without being a revolutionary. His ideology stems from Alexis de Tocqueville, the nineteenth century French savant who wrote that "it behooves moderate men to ensure the success of an orderly republic." In a province of talkers and boasters, he is a careful listener who seldom allows himself the grand gestures and verbal hyperbole that mark the discourses of most Quebec politicians. Our interview turned out to be a kind of episodic progression of questions and answers, slipping effortlessly from one subject to the next, each ex-

154

change completing itself like a slow movie fade-out, while the next topic built up underneath it. In everything he does and says, Bertrand is aware that his government must raise at least $450 million on the bond market this year, and that his province's credit rating fluctuates according to its political climate.

At the end of our talk, I asked Bertrand whether he considered himself to be a Quebecker or Canadian first. "Well, I'm a Quebecker first in areas of provincial jurisdiction and a Canadian first in the other areas. It was said of Daniel Johnson that he was a faithful Quebecker and a loyal Canadian. I hope they say the same thing about me."

[1969]

155

Robert Bourassa

POLITICAL SUPPLICANTS OF ALL SHAPES AND DESIRES crowd the anteroom of Robert Bourassa's parliamentary office. Men with thin moustaches and large ambitions, they hunch their shoulders against the burdens of office they soon hope to carry, displaying their self-importance by puffing cigars, shuffling through briefcases and exchanging whispered confidences. Telephone calls, coming in at one-minute intervals, keep two secretaries busy. Mayor Jean Drapeau of Montreal is put through; others are diverted or delayed.

The only relaxed presence in all the euphoric hysteria is Robert Bourassa himself. He appears even younger than thirty-six, a man so gaunt his neck muscles are taut and his Adam's apple juts out incongruously below a face whose eyes incongruously mirror the sensitivity of a nun. Bourassa is so cool, so without pretension, that in his presence Lesage's former *politique de grandeur* seems an absurdity. His style is almost wholly cerebral. He is laconic, unimpressed with himself, and unemotional. There is about him still the air of the brilliant, bespectacled student who figures he can solve any problem with the application of enough energy and intelligence.

Since Maurice Duplessis died eleven years ago, six men have held what must be the most hazardous job in Canadian politics. Joined by the common ideal of trying to reconcile the aspirations of a volatile population with the insensitivities of an Anglo-Saxon environment, they have behaved as if they were kings, negotiating abroad with sovereign pretensions, moving through the province with retinues of flunkeys and dispensing largesse with an upraised hand. Maurice Duplessis turned Quebec into an isolated fortress; Paul Sauvé briefly bridged the moats; Antonio Barrette equivocated; Jean Lesage attacked; Daniel Johnson schemed; Jean-Jacques Bertrand waited.

But Robert Bourassa, if first indications mean anything, seems to see the salvation of his people through economic prosperity and hence through action. Not for him any misty dreams of refighting the Plains of Abraham. He talks only of *now* and intends to push Quebec into full technological partnership with the rest of Canada. He refuses to endow separatism with any mystique about yearnings for lost nationhood, but sees it strictly as a poison seeping from economic inequalities. "Separatism has at its base economic grievances," he says. "If I make a good showing during the next five years, the separatist threat will be over. By that time the consequences of the lower birth rate will make it easier to meet the unemployment challenge. These will be the tough years but I'm pretty confident. It would have been hard with only fifty-five seats, but with the majority I have and a minimum of luck, I'll succeed."

"You know," he continues, "during the election I didn't have much time to try to destroy the *Parti Quebecois*. But in the last week of the campaign, I kept challenging them, asking what they would do to solve unemployment. And they were unable to reply. René Lévesque was saying the independence of Quebec means economic prosperity. But this was an intellectual fraud."

Bourassa sees himself not only as chief spokesman for French Canada, but as the champion of all the economically depressed regions east of the Ottawa River. "I am ready to assume the leadership of Eastern Canada," he said. "Tariff policies up to now have favoured Central Canada too much and that's one reason for regional disparities. A better deal for Eastern Canada is bound to benefit Quebec and we won't have to ask for special treatment. Only Quebec is powerful enough to put pressure on the federal government on behalf of the East. That's why we have a special role in Confederation. If I don't use that power as the leader of Eastern Canada, Confederation will lose the game."

Bourassa's main interest and dedication is to use the instrument of government to intervene on behalf of the ordinary citizen and in this sense, at least, he is a political radical. "When I was studying at Oxford," he says, "I was a member of the Labour party with Chuck Taylor (the Montreal NDPer). Though I was then a leftist, as prime minister of Quebec in the year 1970, I have to behave like a pragmatist."

157

Bourassa went to Oxford in 1957 after graduating first in his class at the University of Montreal law school. He later studied corporate law and public finance at Harvard University and taught economics at the University of Ottawa. Following a brief period as secretary of the Carter commission on taxation, he became research director of Quebec's Belanger commission on public finance. He moved into active politics by winning the Mercier seat in the 1966 election and became a protege of Lesage's and the Liberals' chief financial critic.

Married to the daughter of Joseph Simard, founder of the huge Marine Industries complex at Sorel, he won the leadership of the Quebec Liberal party in a tough contest earlier this year. "I have the same training as Pierre Trudeau," he says, "and I'll be able to negotiate with him on an equal footing. I don't know him well; in fact, I haven't spoken to him at all in the last four years. But I know Marc Lalonde very well. He is one of my closest friends. On administrative grounds, I think Trudeau has done a good job. But I'm not the same type of person. I'm more austere than he is. But neither of us is dogmatic and I think it will be easy to work with him."

When Bourassa begins his negotiations with Ottawa, Trudeau will discover that unlike Daniel Johnson or Jean-Jacques Bertrand, Bourassa is more interested in economic realities than in constitutional complexities. "I don't like the legalistic approach," he insists. "Look what the Lesage government accomplished between 1960 and 1966 without changing a comma in the constitution. Sure, we need a constitutional revision. Everybody says that. So I'll say the same thing. But I don't think anything will be solved by that. Supposing we say that social security should be a provincial matter," he went on. "We would get control of unemployment insurance, for example, and it would cost us $50 million more. That's not a good bargain for us. The essence of a good federal system is to redistribute revenues from the rich to the less rich provinces. So my view is that we must benefit from the workings of a good federal system to diffuse the economic prosperity of Ontario to Eastern Canada. I'm confident that I can deal with Ottawa because I'll tell them if you're true federalists, you will work for a better sharing of prosperity. Otherwise there would be no raison d'être of a federal system. The test of Confederation will be a solution to regional disparities. This will solve the Quebec problem at the same time."

Bourassa's other demands are likely to include Quebec jurisdiction over the French network of the CBC; reform of the Supreme Court of

158

Canada; provincial participation in the setting of tariff policies; turning over to Quebec of family allowances; and a new formula for distributing medicare funds to take into account unemployment levels, per capita income and tax revenues of the less rich provinces.

One thing he is not at all interested in is a continuation of Quebec's harassment of Ottawa's external affairs policies vis-à-vis France. He is saying, in effect, *Adieu, mon Général* and believes that Quebec should only have a cultural relationship with France, conducted under federal auspices.

Bourassa's first dealings with Ottawa will occur in mid-June during a federal-provincial conference of ministers of finance, a portfolio that he intends to occupy during the first year of his administration. Bourassa is optimistic, but he is also aware that his failure might doom the Canadian experiment. "I've been told that I represent Quebec's last chance, and to some extent it's true," he says. "If I fail in my relations with Ottawa, people will say Bourassa was well prepared and rational and Trudeau is also well prepared and rational. If these two guys can't make the system work, it's impossible. And they could be right."

[1970]

PART FIVE *Campaigning*

John Diefenbaker

THE ELECTION WAGED BY JOHN DIEFENBAKER in the fall of 1965 was not a campaign in the accepted sense. It was a guerrilla war, fought along a four-thousand-mile front in treacherous circumstances with unreliable troops and intriguing generals. Victory was impossible; success would be measured by mere survival.

The Diefenbaker campaign style transcended ideology. The Conservative party became little more than a front for his rhetoric. Even more than winning the election, he seemed obsessed by a need to propagandize his vision of Canada; to hold back, somehow, the mechanized urban society threatening to engulf his world.

From the beginning, John Diefenbaker refused to read the portents or heed the omens of his defeat. Only one explanation seemed to fit the dimensions of his extraordinary campaign. It was as if, sometime after Lester Pearson called the election, John Diefenbaker decided to transform himself into an incarnation of the Canada he knew. He became a figment of his own imagination, a man for whom nothing was impossible, a politician without rivals, who saw himself personifying the national will.

Diefenbaker had to lose. But the odds did not seem fair. While Lester Pearson was firing salvos of press releases from his Ottawa office or the multigraph machines mounted in his campaign aircraft, John Diefenbaker was jolting into small towns at twenty-minute intervals on a punishing coast-to-coast railway tour.

An air of timelessness hung over Diefenbaker's campaign train as he whistle-stopped his way across the country. There was no taste of 1965 in the air, no sensation of progress or reality. The landscape on

163

which the Diefenbaker train moved seemed like a sequence of Krieghoff tableaux run through a Cinerama lens.

Diefenbaker's advisers had warned him that campaigning by train could prove disastrous, because in the age of the automobile, railway stations were no longer a factor in most people's lives. During the first leg of his journey, from Halifax to Montreal, it looked as if his advisers had been right. At Matapédia, Quebec, only five off-duty trainmen and three stray dogs turned out to meet the Chief. At Rimouski, where seven lonely Tories were waiting on the platform, Diefenbaker asked one of them: "Who's the candidate here?" He replied: "I am, sir. My name is Gérard Ouellette." At Amqui, the Conservative leader was introduced to a Monsieur Legris, who in turn presented the young man beside him as *"mon fils."* Diefenbaker smiled and said: *"Bonjour, Mon-seer Monfils."*

It wasn't until the Diefenbaker train was being pulled into the rural way stations of southern Alberta that the campaign began to pick up. The signs that dotted most station platforms on the Prairies – sometimes printed, sometimes scrawled on fences – established the theme of the Diefenbaker campaign: HE CARED ENOUGH TO COME. Nothing else mattered. Diefenbaker cared, and had come. Pearson had not come and, by implication, did not care.

Out of his passion for the homely, awkward and shattering small truth came Diefenbaker's rapport with the people of these small, flat Prairie towns, slanting across time. Here he could feel again the only role he had ever played well: the champion of society's downtrodden, assaulting the proud fortresses of the nation's various establishments. He soaked up the mood of rural Canada and gave it off, like a hot swift fire that burns away the scrub of a hidebound life.

The Diefenbaker train went tumbling through the night of time, its press car filled with the noise of tapping typewriters, the tinkling of glasses and the slap of cards. In his private car, Diefenbaker dictated and signed three hundred letters a day, mostly to well-wishers along the route. Between whistle stops, particularly late in the day, fatigue would dissolve his face into deep creases, like the starved topographical map of some rugged mountain range. Occasionally he would relax by taking off his clothes and stomping around his car in a bathrobe, hunching his shoulders like a prize fighter flexing for the big bout.

The leader's entourage had picked up a canary from a supporter in Richmond Hill, Ontario, and Diefenbaker spent hours trying to coax the bird to whistle, as if its song were some omen of good fortune. The

164

bird never did sing, but on the morning of November 6, between Saskatoon and Prince Albert, the steward was imitating a canary whistle, and Diefenbaker, who thought it was the real thing, got very excited. No one ever told him the truth.

The Prairies became a land to flee across – every town, every village a destination. When would these place names – Rivers, Yarbo, Raymore, Watrous, Wadena, Mortlach, Morse, Maple Creek, Taber, Fort Macleod, Claresholm, Nanton, Vulcan, Barons, Three Hills, Findlater, Aylesbury, Lumsden, Gull Lake, Champion – ever again appear in reports of Canadian election campaigns?

The journey was illuminated with moments of lucid pathos. At Fort Macleod, seventy-eight-year-old Norman Grier confided to the Chief: "Heck, I wouldn't vote for that Pearson. He wants to give away Crowsnest Mountain to Quebec." At Stettler, two raggedy kids were holding up a huge, hand-lettered cardboard sign with the letters: DEIF FOR CHEIF. At Morse, local musicians serenaded him with a wavering version of *The Thunderer* and reporters could not file their copy because the telegrapher was playing the drums. As the train pulled out, the brave little aggregation struck up *God Be With You Till We Meet Again* and John Diefenbaker cried. At Swift Current, twenty-one blue-gowned ladies on the back of a truck broke into *Land of Hope and Glory* and sang *Mademoiselle from Armentières* for an encore. At Taber, Diefenbaker told an audience of hushed school children: "I only wish that I could come back when you're my age to see the kind of Canada that you'll see. So dream your dreams, keep them and pursue them." Somewhere along the route, an old man sat by the tracks in the twilight, holding up a sign that read: JOHN, YOU'LL NEVER DIE.

[1965]

165

Robert Stanfield

I

THE SHEER MAGNITUDE OF THE PROBLEM Robert Stanfield faces in trying to become Canada's next prime minister must have been evident to him last night as he kicked off his 1968 campaign in Winnipeg with a lukewarm reception to a lukewarm speech. The Conservative leader's difficulty is that he is caught in a triangle of frustration. He cannot make any bold promises about the future, because he is too responsible a man, and anyway, the electorate is too jaundiced for any new "vision."

Yet he cannot offset the absence of an exciting program by overwhelming the voters with his personal appeal because his charm is not the kind that is readily projectable from the public platform. At the same time, he cannot whip up much enthusiasm by attacking the Liberals since their unhappy record was made under a now-departed leader and the new one hasn't done or said enough that is worth attacking.

These constraints were very much in evidence in the Winnipeg Civic Auditorium as Stanfield tried valiantly to breathe some life into the lifeless text of his campaign's opening address. By the end of the evening all that was left was the basic integrity of the man.

There is nothing contrived about Stanfield. He refuses to use any of the tricks of political oratory. Even though his address had an emotional closing ("Let this great meeting mark the transition of our time. The years of failure in Ottawa are over, the years of confidence begin"), he hurried through it as though he did not want to be accused of emotionally stirring up his audience.

166

But that was why the people had turned out, forty-five hundred strong, to become involved, to be touched by the Stanfield presence. They wanted to get a good look at him and his gracious wife, Mary, to see how he reacted to compliments, whether he had a sense of humour, what kind of a man he was and what kind of potential prime minister.

None of this happened. Not one of the warm-up speakers, who roared on for ninety minutes, told a single anecdote, introduced his wife or said anything human about the new Tory leader. Stanfield himself never departed from his text, said nothing that might leave his listeners with the warm feeling that they knew him better than before they had come.

The meeting was ineptly managed and exuded an old-fashioned aura. (Not old-fashioned picturesque like John Diefenbaker's rallies used to be, but old-fashioned dull.) It was meant to be the kind of cheerful meeting-hall entertainment that suited a simpler Canada, with the master of ceremonies warming up the audience by suggesting they sing *Pack Up Your Troubles,* and trying to rouse them with lines like "It's not raining inside tonight, folks."

A group of bearded students provided the main excitement of the night by parading around with some mildly funny homemade banners. My favorite was a sign board that read "A VOTE FOR TRUDEAU IS A VOTE AGAINST STANFIELD," on one side and "SUPPORT YOUR LOCAL AN-ARCHIST" on the other.

The best speaker of the evening was former agriculture minister Alvin Hamilton, ("the man who knows how to sell wheat") who scorned Trudeau for his "kissing campaign" and thundered: "I think of the 908 million bushels of unsold wheat – you can't kiss that away." This was the kind of folksy humanity, the identifiable political quality that Stanfield lacked.

Even if the Tory leader could have joked about himself as "Silent Bob" it would have been better than the Gothic mask of unconcern that hides this man from public scrutiny. The audience was full of open, hearty westerners ready for laughter; the leader was a taciturn, close-mouthed easterner, ready for responsibility.

The obvious point of the evening was to boost Conservative solidarity by showing off its regional strength. There were six leading provincial Tories on the platform, three of them premiers. "Ike" Smith, Stanfield's successor as the premier of Nova Scotia, gave a routine speech about regional economic disparity and after praising his predecessor made an unconscious blunder by saying, "Now let me turn to one or two other Canadian problems besides Mr. Stanfield. . . ." John

167

Robarts, the Ontario premier, behaved like a fat, rich cousin at a family reunion, a little patronizing, a trifle remote from the family's problems, but trying hard to be a good chap all the same. "Do not fall into the web, or pit if you like, of believing there are pat answers to tough problems," was his message for the night. Duff Roblin was in top form, boosting his view of Canada as a "land of many cultures, two languages, one united nation." Marcel Faribault proved that he was more than a constitutional expert. He is a man of courage. There were scattered "boos" when he was introduced and after he started to speak in French. But he won his audience by salting his speech with references to his relatives. ("My wife's grandmother was a Mackenzie. . . . My sister married a Polish engineer.") He said that he was "a Quebecker just as you are Manitobans" and this was something his audience could understand.

Finally Stanfield was piped in and he stood in that crowded hall like some misplaced favourite uncle, determined to do no less than the right thing, yet somehow looking as though he would be happier somewhere else. "Our goal," he said, "is to make this country work." You felt he could do it, but that without a keener sense of occasion than he demonstrated at this meeting, he might not get the chance.

[1968]

II

SURELY MOST THOUGHTFUL CONSERVATIVES coming out of Robert Stanfield's unlikely rally in Toronto's CNE Coliseum last night must have been asking themselves some tough questions, beginning with the clincher: What the hell has happened to my party in the last nine months? Could the bungling amateurs who planned and executed that evening of political misfortune have been the same group that excited the nation last fall by staging the most exciting leadership convention in Canadian political history?

Yes, the very same.

There was Dalton Camp, the great master of political machination who had dethroned John Diefenbaker, looking a trifle uncomfortable, but there just the same, a mute witness to the evening's bewildering events. Nine months ago Robert Stanfield's very presence had electrified a packed Maple Leaf Gardens. Last night, he seemed like a figure out of the pre-Edison age.

With all of Metropolitan Toronto to draw on, why couldn't the Conservative organizers have filled the relatively small (seating capacity fifty-five hundred) Coliseum when Pierre Trudeau had a few nights earlier drawn sixteen thousand to a meeting in Hamilton? Why couldn't someone have orchestrated the meeting so that Stanfield could have come on stage with the receptiveness of the audience at its peak? Instead, he got a great cheer when he arrived, then had to visit on the sidelines for at least an hour before he was allowed to speak. Why couldn't John Robarts have arrived on time? The Ontario premier wandered in at the end of Stanfield's speech, mumbled a few platitudes that in no way excused his not being there to introduce his national leader. And what could have possessed the evening's organizers to schedule twenty-two minutes of Ukrainian dancing and singing at the peak of the rally?

Most old-line Tories of the Davisville abstainer variety were furious. I overheard a waspish lady telling her husband: "All this ethnic stuff is colourful and everything. But couldn't they have had a nice highland fling to make Stanfield feel at home, something you could understand?" A bored kid said to no one in particular: "Let's start a rumour that Stanfield eats onions." When the Ukrainians finally bounded off the stage to be replaced by the Sugar Shoppe, a down-at-the-guitar rock group, the waspish lady complained: "All of the crazy stuff with the kids is beyond me. When we were young, we made our own fun at home." Her husband responded with the comment, "That's right, Marg, it's unwholesome."

When Stanfield finally got to speak, the political ardour of his audience had already cooled. The signs reading "SOCK IT TO THEM, BOB" demanded the impossible.

He began well, his voice clear and strong. But after four or five ripping sentences, he resorted again to droning off interest rates, the money market, income tax, saying things like "we will put an end to extravagance" and "we will create a climate of goodwill and rigorous purpose in government."

It is not that his speech was bad. In fact, his delivery was startlingly better than it had been in Winnipeg but his tone and temper made him appear to be expressing a resentment of social change. He kept referring to Conservatism's great yesterdays by invoking "the spirit of 1876," talking about a glorious past when his listeners wanted to hear about a glorious future.

The sad thing was that most of the audience really wanted to listen. They came prepared to like Stanfield, to leave the hall feeling closer to him, a little warmer in their political commitment. But the alchemy never took place.

Perhaps the trouble lies beyond Stanfield and extends to the party he leads. The Conservatives' dilemma is that they have never properly sorted out what it is that governments should and should not do. Their largest group of natural supporters – the businessmen – want the government to do nothing, to leave them alone. There is this strong strain in Canadian Toryism of the Protestant ethic, the feeling that each individual must be left master of his own destiny. This is a difficult faith to sell in an age of collectivism, particularly against an opponent who may not make specific promises but at least excites the potential in people.

Sitting in the Coliseum last night, it was disquieting to remember how many able, talented, progressive men there are in the Conservative party and to realize how badly they are being used in the current campaign by a leader who expects his followers in this time of ferment to enjoy the comfort of opinions without the discomfort of thought.

[1968]

Pierre Trudeau

I

EVEN THIS EARLY IN THE ELECTION A COMPARISON of the campaign styles of Pierre Elliott Trudeau and Robert Lorne Stanfield leads to an inescapable conclusion: unless they are dealt some unexpected blow, the Liberals will sweep into power on June 25 with a majority mandate based on their leader's burgeoning popular support in every province. You could feel victory in the air here on Thursday when Trudeau spent the day touring Winnipeg's conservative suburbs; you could hear it in dozens of casual conversations and see it on the faces in the crowds that turned out to watch his campaign.

Trudeau led a triumphal procession from shopping centre to shopping centre, where he was gaped at, flower-bedecked, sung to, applauded, heckled, admired, all the time being magnified in the public eye by the crowd's intense awareness of his style. The Trudeau crowds are sprinkled with teeny-boppers, running with long manes blowing like banners in the wind, full of vitality, excitement, laughter, shrieking in a kind of ecstacy that rises to a squawk when one of their number is kissed. (Reporter to writhing girl: "Why do you like him so much?" Writhing girl to reporter: "Oooooh, I like his pock marks.") What is probably more significant is the presence of scores of toddlers, held on the shoulders of their parents being admonished to "remember him," the way in other years the very young were brought out to behold royalty. Trudeau seems to enjoy each of these occasions, accepting the flowers thrust at him with a shrug, bounding up on the backs of trucks to give voice to his cause. But he is at his best away from the howling mobs, at press conferences where he is transformed into a first-rate teacher who can turn tentative, vaguely articulated questions into something intelligent, reworking them so that each answer becomes a lucid lecture, a precis of the problem at hand, its ramifications, other possible solutions and the difficulties involved.

He speaks English not just well but superbly, with a mastery of the Canadian idiom and of the language's subtleties. At one brief press conference he referred to "backyards" though "gardens" would have been the learned and less appropriate word. When he was asked a question that implied he might be a socialist, he answered: "I ask you not to judge a man by labels, by the thickness or thinness of his pocketbook – or indeed of his hair – but by his ideas." It was a simple response, yet exactly right because it reminded his audience in a graceful way that he is, after all, a millionaire and how could he possibly be a socialist?

If Trudeau looks like a winner, it is because little in his campaign is left to chance. At the Stanfield rally here last week there could be seen, in a back row, the bent-over figure of Gordon Churchill, once the most powerful Tory in Winnipeg, sitting unheralded and unwanted. Nobody had thought to ask him up on the platform and, except for a mumbled tribute, Stanfield ignored his presence. But Veterans Affairs Minister Roger Teillet, who was in a very similar position within the Liberal party after losing the nomination for his seat on Wednesday night, stood up on the platform at the Crossroads shopping centre at Transcona where Trudeau put his arm around him, as the audience cheered.

The old style-new style contrast has permeated the basics of the campaign, the posters, the slogans, even the music. Stanfield's organizers favour the bagpipes and his Tuesday audience was warmed up with *Pack Up Your Troubles In Your Old Kit Bag*. The Liberals had a group of attractive young folksingers, known as the Trudeau Troop, deployed at each shopping centre, singing *Rock Your Soul* and throwing machine-autographed pictures of Trudeau into the crowd.

The differences run far deeper than the paraphernalia. They are reflected in the way the two men see the issues. The Conservative leader has been going across the country making specific policy pledges, such as a feasibility study for building a tunnel to Newfoundland and the launching of a federal-guaranteed minimum-income plan. Trudeau is making few promises. He is basing his appeal instead on his ability, in this time of national crisis, to become accepted as the indispensable political leader who can take our national anxieties and release them to the surface, where they can be studied and eventually resolved.

172

He does not say how he is going to do it, but to English Canada he looks as though he is the one man who can solve "the Quebec problem" and keep the country together.

The superficial conclusion from all this might be that Stanfield is a bad campaigner because he is withdrawn and not a showman, while Trudeau is a good campaigner because he is an extrovert, a performer doing his thing. Yet Trudeau remains just as private, just as locked within himself as Stanfield. His new role appeals to his imagination and he plays it with great verve, but the blue-ice inner core of the man remains disengaged. If you look closely at Trudeau's eyes, you realize he is about as casual as a computer.

[1968]

II

PIERRE TRUDEAU'S MAMMOTH RALLY in Toronto's Nathan Phillips Square would have been an unqualified triumph if the prime minister hadn't opened his mouth. It was his presence, not his words, that excited the sea of fifty thousand Torontonians who turned out at mid-day to participate in his final visit to the Ontario capital. The fact that even his dismal speech seemed to have little effect in cooling the crowd's ardour left the impression that this – as most of other Trudeau rallies – was not a political occasion at all, but some kind of public rite, new and strange to the Canadian electoral process.

Possibly it was the difference in settings as much as anything else that transmuted the Liberal gathering into a success while the Conservatives' major Toronto rally, held two nights before, was such a misfortune. Robert Stanfield was booked by his organizers in the Canadian National Exhibition's dank Coliseum. It is a building that could almost be a monument to the old Canada of the rural era, redolent of horse shows, prize cabbages, homemade quilts and rhubarb preserves. Stanfield came and departed in the dark.

Trudeau arrived in the sunlight at city hall square, which must be the most urban setting in the country. It is urban in the best sense, full of excitement, gaiety and youth, surrounded by the towers of commerce, by the trappings of culture (Henry Moore's famous *Archer*) and of learning (Osgoode Hall in the background) – a seemingly perfect setting for a leader of tomorrow.

Waiting for the prime minister to arrive, the scene was reminiscent of Expo, with the fountains giving freshness to the air and the wind whipping the boppers' skirts and the matrons' curled hair, making everybody feel part of the environment, free-wheeling and summer-happy. There were kids on top of the concrete arches that vault over the fountains, helicopters, balloons, placards, flowers. Everybody was clapping to the infectious rhythms of the Travellers singing *This Land Is My Land*.

Unhappily what this breathtaking setting inspired from the prime minister was a speech so pedestrian that if almost any other politician had made it, he would have been booed. It was not so much that one expected concrete policy proposals (the Liberal leader has already indicated he is against that kind of thing) or even singing statistics laying the foundation for his Just Society. But one did expect some sort of intellectual content, some significant display that Trudeau believes he is not the only one around with any brains, that he understands *les beaux yeux et les belles fleurs* are only the trappings of style and that style itself must have substance.

Instead he gave a curious speech, part discombobulated sloganeering, part first-year-survey-course-in-history lecture on the role of the city-state in the history of civilization. He made the obvious point that all great civilizations have developed in urban environments and that he hoped there could be maintained in the country "harmonious cities where ideas can be exchanged."

Nobody is going to vote against that. But it was hardly what the people had come to hear. The bulk of the adults in the crowd were office workers skipping lunch to hear him. Many of them had waited nearly an hour in the sun for Trudeau's appearance. They came to feel some broader involvement in Canada's problems, perhaps even to be uplifted, who knows? But all the prime minister attempted was to incite municipal loyalties. Before he was through, most people looked puzzled, many were beating the crowd out the exits; only the boppers were still ecstatic.

This is the great mystery of the current campaign: why Pierre Trudeau is presenting himself as so much less than he is. I have heard him talk beautifully with depth and intuitive understanding about contemporary Canada to an audience of one. All winter long he presented himself on television to an audience of millions as a man with immense respect for the public intelligence. Why now on the hustings when he has audiences of five hundred – or fifty thousand as yesterday – does he not give a little more of himself and demand a little more of his listeners?

174

Perhaps Trudeau knows too well that he is riding the crest of success, maybe he has been infected by the winner's psychology that permeates his camp, and figures that no matter how little he says, nothing can go wrong for him now. Yet it is disappointing that this remarkable man has yet to utter a memorable phrase, that he is treating the electorate with a self-contained arrogance which implies the intellectual's snobbish suspicion that the proletariat will be content with circuses and would not, in any case, understand the issues being discussed.

From here Trudeau moves to New Brunswick, Quebec, rural Ontario and Winnipeg before ending his campaign in Montreal.

The Liberals may be planning some dramatically memorable last-day speech in Montreal, but in Toronto yesterday the kid in the crowd who was holding up a lonely sign that read "FIFTY TO ONE HE SAYS NOTHING" turned out to be dead right.

[1968]

John Diefenbaker

I WENT OUT TO PRINCE ALBERT, SASKATCHEWAN, for a few days during that eccentric 1972 election compaign to report on John Diefenbaker's re-election; to discover what, if any, secrets might still be simmering in the smithy of his soul. I went, too, because it seemed like a good place to get away from the press buses, the handouts, and the crowds. A place where you could still touch the country. But mostly I went because John Diefenbaker was once again in the political ring and I could not stay away.

I found a candidate very different from the frantic Diefenbaker of the great national campaigns. This was a relaxed politician, dancing out the joy of getting back among his own people, the brew of laughter never far below the surface of his outrage.

The Diefenbaker years of Canadian history seemed as distant as the Boer War, but the man whose name they bear was still running hard (because he knows no other way to run) and it was only his tight-faced competitors who failed to understand why, at the age of seventy-seven, he really had no choice. Diefenbaker's life has been so exclusively channeled into his public role that clinging to existence means clinging to office. Watching him "main-street" the small prairie towns, hearing him talk to the farmers in the faded Legion halls, I could feel myself in contact both with the roots of his power and the reasons for his downfall.

The dilemma of most Canadian politicians seriously interested in office is how to stress their marginal differences so they can conceal their basic similarities. John Diefenbaker's difficulty is exactly the opposite: his problem is somehow to make enough concessions to his nature so that he will sound enough like his less individualistic rivals.

176

He sees himself as a man on his knees in a land of political midgets.

This campaign, his fifteenth, began as always with a nominating convention at the Orpheum Theatre, the converted vaudeville house in downtown Prince Albert. Summer had one more week to run and half a dozen Indians dozed on the benches near the Hudson's Bay Company fur depot on River Street. The combines were still out harvesting and Diefenbaker's people worried about packing the eight-hundred-seat theatre.

But the Orpheum filled quickly that night as a seven-piece band called The Cottonpickers (MUSIC ANY WAY YOU LIKE IT) struck up a kind of Hawaiian gavotte, then went on to play polkas and country rock. J. J. Cennon, a local disc jockey, came on stage to warm up the audience: "Did you hear about Trudeau's accident? He was taking his morning walk when he was hit by a motorboat."

Here, in this draughty little theatre, Diefenbaker had first conjured up those grand visions that later claimed the emotional conquest of a decade. And now the man who had refused to sip Napoleon brandy with Winston Churchill, who had called General Eisenhower "Ike" to his face, and who had saved the Commonwealth by standing up against South African apartheid was reduced to this praetorian guard of home-town loyalists. Still, this was *his* army, and there was a rush of sheer happiness (that made you realize how rare joy is in crowds) when the barbaric evocation of the bagpipes heralded the Chief's arrival.

But after eight nominating speeches, itemizing the Great Man's glories, there was a bad ten minutes as Bob Fair, a Saskatoon business-man, nominated his brother, Bill, as an anti-Diefenbaker Conservative candidate. "The PC party has gone from a majority two hundred and eight members in 1958 to a minority of seventy-two members at the present time," he began. "What happened? Who was to blame? The party? Or *the leader*?" It was a chilling moment. Every eye in the house turned on John Diefenbaker and suddenly people were remembering all the tragedies, small and large, that had cost their man his power, understanding a little of why he was being challenged here on his home ground by a spoiler, a young man impatient with the old man and his dreams.

Diefenbaker's speech, the only major address of his campaign, was one of those impressionistic spectaculars in which, like most self-made men, he sets out to worship his creator. He is old, so old now, but the mercurial touches are still there. The half-smile, the devastating scorn for his opponents. By alternating clipped participles with long open

177

vowel sounds he achieves a Biblical cadence, the glancing immediacy of his language enforced by gesture. The right hand swooping down in accusing chops as the whole man sways to the melody of his words. "Why do I continue in public life?" he demanded, then answered his own question: "I still have work to do for Canada. So much to do. So little time to do it."

The most curious part of Diefenbaker's hour-long discourse was the listing of his accomplishments. He said, among other things, that he was the only Canadian ever to be awarded the Princess Olga Medal from the World Organization of Ukrainians for Freedom; he said that he had been chosen an honorary chief by the National Indian Brotherhood; he said that the Canadian Zionist Federation had recently honoured him and that the Free Baltic People of the World were about to do so. But at the end he landed back in Prince Albert: "I'm asking you to mobilize. Let us march together to bring about the changes that you want. Ladies and gentlemen, from the bottom of my heart I thank you. My people residing in this constituency, I shall not fail you. Thank you. Thank you."

The actual campaign began next morning. Word was out that they were going to get Dief this time. (*They* were always going to get Dief but nobody ever did because you cannot defeat a man who assesses himself at his own valuation.) Bill Berezowsky of the NDP, a stocky, energetic socialist with a good, windblown face, put on the best campaign any candidate had ever run against the former PM. His initial slogan aimed at Diefenbaker's age was GIVE YOUTH A CHANCE. Bill Berezowsky is 68. He campaigned so well that on election night Diefenbaker told him: "You scared the hell out of me." But Dief's support cut deeply across party lines and even in this ebbing time he ended up with a 9,678-vote victory margin.

Diefenbaker only left Prince Albert for five brief appearances in his supporters' ridings; he made few formal speeches. One exception was a talk he gave to the students of the local composite high school. He reminisced about his greatness. ("I've lived history. I've made history, and I know I'll have my place in history. That's not egoism.") He relived some of his great moments with his own reading of events. ("President Kennedy sent one million dollars and four hundred operators to defeat me in 1963.") Later he made fun of Pierre Trudeau's contention that Otto Lang was Canada's greatest wheat salesman. ("If Otto Lang had to cross a field with four cowpies in it, he'd manage to step in all of them before he'd make it to the other side.") But his

178

greatest scorn was reserved for Trudeau himself. ("I heard the prime minister. It was a four-letter word. It ended in 'k' and it wasn't 'work'!").

Most of his time was spent meeting small groups of constituents. He seldom paused for conversation. He held open house with himself.

"If it wasn't for you, Mr. Diefenbaker, Prince Albert wouldn't be on the map today, that's what my dad says. . . ."

"Well, thank you, son, and how *is* your dad. A fine man. . . ."

"How are you, Mr. Diefenbaker? I want you to know that I still carry the letter you sent me in 1957 when I was sick in the sanatorium. It sure helped me a lot. . . ."

"Ah, that's very kind of you. There aren't many letters like that still extant you know, not very many."

To a bystander: "Isn't it remarkable that in this violent age, I, a former prime minister, can walk around among all sorts of people with no bodyguard, no fear. Isn't that remarkable?"

A hot politician in the age of cool, Diefenbaker is always in a hurry. Time pursues him. To cover the most territory in the shortest period he rented a helicopter to tour his riding. He descended from the sky through the autumn haze and people flocked to meet him. At Ethelton, with a population estimate of twelve families, sixty people were waiting. At Meskanaw, school kids were out waving a big Union Jack. The farmers drove in from four directions drawn by his presence, many still in their coveralls, a few of the ladies dressed up with crowns of small afternoon hats. Talking at first, they grew still as he landed, the chopper's blades stirring up a wind that blew about their faces, fluttering the hair of the women, making little jib sails of the vents in the men's jackets. "We'd circle a little town in this damn helicopter," said Dick Spencer, the local PC association president who rode along with him, "and I'd pull myself up and think, 'Oh God, if you're there at all make us a crowd,' because I couldn't bear to see Dief disappointed. Then I'd sit back and wouldn't look at him till I'd checked the school yard and seen maybe thirty cars, which would mean maybe sixty people, and then I'd look over at him and the eyes would be sparkling and he'd be getting ready to speak."

Talking afterward to some of the farmers who had met him – though *touched* seems a more appropriate word – I could see why Diefenbaker still inspires such loyalty in most of Western Canada – and why the Conservatives made such impressive gains here. What he understands so well is that there is only one issue that matters in the

179

West: the idea of *control*. The Liberals, whether under Louis St. Laurent, Lester Pearson, or Pierre Trudeau, tend to equate the political satisfaction of the Prairies with wheat sales. Otto Lang, the former dean of the University of Saskatchewan law school, appointed by Trudeau as the minister in charge of the Canadian Wheat Board, kept stressing throughout his campaign that prairie farmers would market at least one billion bushels of grain this year. The strategy failed because he never recognized what John Diefenbaker has known all his life: that wheat sales mark only the beginning of most farmers' concerns.

There is money on the Prairies this year. Net farm income in Saskatchewan is expected to reach $480 million for 1972 and Ford dealers are reporting truck and car sales increases of 23 per cent. But the farmers know, too, that in another year or so they may be poor again. (In 1970, Saskatchewan's average net farm income was $2,500.) They realize that their economic existence is governed by forces over which they exercise little *control*. That is why the West has always needed champions (and not just wheat salesmen) inside the larger circles of power in Ottawa. And that is why they love John Diefenbaker. As prime minister he granted them a measure of self-determination by sponsoring laws to help even the odds.

This is a land of long memories. During the Thirties Saskatchewan suffered the severest curtailment in material living standards of any area in the civilized world. The older farmers fear it can happen again unless they're able somehow to gain *control* over their future. Basic incomes will always hinge on how the weather affects crop yields and no man can guarantee that. So when they talk about *control,* Westerners really mean getting away from the stifling influence of the commercial, industrial and transportation interests of Eastern Canada, anxious to turn the Prairies into an exploitable hinterland. Westerners admire John Diefenbaker for the enemies they share: those nameless Eastern interests who, looking down from their penthouses of power, always regarded the man from Prince Albert as some kind of unfathomable electoral accident, a political street-singer to be silenced.

As I talked to farmers, letting uncounted cups of coffee grow cold between us, they speculated about their lives. It is not envy they feel. They have little desire to emulate the slickness of the East, no wish to inhabit the smooth apartment towers that stab the sky around the great urban centres. It is anger that fills their minds and resentment that motivates their politics. Not so long ago they were at the forefront of Canadian civilization. They won this country from the wilderness and

180

now they have lost it to the moneyed navel-gazers and midnight philosophers from Toronto and Montreal who never had to serve their harsh apprenticeships. The older generation mourns the decline of religious faith and is furious with Trudeau's sacrilegious wisecracks. They regret the disappearance of simplicity, fidelity and all the homely virtues. They want to return to a time when people did a little business so they could socialize, not socialize in order to do business.

By helping them celebrate their past because he himself is so much a part of it, John Diefenbaker became a kind of thundering reminder of the Prairies' missing alter ego. He moved through the knots of farmers who turned out to see him, savouring the sights, the sounds and the smells of the land, looking into men's eyes and women's feelings, measuring their distances and their closeness, understanding their protection of each other, their sense of shared loneliness. His brief blessings didn't bleach the color and meaning out of words, like the benedictions of most politicians on the stump.

Here was a rare communion of instincts. The old man living out his legend. The people responding to the spectacle of his presence with a deep folk wisdom that saw him as a final link with their hopeful origins, a touchstone against the baffling present and the frightening future. And that was why the Diefenbaker magic, long a spent force in the rest of the country, still meant something here.

[1972]

181

PART SIX   *Music*

Stan Kenton

WHEN I FIRST EMIGRATED TO CANADA from Czechoslovakia in the early Forties, I used to put myself to sleep listening to the Eaton's catalogue radio I got for my eleventh birthday, and it turned out to be one of the most important formative influences of my life. I could not speak much English then, but I soaked up the earnest CBC documentaries about Canada, turning myself into a loving nationalist in the process.

And late at night, long after my parents thought I was asleep, lying there with the radio tuned right down (its dial light removed so there would be no telltale glow), I tuned into other, more exciting worlds. The midnight airwaves were filled with remote pickups from ballrooms all across North America where the big bands were swinging high, and it was their music that first opened the way for me into the culture of the continent to which I had so lately and luckily come. When I finally fell asleep after three or four hours of CBC documentaries and the big bands, I would dream about Sir John A. Macdonald, Glenn Miller, George Drew, Tommy Dorsey, Mackenzie King and Charlie Barnet, somehow sure that this would always be my country and my music. And then one night in the late summer of 1941, I picked up a Mutual Broadcasting Company remote from the Rendezvous Ballroom in Balboa Beach, California, and heard Stan Kenton for the first time.

The music come pouring out of my little radio like a hailstorm. The sound engulfed me with its azure beauty, the soloists cutting into the static of my radio in dissonant outbursts, like voices shouting into the wind. Right then and there began my obsession with Kenton's music. I performed it, studied it and played it ever since. I had tapes of it along with me during those incredible train rides of the Die-

185

fenbaker campaigns; I listened to it when I was reporting the Israeli wars crouched in foxholes along the Suez; and now, when I find myself besieged by visiting American journalists trying to find out what Canadian nationalism is all about, I never completely turn down my office phonograph, hoping that one of my American visitors will share my passion. Not one of them has, though I think I detect in them relief, as they listen to my Yankee music, that we nationalists might just be a bunch of sycophantic crackpots after all.

I have every one of Kenton's 134 albums which encompass just about all the musical tempos known to man, including belly-dance Egyptian, passacaglia (a stately eighteenth-century Spanish dance), fugues, spirituals and Christmas carols. (Kenton once recorded most of Richard Wagner's *Lohengrin,* not as a jazzed-up version of the opera, but as it would have sounded had Wagner scored it for *his* orchestra.) It is a tribute to his integrity as a musician that Kenton managed to move deeper into semiclassical impressionism without ever losing his feeling for jazz as a hot, existential, get-it-off music. Kenton plays piano, but the band has always been his real instrument and he has used it like a playwright with his own versatile stock company, to extend his reach and develop the vitality of his art.

All of this sounds as if Kenton and his music were part of some nostalgic rite, kept alive by a few grown-up kids with long memories like myself. But even nostalgia is not what it used to be. Kenton in the Seventies is so much more exciting than he was in the Forties, that when you hear him he blows those days and those bands right out of your mind. For the past year, Kenton has been on the road with nineteen musicians, crisscrossing the United States, with occasional side trips to Canada and Europe.

Kenton's recent albums of concerts played at university jazz workshops across the continent are, quite simply, the best big band music ever recorded. The most interesting tracks are the works of arranger Hank Levy, whose *Indra* and *A Step Beyond* (written in alternating 7/4 and 14/8 time) have the band soaring in full throated harmony. In his *Ambivalence* Chris Galuman's flute dances above the loose clusters of sound (played in 5/4 time) until the band switches into a 20/16 tempo, cascading behind the chant of John Park's alto. In *Blues, Between & Betwixt* Levy extends the blues form into alternating 7/4 and 7/8 time, while Richard Torres blows a *macho* salute on his tenor. *Of Space and Time* (written in 5/4) has each of the orchestra's sections fanning in and out in a kind of inexorable succession of salutes to the

186

proposition that with enough talent and commitment jazz composition, however intricate, can produce an ensemble sound that just plain swings. Such romantic themes as *Tiare* and *Rainy Day* come on with a grieving, introspective quality, tingling and nebulous in the trampoline-like tensions they stir. Ken Hanna's brooding *Twilight in the Favelas* is a rain dance that evokes a sense of decay; the smell of late-season mushrooms.

It was Kenton who first moved American music beyond its "polka dots and moonbeams" phase into meaningful rapport with the changing fluorescent environment of the late Forties. He believes that rock will eventually evolve into jazz because that is the only direction in which it can grow.

The young have turned music into an expression of their defiance. You can hear them in the dives off Yorkville and at the rock festivals, paying homage to dissonance, and their parents have responded with a mixture of fear and embarrassment. But Stan Kenton's music transcends the generations, not as a music that expresses the smugness of the balmy Fifties or the protest of the frantic Sixties, but as an enduring interpretation of our times.

[1971]

II

THE PALAIS ROYALE IS A DECREPIT BALLROOM on the edge of Toronto's Lakeshore Boulevard. It looks and smells like some shoddy papier-mâché invention of a madly nostalgic Hollywood director, anxious to recreate the cheapest possible set for a movie about the Fabled Forties. One good shove and the whole peeling structure would float out into Lake Ontario and dissolve in a burst of giant technicolor bubbles, Panama ceiling fans, coloured light bulbs, cracked mirrors and all. But half a dozen times a year, one of the big bands still cruising the continent stops there and for a brief evening, the Palais Royale is alive again.

Into this time-machine atmosphere, one hot Tuesday evening in July of 1970, came Stan Kenton and his nineteen-piece orchestra. It was their first Toronto visit in seven years, and as the Kenton crew shambled onto a stage that ordinarily accommodates a five-piece polka group, the omens were not good. The boys in the band had not bothered with the matching suits that used to be a swing-era trademark, and unlike most big band configurations, this one had two baritone saxophones and a tuba, for God's sake. "Looks as if Stan picked them up on his way through Guelph," a small sleek man muttered.

187

Along with most of the twelve hundred Torontonians in the hall, he had obviously come down to the Palais expecting an evening of instant nostalgia – a recreation of the time when he was young, twenty-or-so hectic years ago. A time when everybody thought Studebakers were the sexiest thing on the road, people were laughing at L'il Abner, buying fountain pens (remember the Parker 51?), voting for George Drew, listening to the Make Believe Ballroom and worrying about teenagers' petting. When "going steady" was a new craze, girls not only had bosoms but wore bras, only cellists had long hair, lipstick was bright red, and kids put nickels in their loafers, danced cheek to cheek, and The Pill ("that rules the waves") was a seasickness remedy.

Before the music started, you could almost imagine through half-closed eyes, that everything was the same. The men had mickeys in brown paper bags, the women stood on the slanting terrace in summer dresses, and one barely noticed that too many of them had midriff rolls and dye jobs.

But then Stan Kenton comes on stage, gives the countdown for *Aquarius,* and suddenly all of us stop believing we wanted to be young again and start feeling, quite simply, alive. Awareness has replaced nostalgia.

The flash, the flair, the sensuous thrust of the Kenton sound has more than survived; it has conquered two decades of decline in jazz to become classic. There is the brass section – blowing as if it were suspended ten feet above the rest of the band – counterpointed by the lyricism of the saxophones, pulling from underneath, modulating the mood. The music's total effect is to engulf its listeners with the same feeling of decompression that comes after a deep scuba dive.

After thirty years of travelling with just about every format into which the jazz orchestra can be expanded, he has returned with, of all things, a genuine road band, young and airy and free. Somehow, Kenton manages to recreate that indefinable magic that makes the band sound as if it had been created especially to fulfill this particular one-night stand. That is artistry of a rare calibre.

Setting up the living environment for the Kenton sound has always been the drummer's assignment, and this one (John Von Ohlen, last heard backing Woody Herman's 103rd Herd at the Monterey Jazz Festival in 1967) takes his job seriously. A square-looking gent with the air of a small-town barber, he pushes and lifts the music with complex syncopations of cross-rhythms, punctuating, goading, catapulting the band with an endless variety of fill-ins, regulating its volume

188

and intensity according to his predetermined flight plan.

Kenton has always had the rare ability to fuse a collection of raw young musicians into a polished, pulsating band. And this new orchestra is no exception. He leads from a half-crouch at his piano bench. There is a sinus-clearing blast from the brass section – ten men loud and true. He turns them off with a twist of the elbow; a saxophone player blows a clinker and Kenton's head withdraws like a turtle's in mock horror between his shoulders. He gives a downbeat, the long slender fingers of his hand cutting the air like dinner knives. He smiles, slouches over the piano, watching his men, leading them home, projecting once more to his audience the effortless truth: this is not just a big band, not just jazz, but eternal music with the great inner authority of a work of art.

[1970]

III

THE LEGEND OF JAZZ IS DEATH. Death by drowning, sometimes in alcohol, sometimes in drugs, but more often in the existential demands of creating new sounds out of used-up ideas. Jazz breeds such brief lives that only a few talents survive first maturity, their resonances siphoned off by fresher disciples while they descend into silence, or worse, die on their feet thumping out swizzle-stick music on cocktail bar circuits. To transform jazz into a classic art demands what Albert Goodman, the New York music critic, calls "the emotional depth, technical assurance and vast experience of a man with a million miles on his meter."

Jazz these days is in a period of minor renaissance and one of its major sources is the revived creativity of Stan Kenton, the pianist-leader who has influenced and haunted contemporary American music since his first band opened the 1941 summer season at the Rendezvous Ballroom in Balboa, California. His current reincarnation marks a curious turn in the long lifetime of a man who has more than paid his dues, but until recently was being dismissed as a pre-bop phenomenon, never quite in tune with the rhythms of his time. He has moved through our musical lives as a kind of noisy ghost, a half-forgotten reminder of unrealized potential, defying not only musical fashions but the inexorable erosion of the chivalrous fantasies that his bravado orchestrations have always inspired.

Now Kenton is back, if not in the mainstream where he has never wanted to be, at least to claim the musical legitimacy that has always eluded him. Every age has the good fortune to produce artists who

189

work against the grain. Where there is disorganized noise, they create harmony and melody. Where there is ugliness, cruelty and an apathetic acquiescence to both, they create art forms of remarkable beauty and feeling. With his new orchestra Kenton emerges as such an artist, and his many critics will have to reassess their harsh verdicts of his contribution to contemporary music.

The Kenton band started as a hybrid offshoot from the rhythm machine put together by Jimmie Lunceford in the late Thirties, while Kenton's own piano style descended straight from Earl Hines. His charts quickly, perhaps too quickly, introduced harmonic values alien to jazz, as Kenton moved toward the polytonal inventions of Bartok and Stravinsky, the Afro-Cuban rhythms of Johnny Richards and the intricate harmonies of the French modernist, Darius Milhaud, as adapted by Pete Rugolo. London's Sadler's Wells company experimentally choreographed some Kenton arrangements and several French and Italian art films were built around his music. His influence began to be felt on the thematic pseudo-jazz that served to background avant-garde films and TV detective series. Then came the forty-piece Innovations orchestra which took two hours to unload out of four buses and mercifully collapsed under its own weight.

In September of 1970, after 27 years with Capitol records, Kenton left to establish his own Creative World label which has since issued sixty-five albums. His most interesting new works have been drawn from Hank Levy, a jazz educator at Towson University in Baltimore, Maryland. By using time signature changes based on the goading, mystical punctuations of far eastern, especially Indian music, Levy's scores achieve a sense of dramatic imbalance that keeps listeners and musicians constantly on the edge of about-to-be-fulfilled expectations.

The fundamental intent of jazz is to entertain and recharge the spirit with new sensory awareness. No music depends so much on the individual performer and his ability to improvise. Ideally, the jazz musician is a spontaneous, non-repetitive poet expressing himself through his instrument. What Kenton has always demanded of his musicians is that they broaden the harmonic, rhythm and structural boundaries of the band's charts, so that they follow not only the letter but the *spirit* of the composer's intent. This is more difficult than it sounds because the more conventional styles of jazz require only that a composition trigger a musician's own ruminations. "Each time we play," Kenton says, "I like it to be a new experience, even though it may be a piece we've performed time and time again. It must be a balance of complete freedom

190

and discipline. I want our music to express the widest range of emotion, from the most intimate, delicate form of communication to a roaring, intense organized expression of human energy."

This orchestra projects exciting new dimensions to Kenton's theories of collective improvisation. The broad, vibrant voicing, the staccato phrasing, the showers of open, scalding notes engulf the listener with a sense of shared loneliness which is exactly what Kenton's music is all about.

But there is a difference. The biblical cadence once so characteristic of Kenton is missing. Gone is the syrupy commercialism of his muddled middle years when Kenton was sounding pointlessly fussy and decorative in a desperate attempt to keep from becoming an anachronism in a musical time he helped to create.

Instead, Kenton has returned to his roots, to depend on the intuition of the moment which night after night is all the jazz artist can really trust. All the abstracts of his craft – timing, harmony, phrasing – have fallen into place so that the music Kenton is now playing at peeling dance halls, university auditoriums and shopping centre plazas across North America and Europe can claim that essential art of surprise absent from some of his past congregations.

What is really impressive and unusual about this particular Kenton band is that despite (or could it be because of) their leader's high expectations, it is a relaxed group of musicians, and they sound like it: nineteen kindred spirits out to convince their audiences and themselves that in big band jazz the whole can be greater than the sum of its parts. The happy mood is infectious. (Kenton opened one recent concert, recorded on the Phase-4 London label, by excusing his informality: "We usually come on stage and the band blows about ten fanfares before I come on, then I'm wheeled on in a chariot. Sometimes I use a bicycle. . . ." – then broke up as he gave the downbeat for the opening number.)

Unlike some past Kenton ensembles, which evoked the sterile perfection of musicians reading their arrangements off punched IBM cards, this one sounds as if the charts were pages torn out of a late Dostoyevsky novel. The pillows of sound and the swirl of tonal colours combine into a kind of deep-mouthed empathy – not so much a remembrance of sounds past as a revelation of jazz's future.

Late in his middle age, Stan Kenton has come home at last, plying his craft with dignity and humour, a man and a musician firmly in command of his worth.   [1973]

191

PART SEVEN   *Departures*

Ralph Allen

I WAS IN QUEBEC CITY YESTERDAY MORNING when I heard the CBC announce that Ralph Allen had died in the night. When that cool voice delivered this stunning news I thought, how can they presume to sum him up in five lines? Now I am trying to sum him up in five hundred and that, too, is a presumption.

I cannot write about Ralph the war correspondent or Ralph the fisherman or Ralph the raconteur. In the decade I knew him we had what he once called "the tough relationship between editor and writer;" and we were very different men, of different generations, different backgrounds, different personalities. But I don't expect ever again to know a man I can so implicitly trust and so unabashedly revere.

When I first went to *Maclean's* in 1956, it was that golden time when Ralph Allen was its editor. He made all of us who worked for him then seem special, bigger than we were, better writers than we knew how to be. He made us feel part of an admirable human adventure. He sat, fat, freckled, red-headed, quick-tempered – and irreplaceable – in a corner office and the world outside looked manageable. When I look back on it now, I realize we were only basking in his reflection and the world was not manageable and we were not golden and never will think we are again.

As an editor, he was no hot-eyed radical, but a man of reason, a man of civility and no cant. His natural enemies were poseurs of every description – war correspondents who hadn't gone to the front lines, public relations men, journalists who talk better than they write – and mediocrity in all its aspects.

He sought excellence relentlessly. He was a hard and exacting

195

editor. But once he hired you, he believed in you, and when he believed in you, you believed in yourself. In some ways he did not fit the temper of his times; he was something of a puritan (although no prude) and, for a journalist, uncharacteristically dedicated to defending the individual's right to personal privacy.

He was a man for all seasons; a man whose sense of integrity and instinct for fairness were such a large part of his character that it was easy to overlook his personal courage, his sensibilities, his wit and his vitality. He could transform the banter of a ten o'clock coffee break into a memory you would savour for a decade.

He was one of the best natural writers I have known; even his interoffice memos were graceful and as he got older, he overcame more and more of his natural shyness and began to talk as he wrote, in flawless cadence. His most serious writing went into his novels. They were autobiographical only in the sense that in each of them there was one character vainly standing up for reason in a mad world.

He found uncharacteristic joy in his books and I remember on the heady day after he finished his last he phoned me and said that it was "damned good." When a book of mine was published he sent a note in which he said that "writing a book has always struck me as a very close parallel to going to a war; a great place to have been and a great place to be back from."

"God bless" was how he said goodby to friends, and somehow it was a benediction worthy of a pope, although Ralph himself had a Presbyterian conscience and claimed he was a lapsed Unitarian.

Ralph Allen was a good man. When I met him first I was very young and I thought there were lots of good men, that my world would be full of them. But now that I am not so young, I know two things: that there are not many good men and that I am forever lucky and forever different because I knew one.

Ralph, God bless.

[1966]

Robert Thompson

THIS IS A REQUIEM FOR A LIGHTWEIGHT.
The resignation of Robert Thompson as leader of the Social Credit
party is a matter of no great national consequence, and certainly
no occasion for lament. Yet within his own terms of reference, Thompson for six frustrating years and without slackening energy did what
was asked of him, and his failure says something significant about the
political system in which he operated.

Robert Thompson's great difficulty and the cause of his downfall
was simply that he tried to master the technique of Canadian politics
without understanding its principles. It was not just that he remained
committed to an unworkable ideology. Unlike other party leaders,
Thompson was always seeking not just ballots, but converts.

That there was little logic or structure in his appeal was not due to
any lack of conviction in Thompson himself. Rather, he believed his
own doctrine too well. His faith dated back to his 1934 conversations
with the mystic Bill Aberhart, when as a twenty-one-year-old student,
Thompson became an enthusiastic adherent to the economics of Social
Credit.

A sad-eyed introvert, Thompson presented a sharp contrast to the
not-too-distant past, when his party used to rave against the international conspiracy of bankers and Zionists. But if he wasn't anti-Semitic
Thompson often gave the impression of being anti-semantic, especially
when trying to explain the theories of Social Credit. With a dogged but
curiously impersonal fluency, phrases spilled out of him in an unanswerable gush that left his listeners either totally convinced or totally
baffled. ("For every dollar in circulation, we will create a matching

197

dollar of consumer goods, so that production to satisfy the wants of the people will control the money system, instead of money controlling production.")

He advocated many things that few responsible Canadian politicians would oppose, but most of his declarations somehow came out as convoluted cliches, flavoured by a wistful candour that made it impossible to dislike the man. Certainly his most memorable contribution to Canadian politics was the statement that "the Americans are our best friends, whether we like it or not." Another Thompsonism was his comment that "Parliament is being turned into a political arena," and he once attempted to silence an interjecting MP by telling him: "You've buttered your bread, now you have to lie in it." During a debate on February 1, 1965, while trying to explain why Social Credit could not take the same position as it had with the Diefenbaker minority administration in 1963, he declared: "We've had not one but two elections since then, and two rights do not make a wrong."

It seems much more than five years ago now that Robert Thompson was a political figure to be reckoned with. The leader of thirty MPs who held the balance of power after the 1962 election. On June 22, 1962, Thompson flew to Rouyn and went for a motorboat ride with Real Caouette, his deputy leader. It was then that Thompson confided to Caouette their party would probably form the government after the next election. If that happened, he proposed to resign in favour of Ernest Manning, who would then become the first Social Credit prime minister of Canada. But Thompson's relations with the mercurial Caouette began to degenerate soon afterwards and the hold over his followers grew ever slacker, until after the 1965 election, he came back with only four colleagues.

Everything went wrong in that last campaign. Thompson was fogbound over Toronto airport during the press conference called to announce his party platform, and later, on a flight to Calgary, his baggage wound up in Chicago. At a small rally in Regina on October 3 he begged for votes with the appeal: "You can't be any worse off than you are now."

His party printed a million comic books glorifying his career, distributed recordings of his voice and handed out pills labelled "Social Credit – your prescription for curing Canada's ills."

He even had his own brain trust of fifty bow-tied BBBs (Bob's Bright Boys) helping him, but nothing really helped, and at the end of his campaign, there was only the sense of an exhausted man with blood running through his shoes. "People haven't quite accepted the notion of giving us power," he confessed, then added wistfully: "But they're toying with the idea."

During his long, lonely years as party leader Thompson had to compromise so many contradictions that in the end he no longer seemed to have the stamina to match his convictions, so that when the provincial Social Credit cut off his supply of party funds recently, what was left of his spirit went out of him. At the end, he stalked the country like a ghost, still reminding blinking audiences that "Social Credit is above politics." But nobody was listening.

[1967]

Leon Balcer

WHEN LEON BALCER, THE MEMBER OF PARLIAMENT for Trois-Rivières, crossed the floor of the Commons, he was giving up a lifetime struggle against the political odds of being a loyal Conservative in the province of Quebec.

An intense 47-year-old ex-naval officer who still walks with a nautical gait, Balcer epitomized the crushing dilemma faced by the few French-Canadians who have survived in the Conservative party under the leadership of John Diefenbaker. "At first, I thought that Mr. Diefenbaker just didn't understand Quebec," Balcer told me a few hours before he took his fatal step. "Now I'm convinced that he's genuinely against French Canada, and that as a political expedient, he's trying to whip up an English backlash for an election campaign."

These are bitter words from a man who achieved more within the ranks of the Conservative party than any other French-Canadian in this century. Leon Balcer is no ordinary MP. He held his Trois-Rivières seat for sixteen years – winning six elections – more than any other Quebec Conservative in Canadian history. At a time when it meant nothing, literally nothing, to be a Tory in French Canada, he stubbornly stuck to his political faith, insisting that it was possible to be both a good federal Conservative and a good French-Canadian. He was rewarded by his party with two of the highest honours it can offer – presidencies of both the YPCS and the PC Association – and became the first French-Canadian to hold either of these positions.

He served as a competent minister of transport during the Diefenbaker years and in February, 1964, the party's annual meeting proclaimed him "provincial leader and chief lieutenant to the national

200

leader." Diefenbaker promptly hailed Balcer as "a second Sir George Etienne Carter" and pledged that he would consult with him on national as well as Quebec policies. The arrangement was stillborn. Not only did Diefenbaker fail to consult Balcer on national affairs and party policies, but intimates of the Trois-Rivières MP claim that in the past fourteen months, their man was not once invited into Diefenbaker's office for a private conversation. "Mr. Diefenbaker has put me in a position where it would be false representation for me to stay," Balcer complains.

Many Conservatives in and out of Ottawa have been trying to dismiss the Balcer defection as not being really significant because they regard him as a political lightweight. Balcer is not the kind of politician who could ignite a Tory resurgence in Quebec – with or without the burden of the Diefenbaker leadership. But this does not alter the fact that a man who has devoted his life to the Conservative cause has now become so disillusioned with the Diefenbaker brand of leadership, that he felt compelled to leave the party and is willing to ostracize himself into political limbo by sitting as an independent.

The steps Leon Balcer took across the floor of the Commons represented more than just the leavetaking of yet another senior Conservative, disillusioned by the leadership of John Diefenbaker. It was a warning of the disintegration of a great Canadian political party as a national force.

[1965]

Jack Pickersgill

T HIS WEEK OTTAWA BIDS POLITICAL FAREWELL to the Honorable John Whitney Pickersgill, that peripatetic son of Newfoundland whose unusual career has spanned four political eras and left a deep imprint on each. It is perhaps typical of Pickersgill that he plans to end his days in Ottawa the way he began them thirty years ago, as a member of the public service, and that he regards without qualms his transition to politics and back again. It is entirely in character that as the new head of the Canadian Transportation Commission, he will be occupying a $40,000-a-year job created by himself for himself – a plush sinecure from the political wars that have occupied his talents since he became secretary of state in the St. Laurent government on June 12, 1953.

The new job, which will make him one of the most powerful members of the Ottawa bureaucracy, is Pickersgill's fifth incarnation on the national scene. Between 1936 and 1948 he functioned as Mackenzie King's most powerful advisor and "check it with Jack" became a password to power in Ottawa. He was an even more influential backstage influence in the administration of Louis St. Laurent until he emerged, full-blown, as a cabinet minister and MP for Bonavista-Twillingate. His next role was as one of the most effective of the front benchers during the Pearson Opposition period – enjoying what he once described as "a reasonable sense of irresponsibility." When the Liberals regained power, Pickersgill grabbed centre stage once more as one of the new administration's most important parliamentarians. Now, finally, he has drifted back to the safer confines of the civil service.

It may not have been exactly a noble career, but it was, well, cohesive. Pickersgill's approach to government was so uniquely his own that his name found a place in Canada's political dictionary. The expression "Pickersgillian" came to signify any partisan ploy that was too clever by half. The qualities which helped him survive so long in the heady upper reaches of Canadian politics are difficult to isolate. Grant Deachman, a Liberal backbencher from Vancouver, took a good run at defining them when he quipped: "Pickersgill can knit you a stove if you give him a ball of steel wool."

Like Mackenzie King, Jack Pickersgill has never seen much scope for public service away from power. More so than any other Liberal, he has always considered his party not so much an organ of the people as an organ of the state, and in private he often refers to the Liberals as "the government party."

Though he was once considered an impatient reformer – and played a large part in persuading Mackenzie King to accept the desirability of the family allowance idea – in recent years he was one of the Liberal cabinet's most ardent reactionaries, urging the undertaking of social reforms only if there was less danger in passing them than in turning them down. "Jack is so firmly hooked on the past I sometimes think he's wearing cement boots," commented one of his colleagues. A fellow minister swears that there have not been more than half a dozen cabinet meetings in the past four years during which Pickersgill has failed to mention the way Mackenzie King solved the crises of his day. He is full of irrelevant historical trivia (for example: Bracken's Manitoba cabinet of 1922 was composed entirely of Presbyterians), but has little contact with the society he has had such a prominent part in governing. He grew up on a Manitoba farm, attended university and then, except for summer holidays on the coast of northern Newfoundland, spent the rest of his life entirely in Ottawa, so that the world of urban, contemporary Canada has remained entirely outside his experience.

What allowed Pickersgill to prosper so long at such levels of influence within the Ottawa hierarchy was his uncanny ability to manipulate the gears of bureaucratic control. His three long decades within the federal power structure taught him all the tricks both of how political control of the civil service could be exercised and how bureaucratic methods could be used to drain the will of the politicians. He had the habit of power and knew the mechanics of the game.

Pickersgill's career and opinions made him the quintessence of Ottawa's Liberal establishment. He acted as though he really believed that, by accepting the burdens of office, the Liberals were bestowing a

203

benefaction on the nation at large, and that any criticism of Liberalism was a distinctly unpatriotic activity. Just before the 1957 election, Pickersgill declared with a straight face: "It is not merely for the well-being of Canadians but for the good of mankind in general that the present Liberal government should remain in office."

His party affiliation seemed so close to a religion that one wondered whether faith alone and not reason informed him. Questioned by a reporter about the characteristics of Liberal prime ministers, he replied: "They never, any one of them, ever told a conscious lie or allowed anything that was calculated to give a false impression. Mackenzie King, for instance, was meticulous to the point of being tiresome about it, putting in all sorts of qualifications so that nobody in any conceivable circumstances could ever show that there was anything about his statements that was untrue."

If the Liberals were lily white in the Pickersgillian lexicon, the Tories were jet black. "The real trouble with the Conservative party," he once said, "is that basically it has been a party of Anglo-Saxon racists. They really don't believe in the equality of all Canadians. They really don't believe the French have any right in this country, unless they act like a conquered people." On another occasion he remarked that Conservative governments are "like having the mumps – something you have to endure once in your lifetime, but when it's over you don't ever want it again."

Though Pickersgill's influence was exercised in the hush of his office and the privacy of the cabinet chamber, he was best known for the displays he put on in the House of Commons. His penguin shape was constantly bobbing up and down during the excitement of debates. Physically clumsy, he was utterly incapable of sitting still. When he was a youngster, his grandmother had made him a standing offer of five cents for every five minutes he could keep quiet. "I needed the money badly, but I never earned a penny of it," he liked to recall. (It was during his youth that Pickersgill also learned a thrift that became the habit of his lifetime. He still does not part easily with the coins he carries in a black clasp-type change purse stuffed into his right hip pocket, and uses pencils until they are inch-long stubs. He once complained at length in the Commons about losing fifteen cents in an airport stamp-vending machine.)

Because Pickersgill performed so effectively between 1957 and 1963 when the Liberals were in opposition, his authority within the Pearson retinue continued to expand and when the Liberals moved back into power he was named to the key post of House leader. One of the few ministers Pearson's secretaries would unhesitatingly put right through to the PM any time he called, he was a key influence throughout the Pearson period, particularly after Walter Gordon (following Pickersgill's whispered advice) proved so inept in defending his first budget.

Pickersgill extended his power by adopting Guy Favreau as a kind of political protege. It was Pickersgill who persuaded Favreau to bring Leo Cadieux and Jean-Pierre Côté into the cabinet, mainly because they were colourless, politically neutral French Canadians who would cause no trouble but would back the Pickersgill-Favreau axis. In the winter of 1964, Pickersgill recommended to Pearson that Guy Favreau succeed him as House leader because it would enhance his prestige when he became Quebec lieutenant. This was a disastrous appointment, for both Favreau and the Liberals, but despite these and other errors in judgment Pearson continued to heed Pickersgill's advice. Part of the reason may have been that to Pearson, Pickersgill represented those happy, placid days when the government had been really in charge of Parliament and Parliament seemed in control of the country. Surely this man who had advised Mackenzie King and Louis St. Laurent in the delicate art of keeping the political lid on could do the same for him.

The trouble was that while Pickersgill remained the same, the country in which he was operating had altered. In terms of the federal administration this meant the unruly, sometimes agonizing passage from the old, interest-group, elite-conducted approach to government (which had allowed a Pickersgill to thrive) to a new and very different kind of politics. Mild welfare plans tailored to keep the voting public at bay were no longer effective. Issues and challenges became more sophisticated, far less amenable to the old calculus of behind-the-scenes deals conducted by a self-selected hierarchy, of which Jack Pickersgill had been the most experienced member.

His world was vanishing but Pickersgill was shrewd enough to recognize it and proceeded to plan himself a new career. In the summer of 1967 Pickersgill as the minister of transport was busy piloting through the Commons the National Transportation Act, designed to regionalize Canada's obsolete railway system. Few MPs noticed that the presidency of the new Canadian Transport Commission set up by the legislation was made particularly attractive. The annual salary was set at $40,000 a year and the retirement age (Pickersgill was then sixty-two) was not the usual sixty-five, but seventy. The position was never

205

advertised by the Civil Service Commission. Having written himself a job description, Pickersgill resigned from cabinet and recommended himself for the opening. Pearson accepted and "Sailor Jack" launched himself on his new career.

The circumstances that allowed Jack Pickersgill to flourish were part of a cynical old-style approach to Canadian politics. But even in that context he was one of a kind.

Walter Gordon

A S THE DAYS DROP AWAY and the implications of Walter Gordon's leave-taking become apparent, even the former finance minister's critics concede that the Liberal party has been turned inside out. Gordon was that rare creature in Canadian politics: a man whose passion was in the pursuit of ideas rather than power. In his brief political flowering, he tried to alter not just his party, but his country.

The legacy of Walter Gordon is a large one. By becoming (with a few personally chosen associates) the main supplier of political ideas to Lester Pearson, he re-oriented the Liberal party from its pro-business outlook of the St. Laurent period to a pronounced social welfare emphasis. But his most enduring contribution will be the alarm he sounded over the potential dangers of large-scale American investment in Canada. Instead of following the example of most politicians and merely preaching that Canadians must acquire a greater measure of control over their economy, Gordon was imprudent enough to actually try and do something about it.

This roused cankerous irritation in the country's various establishments because Gordon was pointing up explicitly a situation which could not be solved in the neat grey way that Canadians prefer in dealing with their problems. Because there is little evidence that American ownership of Canadian industries and resources threatens our individual liberties, Gordon's message drew little support from the nation at large. But Gordon believed that American capital, if unchecked, would eventually threaten our collective freedom by turning us into a political as well as an economic dependency of the United States.

Gordon's aim was statesmanlike: to alter the Canadian economic

207

setting and gradually draw the people behind him in a crusade to recapture control over the nation's economic destiny. But he never managed to warm up to the people, or the people to him. This was a failure partly of method and partly of personality. His early attempts (notably the disastrous 1963 budget) were judged to be administrative monstrosities and did much to discredit his cause. The kind of man he was tended always to be obscured by the kind of man he seemed to be. Witty, intelligent, contemporary and humanitarian, he looked merely overprivileged, the very model of an upper-middle-class WASP in pin-striped suit and regimental tie. He liked good food, fine wines, paintings, antiques, travel and the company of his peers. He could be warm and amusing with close friends, but remained an intensely private person who abhorred the little arts of popularity and the comforting generalizations that are the touchstones of politics in western democracies. His language was that of his class – cool, reasonable, passionless. He could never transform himself from an ideologue into a revolutionary and in the conduct of his nationalistic crusades he remained a sort of Garibaldi without a horse. Even his books, with their revolutionary implications for Canadian society, read like dry texts on bee-keeping.

He never took his crusade to the people. In the 1965 election, instead of making economic nationalism a dominant issue of the campaign, he sat around Liberal headquarters, hardly venturing out to make a speech. Gordon's intimates insist that this strategy was based on a fear that never ceased to haunt him: that economic nationalism as a definite issue might be rejected by the voters. American business would then be free to expand its objectives in Canada, safe in the assumption that economic independence had been repudiated by the Canadian people.

Gordon's unsuccessful drive for domestic control of the economy tended to overshadow the fact that in the day-to-day administration of the nation's fiscal and monetary policies, Gordon was an outstanding success. It was a blow to his prestige that in the letter accepting his resignation, Lester Pearson wrote that he had hoped to persuade Gordon "to take another cabinet post where the responsibilities would not be so heavy and continuous as they have been in Finance." The stated purpose of Gordon's resignation was to absolve his old friend from responsibility for the Liberals' disappointing performance in the 1965 campaign. Instead, the Pearson statement seemed to cast doubts on Gordon's whole performance in finance by implying that he could better handle another portfolio.

The former finance minister's absence from the inner circles of Canadian Liberalism is bound to produce a major re-orientation in the party's policies. It is the final irony of Walter Gordon's strange political career that the extent of his influence should not become fully apparent until his departure from the corridors of power. Still, despite the limited success of his nationalistic crusades, Walter Gordon's time in public life enlarged not just his party, but the nation as a whole. He had three qualities rare in politicians – courage, simplicity, and selflessness. They made him for a time the conscience of his country.

[1965]

George Vanier

THE EIGHT STOUT SERGEANTS who acted as George Vanier's pall-bearers carried more than a hero to his grave. In a very real way a nation seemed to be in mourning for itself.

By the act of dying, this good man provided us all with a spiritual occasion to celebrate the virtues for which he lived, the traditions that gave Canada its existence and meaning.

George Philias Vanier was born three years before Sir John A. Macdonald died. His life literally spanned the history of this nation; his accomplishments were intertwined with its great affairs.

He fought in two world wars, and as a delegate both to the League of Nations and the United Nations Assembly took part in fashioning the uneasy peace that followed each. As Governor-General what he gave this country was a mood – a sense of earned dignity, of grace without pomp.

The plumed assembly of bishops, monseigneurs, premiers, ambassadors, admirals, generals, air marshals, and splendid Legionnaires turned his state funeral into a moving occasion. The shiver of swords, the tolling of bells, and the booming punctuation of saluting guns all spoke of an age of heraldry, when individual courage could still change history.

But it was the naval ratings drawing the coffin, slow-marching sixty steps to the minute down Ottawa's Wellington Street, who really caught the mood of the occasion. Their formal, inexorable pacing brought the prick of tears to many faces in the crowd.

The tears were for George Vanier, but the sadness in part was for the end of an era. The men of power who walked in the funeral cortège were the captains and the princes of yesterday. They tamed this country and brought us this far in our history.

But the time of their time is passing; their world is being adulterated, transformed into a surrealistic universe which marches to different drummers. The qualities of ideas, the priorities of concerns will never return to the benign impulses that granted them an honoured place in this procession. The landscape is changing and it will take other men with different tempers to complete the forging of this nation.

[1967]

Lester Pearson

THERE WAS SOMETHING INNATELY GRACEFUL about the way Lester Pearson chose to give up the prime ministership of Canada yesterday (December 14, 1967). He has never been a politician with flair, but he has always been a man of taste and when he decided to step down, he did so in a characteristically civilized manner. There was no oratory, no hint of sadness or even regret, and yet he must have known that he was merely putting the best face on what was becoming an ugly situation.

He surrendered the leadership of the Liberal party with his dignity intact, and he is now able to put behind him all of the wheeling and dealing of politics so alien to his nature. Still, the poignant fact remains that for the past few months he has psychologically ceased to be regarded as the prime minister of this country; his leadership was eroded by too many compromises, too few commitments and he had at last come to realize this.

While the suddenness of his departure caught Ottawa and the nation by surprise, he had always maintained in private that he intended to leave by the end of the centennial year. Several political factors and one personal consideration motivated the choice of December 14 for his retirement announcement. The personal touch was that on Wednesday evening of this week there was a small family party at the PM's residence to celebrate his wife Maryon's birthday, and he decided to give her the birthday present she had so long wanted: his promise to retire from the Liberal leadership the next day. His political reasons included a judgment about his possible effectiveness at the constitutional conference to be held in Ottawa on February 5. Some of his advisers, aware that he

212

intended to retire soon, had insisted that he would be in a stronger position at that conference as prime minister with the undiluted power of his office behind him.

But this opinion changed radically during the federal-provincial conference on housing held at the beginning of this week. It became evident there that his former mastery of such gatherings had somehow spent itself and that he could no longer count on his prestige as prime minister to carry him through the much more perilous enterprise of trying to hammer out a consensus on constitutional reform. It was consequently decided that it might increase Pearson's effectiveness, if he came to the conference as a man shorn of the partisan motives that would be attached to a prime minister, attempting what will amount to a renegotiation of Confederation.

Pearson leaves the prime ministership as he entered it: an unknown political quantity in search of a ill-defined Canadian future. He was a good man in a wicked time; a compromiser in a nation crying for leadership; a prime minister who did not seem so much to be governing Canada as presiding over its survival.

The combination of Pearson's high purpose with his ability to lead made it difficult to fit him into the stereotypes of Canadian politics. That he is an attractive human being with decent instincts is beyond dispute. His humility, his abhorrence of pretence, his restless hopes for a peaceful world and a united Canada made it impossible even for his bitter political enemies to hate him. He was not a man corrupted by power, mainly because he so seldom used it. Pearson accurately personified the confused state of the country he was trying to rule: a Canada grown uncertain of its domestic and external purposes in a rapidly changing world. And even if his personality never firmly stamped itself on the national conscience, when he resigned this week, Canada seemed a noticeably different place. There was something heroic about some of his political crusades (such as his advocacy of the flag) in which he persisted in acting as midwife for a modern, new Canada which refused to be born.

Despite his accomplishments and his sponsorship of the many welfare measures that decorate his record, a curious gap has always existed between his reputation and his performance. During the fifty-six months of his prime ministership, most Canadians felt nothing so much as disappointment – in his capacity to exercise political power, in his ability to judge the integrity and competence of some of his colleagues, in the nature of his ultimate goals.

Even when the Liberal government did the right thing, it managed to look awkward. Its whole performance was reflective of the Pearson mood and strategy: the notion of never-ending conciliation, minimum risk and vacillation – breath-taking triumphs of compromise over conviction.

This really must stand as the ultimate condemnation of Lester Pearson's time in office: that he failed to provide any frame of reference in which not only his own party but the people of Canada could operate. Although the Liberal propaganda machine heralded the Pearson legislative program as the political redemption of a nation in transition as more and more Pearson proposals became law, it was never clear what kind of society was being constructed and what, if any, ideology was at work. The Pearson legislative record is long and impressive, but the Liberal accomplishments do not seem related to one another and certainly do not add up to any recognizable whole.

During his time in office – as in his diplomatic career – Lester Pearson was always the nimble-footed man trying to forecast the possibilities and probabilities of an unpredictable future. His negotiable approach to leadership made him appear to be a politician drifting with the tide of events.

Perhaps the problem was that Pearson remained one of the few prime ministers in Canadian history who never really had a constituency of his own. He reflected the aspirations of no region of the country or block of its population, except perhaps bureaucratic Ottawa. (It seemed only natural to label John Diefenbaker the man from Prince Albert, but patently silly to call Lester Pearson the man from Algoma East.) Pearson was never really involved in this country at its grassroots level; his ideas of Canada were formed at universities and in foreign embassies. He came to the nation's highest political office too late in life to change his ways and could never find the necessary resonance with the people that must nourish the successful politician.

Lester Pearson's leave-taking will invariably be coupled with John Diefenbaker's departure from the Conservative leadership, a few months ago. There is no better illustration of the difference between the two men than the manner of their going. For the Conservative leader, his departure was one long bloody battle ending in humiliation. Lester Pearson's dignified withdrawal was a fitting last act to the career of a politician who is superficially gregarious, yet possessed by a profound sense of personal detachment which has allowed him to move through many worlds without belonging to any but his own.   [1967]

214

Frank Underhill

THERE CAME A MEANINGFUL MOMENT last night during a dinner given at Ottawa's Rideau Club in honor of Frank Underhill's eightieth birthday when he said, "I simply cannot understand the view prevalent today that there is something vicious about the Liberal establishment." Looking around at that establishment sitting comfortably in the club's barnlike reaches, peering at their guru through the cigar smoke, it was hard not to agree.

The people who were there, however far they may have strayed on occasion from Underhill's ideals, have made this country what it is. The good things and the bad things about it are all their doing. They sold it to the Americans (in order to retrieve it from the British, they are at pains to point out) but they also put into partial practice their ideal of a humane and relatively progressive society.

The Underhill dinner was a moving and very Canadian occasion, with a hundred or so of his friends gathered to pay tribute to one of the most influential thinkers this country has produced. But what was meant as a salute to a great man seemed at times more like a self-congratulatory farewell to a political generation.

They were all there, the big-L and small-l liberals – Lester Pearson, Frank Scott, Eugene Forsey, Bob Bryce, Escott Reid and Graham Spry among them, all moving out of public life now and watching their ideology being assaulted – on the outside by the radicals and on the inside by the technocrats. It was a cerebral faith in the power of intellect, a kind of unshakable trust in the reasonableness of man, that held this group together and allowed it to transform the country.

But intellect and good intentions no longer seem to be enough and

215

Canada is moving out from under them. Pierre Trudeau (who was not included on Underhill's personal invitation list) is cast in a very different tradition and it is doubtful if his group of the hundred most influential Canadians would include many of the same faces.

Of all the people there, Frank Underhill himself seemed to be most aware of the fundamental shift in the power structure that is taking place, and with the effortless erudition of a great classical scholar, he delivered the class valedictory. He recounted how, as a young student from Stouffville, Ontario, he had gone to the University of Toronto and discovered the writings of Thomas Hobbes: "I'd give anything if I could open the magic pages of Hobbes again for the first time. It was a genuine conversion. I had seen a new heaven and a new earth. It dawned on me then that I could spend the rest of my life studying politics and that's what I've done. . . . When I look at all the permanent adolescents in the universities now – the undergraduates, postgraduate students and young staff members who are seeking their identities in confrontation and protest instead of getting down to the tough clarity of books – I can't be thankful enough that I was born in 1889."

In solid establishment tradition, Underhill gently chided Lester Pearson for having attended the wrong college at Oxford. "If Mike had only gone to Balliol instead of St. John's, he would never have allowed that loud, rowdy demagogue from Saskatchewan to get going," because, as he reminded all those present, "the mark of a Balliol man is the serene assurance of an effortless superiority." While at Balliol himself, from 1911 to 1914, Underhill joined the Fabian Society and came under the influence of Bernard Shaw and H. G. Wells. After spending the war as an officer with the British infantry, he came back to Canada and became a history professor at the University of Saskatchewan, later moving to the University of Toronto. "I returned from the war to find the Prairies on fire with Progressivism and that, in turn, swept me off my feet."

Along with half a dozen men who attended last night's dinner, Underhill drafted the original Regina Manifesto which launched the CCF. He broke with socialism twenty-five years later and became a reluctant Liberal. ("At times I have had to hold my nose while marking the ballot.")

Though Underhill has written hundreds of provocative articles and reviews, the comment of his which caused the most controversy was an offhand remark he made to the 1940 Couchiching conference. "We now have two loyalties," he said, "one to Britain and the other to

216

North America. I venture to say that it is the second that is going to be supreme now. The relative importance of Britain is going to sink no matter what happens." This mild downgrading of the "mother country" caused such an eruption that the university board of governors nearly fired him and the Ontario legislature talked of cutting the university's provincial grants. (One MPP called him "a rat trying to scuttle our ship of state.")

The case blew itself out when no one could find a stenographic record of Underhill's remarks. Twenty-two years later the University of Toronto officially exonerated him by awarding him an honourary degree.

At eighty, Frank Underhill looked back at some of these incidents last night and his conclusion was that while his generation accomplished much, it failed to live up to its own ambitions. "We men of the 1930s," he said, "put too much faith in politics. You can't have a great politics without a great culture at its base and we were attempting a great politics with a colonial culture."

What he did not say was that you also cannot have a great politics without great minds. Frank Underhill is certainly one of them.

[1970]

John Diefenbaker

I

WHEN JOHN DIEFENBAKER SAT DOWN LAST NIGHT (November 14, 1966) to small applause, after delivering his keynote speech to the Conservative convention, everybody in the audience looked somehow smaller and meaner.

The evening had begun a couple of hours earlier in high cheer. The hall in the Chateau Laurier was packed with Conservatives, the most vociferous of them, Camp supporters, who were young and loud, with bangs of hair and blue-and-white placards, and they gave a noisy welcome to their lion tamer, Dalton Camp.

He then delivered a careful speech, a thinking ad man's speech, in both measured English and hideous French and he was heckled often but ineptly by men with hog-calling voices. Camp was followed by a woman Conservative and a young Conservative and a student Conservative, and then by the national organizer, the Diefenbaker man, James Johnston.

All the time these functionaries were speaking it was hard not to wonder how Diefenbaker was feeling, what thoughts were running through his mind as he prepared to face, yet once more, the insurrection. When he came up to the platform unannounced and without fanfare, with his gallant wife smiling behind him, even his opponents could not help feel how sad is his story, how terrible the lost opportunities, how really dreadful it is for a politician to be unintelligently indomitable, to lose his rapport with his followers.

He was introduced by the resonant professional voice of Joel Aldred, who began by praising himself and continued to say nothing

218

much, but to say it surprisingly well. His was a pure voice from the right; it could have been a Ronald Reagan, talking with cardboard charm in the accents of reaction. "Some things are considered old-fashioned and to some even loyalty has entered that category" – a line that caused two long-haired Camp boys in front of me to whisper: "Doesn't that make you sick?" This in turn caused two old ladies from the Maritimes behind me to say, "Listen to that kid, he's still wet behind the ears" and though the distance between the pairs was only one row of folding chairs, the gulf of misunderstanding was as wide as the forty years that separated them.

Diefenbaker got up to talk then in a strong voice, shaking only a little, controlling himself with the magic of his own words, sounding as young and clear as anybody who talked before him. The speech was a ragbag of past triumphs, tragic lyricism and vanished appeals.

John Diefenbaker can, even now, squelch a heckler by the simple act of removing his glasses. His voice continued resonant and strong but the total effect was that of a stuck record. He could no longer endow his passions with the practical force and symmetry of ideas. The one passage of his speech which alluded to policy sounded as dry as a laundry list. When he kept repeating "we stood" (as in, "we still have the coat of arms because the Conservative party has stood") it came out not as some courageous stand on a controversial issue, but simply as a position of immobility. When he trotted out the old memories and the older cliches ("I said I would make this a people's party in nineteen hundred and fifty-six. . . . Do you remember the days of Bennett and Manion? . . . ") he left his audience dazed and indifferent. A sleek young Tory near me asked a friend in facetious boredom: "David, do you suppose he's going to tell us about Lord Salisbury?"

Diefenbaker reminded them how far they had come under his leadership. ("Oh, I remember through the years. . . . I am able to come before you now and say that I kept the faith.") And an old lady in a black crepe dress and white fake fur hat and a diamente pin, murmured, "You tell them, John. . . . That's right, these kids are wet behind the ears. . . . Why don't they get their hair cut?"

For a brief few minutes he gained a rapport with the audience when he started to rib Camp, by using his own statements against him and the audience howled with delight and one could remember when he was sharp and witty. But now he goes on too long, his timing is off. He reminisces about "the dinosaur days" when the party had thirty-nine seats or forty-one seats under Bennett and under Meighen and under Drew – and a heckler shouts "don't talk about the past, we want to go forward." He implies that his enemies are Liberals at heart: "Why do they attack me? For the benefit of the party, they claim, yet thousands of Grits too are willing to say a new leader is what we need. Why? They hope to carry us back to the days of forty-one seats." He charges that the Liberals are "a government that has been arrogant in its arrogance." He keeps harking back to his successes, but to the kids in the audience, and the Camp group has packed the floor, 1957 might as well be 1937, it is *history* for heaven's sake, and they belong to *now* and half the electorate is under thirty-five and here they are, impatient and yearning (the young are always yearning) and they did not come to follow John but to bury him. The audience shifts in embarrassment and boredom and next to me a boy letters carefully on the back of an old Diner's Club envelope "I was a teenage Diefenbuddy" and holds it up over his shoulder.

Diefenbaker rambles on to talk of policy, returning again and again to the past, as though it were full of promise for the future. There on the platform behind him are the lesser party chieftains, still confident in their power – John Robarts of Ontario, looking as bored as a company president at his annual staff picnic and Robert Stanfield of Nova Scotia, his skull-formed face drained of emotion.

John Diefenbaker is not a man I cherish but there was in the sight of him while he spoke last night the painful recognition of a human being cruelly used both by himself and by his party. His audience was lost to him half-way through his too-long speech. Yet he went on and on and on, his enemies were Grits, the press was Grit, but he stood, he would stand, he would not falter, he had followed the course. Finally, mercifully, it was over and the Camp kids sat on their hands and the old man sat down, finished.

[1966]

II

JOHN DIEFENBAKER MUST HAVE KNOWN that he was beaten, his brand of politics dying, but custom and courage can outlast reality. When he walked into Maple Leaf Gardens that Saturday, (September 9, 1967), he was going out on his particular path to the end. All of the sweetness and all of the bile that he inspired had by now been expended; he had become one of history's truly irrelevant figures and the whole elaborate

220

drama of his candidacy for the party leadership was pointless, even as a gesture.

Through the long afternoon he sat in a tier of box-seats, just left of the stage, with his wife Olive and her ten-year-old grandson, while his aides, Gordon Churchill, David Walker and James Johnston, came to report the fragments of conversation and miasma of rumours enveloping the Gardens. Directly in front of him, an arm's reach away, two dozen reporters, television cameramen, and radio beepers watched his every gesture, their metallic voices demanding his comments, flashing lights and thrusting microphones at their victim. Diefenbaker's face showed the strain; his eyes were hooded in apprehension. But he remained composed throughout the ordeal, talking during the two-and-a-half-hour delay before the first ballot the way a hungry man eats, for comfort as well as nourishment.

"You've done what you had to do," Olive is saying.

"When does the vote begin?" Diefenbaker replies, just as a convention official makes an announcement in French.

"He's speaking in the language of the second nation," remarks Olive.

"Yes. The Queen's picture isn't even here."

"What d'you think of the convention?" asks a radio man, pointing to the voting machines, holding up his mike to catch the reply.

"Remarkable. In past conventions things moved faster without all those gadgets. But they do *look* impressive."

"Will all this hoopla rejuvenate the party?"

"If the balloons that are up there attached to the ceiling bring on rejuvenation, bring on more balloons!"

"Watcha gonna do when this is over?"

"Go fishing in the north of Saskatchewan. I haven't had a successful fishing trip in years."

"You like fishing with a bamboo pole?"

"What about you," Diefenbaker is suddenly angry. "Do *you* have a bamboo pole? Are you a bambooer or a bamboozler?"

"You gonna write your memoirs?"

"I never think of memoirs. I'm still making history."

"What about the voting delay?"

"Everything's electrified today. But they can't find the plug. That's for sure."

"You read anything by Marshall McLuhan?"

"Oh, that's a very interesting thing. When I was in Regina the other day. . . ."

A reporter interrupts: "When did you *really* decide to run today?"

"When I knew that the decision was reached, determined upon, that this two-nations resolution would be quietly put away."

Finally, at 3:21 Eddie Goodman announces that voting can start. Diefenbaker makes his way toward the machines. He gets bursts of applause along the way. He has trouble with the machine, has to be shown how to use it, and when he returns to his seat is asked about the experience. "If that be not complication, I know not what complication is," he says.

"Do all those telegrams you've received reflect Canada's opinion of your view of the two-nations policy?"

"Oh yes, oh yes, there's no question about that. And that applies to the province of Quebec, with the exception of a vociferous minority."

"You won't change your mind?"

"Absolutely not. To do so would be to deny the trust of every prime minister and leader of this party since Confederation."

"Have you tried to get support from other candidates?"

"I've never discussed support with anyone. I've never spent any money on this convention. Accept me. Here. That's all."

"Did you get a chance to look at your tray? Is it engraved, the silver tray they gave you?"

"It's not engraved."

"It's not, eh? D'ya know where they got it?"

"I don't. They say it's a Macdonald tray."

"How much d'ya think it's worth?"

"I don't look at it from a collector's eyes. It's a question of value, intrinsic value, not a matter of consideration of dollars, when the smallest of things have behind them tradition."

It is time, now, for the results of the first ballot, and the circle of reporters tightens: "How d'ya feel, Mr. Diefenbaker?"

"I'm one of those who believe in the democratic process. You have never heard me exult in victory. I was never craven in defeat. . . ."

"You never were WHAT?"

"Craven in defeat. If you stand for a principle and the principle is right, ultimately you triumph."

"There's a gorgeous colour story in the old boy," says a smooth radio voice.

David Fulton comes, for a moment, to perch beside Diefenbaker, and asks: "How did you like the voting machines?" There is no reply and Fulton, looking like a spoiled boy caught trying to curry favour from his school principal, sneaks away.

Gordon Churchill follows with a fistful of telegrams. FOR CANADA'S SAKE KEEP FIGHTING he reads, and passes it on. GLAD TO SEE YOU BACK IN ACTION. KEEP ON KEEPING ON. The two men smile, and give each other a playful elbow poke.

There is yet another delay, and a reporter asks again: "What about the two-nations policy?"

"I have a great sense of satisfaction today. If it hadn't been for me, we would have had that resolution that went through the subcommittee two hundred, what was it, to one, and then through the program committee, with the platform committee. They didn't dare bring that before the convention. They had it all arranged. It was going to be done well."

"How d'ya mean, 'done well'?"

"Put through, and everything was going to be dandy. Macdonald or Borden or Bennett or Meighen. If they looked down here, they would say: 'What is this?' And Langevin and Cartier. . . . No, great principles must never be subverted to the hope or expectation of political gain. In 1948 I was alone in this party standing against outlawing communism. I said: 'You can't outlaw thought!' They brought it in as a policy. They said you can't do it; I was booed for that. You can in-law wrong-doing but you can't outlaw thought. Once you start outlawing thought, you place everyone in a position who has association with a Communist of having to swear that he isn't a Communist. You can't get votes on a principle that's all wrong. They were going to sweep the province of Quebec – two other provinces were mentioned – if the people wanted it. I said whether they want it or not, it stands. Does anyone talk about outlawing communism any more? You've got to take your stand. Oh, here we are. . . ."

It is Eddie Goodman, announcing the results of the first ballot: "Diefenbaker, 271; Fleming, 126; Fulton, 343 (CHEERS); Hamilton, 136; Hees, 295; Maclean, 10; McCutcheon, 137; Roblin, 349 (CHEERS); Sawka, 2; Stanfield, 519 (CHEERS); Starr, 45. That's it, thank you, ladies and gentlemen."

John Diefenbaker leans forward, writing the figures on a pad. They show that after eleven years of leading his party, he has retained less than twelve per cent of its support. The pouches under his eyes seem suddenly heavier, like purses containing the remnants of a played-out life.

"How d'y feel now, Mr. Diefenbaker, huh? How d'ya feel right at this minute? Huh?" a voice persists.

The Old Chief draws himself together. "I feel as I've always felt," he begins. Then he asks the reporters his one question of the afternoon: "What would be your summary of me, if you were being entirely objective?"

The same voice but in subdued tones: "I'd say you're bearing up extremely well under the strain."

"I've served my country. I shall continue to take those stands that I believe to be right."

Pierre O'Neill of *Le Devoir* turns to a colleague: "Ours is a disgusting trade. We watch a man die slowly and every now and then we say 'You've had it. Now, how do you feel since the last time we asked you?' "

Diefenbaker leaves his seat to fetch some soft drinks for Olive and her grandson. An elderly delegate reaches out for him. "John, you'll always be *my* Chief," he cries, trying for a little while longer to keep alive the Diefenbaker legend. (Maple Leaf Gardens is filled with loyal Conservatives who still believe the legend. But they can no longer support the man.)

The second ballot. Diefenbaker goes to vote and when he comes back, there is joy in his gloating. In silent mime he shows how he pushed and pulled the voting machine's lever, and comments sarcastically on the long time it takes to count the ballots: "Well, it certainly shows what technical advances can do." Then he suddenly seems distracted and tells Gordon Churchill beside him: "Nasser says, next time his people are going to understand who to vote for."

The microphones and the lights are still there, but the questions have stopped. The reporters are looking at Diefenbaker as if they expect him to begin haemorrhaging at any moment. It is now Diefenbaker who leans forward, trying to engage their attention with the story of a Tory convention held in the late Twenties: "That was the first time they ever had loudspeakers. There were about twelve hundred delegates, as I recall it. . . . That was the occasion when the big fight took place between Meighen and the premier of Ontario, Ferguson. It was the first time any of us had ever seen loudspeakers. The loudspeakers were just horns, oh, eighteen inches in diameter, placed at strategic points around the walls, mainly behind the audience. And in the audience, there would be about three thousand. They filled the rink portion of the amphitheatre in those days. There were joint chairmen. One was

Senator Beaubien, who had a very large, loud voice. And Tommy Church, who was Mayor of Toronto several times.

"Tommy was the only person who could make a speech that was totally incomprehensible when it was delivered but was a literary masterpiece when it came out in Hansard. Because nobody knew what he was talking about. Every now and then he'd put in 'British Navy,' 'Empire,' and so on. The matter before the assembly was resolutions on the tariff. Tommy got up, way back, oh, possibly sixty feet from the podium. 'I'm entirely opposed to this business,' he said, 'of a navy for Canada. The *Rainbow* and the *Niobe,* that's all we've got. One's in a garage in Halifax and the other's in a garage in Esquimalt. I'm entirely opposed to that.' The chairman said: 'You're out of order, we're dealing with the subject of protective tariffs.' 'Oh,' Tommy said, 'oh, that's what we're on. Then I can tell you immediately. Let this be perfectly clear. This idea of sending ambassadors . . .'."

The monologue is interrupted by an announcement from Eddie Goodman.

Diefenbaker picks up the story exactly where he left off. "He said, '. . . as far as I'm concerned, this sending representatives down to Washington is nonsense. I wouldn't . . .'."

Again there is an interruption, this time for an announcement by Roger Régimbal, the convention co-chairman.

Diefenbaker picks it up again: ". . . he said: 'It's the biggest nonsense I ever heard in my life.' The chairman replied, 'You are out of *ord-eur.*' That was Senator Beaubien with his big voice. 'We are dealing with the tariff. You are out of *ord-eur.*' 'Oh,' Tommy said, 'it's a simple thing, this business of social security.' He said, 'I'm opposed to that a hundred per cent.' He said, 'This idea of giving pensions to the old. I'm against that. Not yesterday, today and tomorrow. . . .' And with that Beaubien became very annoyed and he said, 'You are out of *ord-eur.*' From out of this loudspeaker up there comes 'You are out of *ord-eur.*' Tommy turns around to the audience and says: 'Shut your damn mouths, you're not even delegates here!' "

The reporters laugh, a little too loud, and the group waits for the announcement of second-ballot results: Diefenbaker, 172; Fleming, 115; Fulton, 361; Hamilton, 127; Hees, 299; McCutcheon, 76; Roblin, 430; Stanfield, 613; Starr, 34.

Now the Diefenbaker smile becomes a grimace, without its adornment of the afternoon's brave joy. He has dropped a hundred votes. He is asked if he will withdraw.

225

"I have no observations to make."

"Well, never mind, Chief," says Senator Walker gently, "maybe we'll go for a little walk and maybe you can get a glass of ginger ale."

Walker and Churchill lead Diefenbaker out to a room under the Gardens galleries. After quick, dismal consultation, Diefenbaker decides to withdraw. Douglas Bassett, a young Hees supporter, flashes in to say that George will give the Chief anything for his support.

As always, Diefenbaker has waited too long to act. It is now too late to withdraw. The third ballot has started. Diefenbaker goes to vote, and the applause he gets is thin, the polite clapping of a cricket-match crowd. Back in his seat, he looks at the reporters and they look at him. No one says anything. Then Roger Régimbal is announcing the results of the third vote: Diefenbaker, 114; Fleming, 76; Fulton, 361; Hamilton 106; Hees, 277; Roblin, 541; Stanfield, 717.

John Diefenbaker is down to five per cent of his party's support. "That's it," he says, and suddenly he is going.

He is still somehow holding himself together, like a sheet of broken safety glass. The conductor of the house orchestra catches the occasion and begins playing *Hail to the Chief.* But there is no music left in the old man, as he makes his way out of that hot hell of a hall, jammed with shamefaced reporters, ungrateful Tories and broken illusions.

[1967]

226

PART EIGHT *Home Country*

Noises from the Attic

HEN I WAS APPEARING ON A VANCOUVER OPEN-LINE radio show
recently, I was moved to make the passionate declaration that
"I love Canada." Five seconds later, the station switchboard lit
up like a birthday cake and the first caller breathing aggressively, demanded that I explain myself.

"You say you love Canada," she snorted (she really could talk and
snort at the same time, a rarity even in the Canada I love), "Well, tell
us, Mr. Smart-Apple Newman, why are you so anti-American? Eh?"

Now, I had said nothing at all about being anti-American. In fact at
the time I was consistently at pains to explain that I really respected
Americans for their strengths, sympathized with them in their woes and
wished them well – though I hoped they would not overrun my country
completely.

But in the months since Richard Nixon's trade offensive came into
being, this attitude of polite moderation has been increasingly hard to
maintain for reasons I would like to explain with a little story we Canadians use to warm our spirits these cold Arctic nights.

It concerns President Richard Nixon and a remark he made at a
White House press conference on September 16, 1971. I am repeating
it in full because I want to make it perfectly clear: "With regard to the
Japanese, I think I can summarize our dilemma in this way. After the
Japanese were here I found that, both from the information they gave
and the information we had ourselves, Japan is our biggest customer in
the world."

The fact is that in 1970 United States-Canadian trade exceeded the
value of United States-Japanese trade by some ten billion dollars. Our

229

purchases from the United States (and if this sounds like north country boasting, forgive me, for it is the absolute truth) have for many years approached in value the total of the combined purchases of America's four next largest trading partners – Japan, West Germany, Britain and France.

But at a time when he was painstakingly examining his country's trading position the American president did not know any of this. Now, four months later, we are still asking ourselves in bumpkin bewilderment – how could he not know it? And the answer that keeps coming back from the void is: Because he does not realize we exist.

In another time, we would have shrugged off Nixon's howler. But Canadians today are experiencing a mood of surging self-assertion, and the idea that to the American president we are a noncountry makes us bloody mad.

What has finally aroused us from one hundred years of political self-effacement is the realization that has come so lately, and so late, that American capital is taking over the Canadian economy, leaving us in control of a smaller portion of our productive wealth than the citizens of any other industrialized nation on earth not actually occupied by a foreign power.

United States investment already here, which has been pouring into the country at a gross rate of three million dollars a day since 1945, is in danger of reducing us to the status of squatters on land we feel is our own and like settlers in the old-time Westerns, we are now searching, if not yet for a hired gun, at least for some way of challenging the intruders.

Our situation is made no less poignant by the fact it was mainly our own greed, naïvete and mute support of a long line of week-kneed political and business leaders that landed us in this mess. And now, some of these same careful quitters are advocating that we join the United States to form a North American common market. Though superficially appealing, such a scheme would inevitably be the first step in our political absorption. The end of the Canadian dream.

Canadian nationalism, the kind I support anyway, means resisting this kind of temptation and asserting instead our national identity, dignity and freedom of action by placing restrictions on foreign investment.

Nearly two centuries ago, Canadians chose to stick with Britain rather than join in the American Revolution. After peacefully, if painfully, acquiring the attributes of a nation, we find ourselves facing a no

230

less definite challenge to decide where we stand in relation to the United States.

And so, Mr. Nixon, what we want to make perfectly clear is this: We are alive and well, and if you should hear some rattlings down in Washington from up here in the continent's attic, it is just us Canadians murmuring the line of another beleaguered American neighbour, former President Diaz of Mexico: "So far from God, so near the United States."

[1972]

Expo Opens

THE CANNONADE OF FIREWORKS WHICH MARKED THE OPENING of Expo bursting in a technicolor tattoo over the St. Lawrence on an April afternoon may in retrospect turn out to have been one of those rare moments that change the direction of a nation's history.

How, after sponsoring this world's fair, can we ever be the same again? This is the greatest thing we have ever done as a nation and surely the modernization of Canada – of its skylines, of its tastes, its styles, its institutions – will be dated from this occasion and from this fair.

At the very moment when the Governor-General, a sombre presence amid the gaiety of the day, declared Expo '67 officially open, I was standing in front of the United States pavilion, which was shimmering and soaring in the sun like an aviary fit for eagles. Beside me, a young Expo hostess, all done up in white leather and a blue beanie, shrieked in pleasure at no one in particular, "*C'est merveilleux.*"

And it was marvellous. All of it. Not just any one building or exhibit; not just the zooming helicopters and purring hovercraft, but everything. It is a wow of a fair. It is fabulous. It is the sun and the moon and the stars. And the more you see of it, the more you are overwhelmed by a feeling that if this is possible, that if this sub-arctic, self-obsessed country of twenty million people can put on this kind of show, then it can do almost anything.

The $650 million Expo will cost is a small price for the impression of Canada its thirty-five million visitors will take away with them. Never again will they need think of us – or will we need think of ourselves – as an impotent appendage of either Britain or the United States. They may not learn much about our history (even though the Canadian pavilion makes it as alive and interesting as it deserves to be) but they will know that we are a nation which has joined the twentieth century and is heading for the twenty-first.

A kaleidoscope of impressions of the first day at the fair crowds in: Passing a pale-blue Buick lonely in the morning on the Ottawa-Montreal highway and in the back seat the upright and somehow gallant figure of John Diefenbaker on his unheralded way to the fair his government first sponsored and brought to its tremulous beginning . . . Louis St. Laurent looking like a kindly effigy of himself, being escorted to a seat in the distinguished visitors section at the Place des Nations by an Expo hostess and the crowd around him, suddenly alert to who he was, bursting into spontaneous applause . . . Jack Pickersgill, nervously removing his fedora, just in case the tune the Expo band was playing happened to be some country's national anthem . . . George Hees, striding into the stands where the opening ceremonies were taking place, flexing his shoulder muscles like a tired but still game quarterback . . . The provincial premiers like wedding cake figures stepping up to the dias in morning clothes . . . Jean Drapeau, triumphant, the founder and moving spirit of the fair.

This was the establishment gathered together in mink and millinery to offer itself ponderous congratulations. Outside was the fair that had so far exceeded their dreams of youth and gaiety that it made the middle-aged spill laughter. Everywhere there were pretty girls, all miniskirts and smiles, German girls in pearl-gray boots and orange tights; British girls striped from top to bottom in red, white and blue; Czech girls with open Slavic faces and scarlet wool suits; Pakistani girls demure in saris.

One of the biggest surprises of this astonishing fair was the British pavilion, so stodgy on the outside, so witty within, a celebration of the history of the English-speaking peoples presented with unexpected flair and self-deprecating humour. In the middle of industrial marvels, literary giants, historical pageants, there is an untidy line of bushes with burrs and birds singing and a sign that proclaims: "Is there under heaven a more glorious and refreshing object than an impregnable hedge?"

In the mini-rail that rings the fairgrounds and provides a breathtaking over-all look at the fair's marvels, people were poking each other and saying, look at Greece, look at Cuba, look at France, taking pleasure in everything, in every nation's accomplishments.

It was a day to be remembered for a lifetime. I came to the fair, a nationalist, full of pride in Canada. I left it, a humanist, full of hope for man. [1967]

Western Skies

THEY HAVE SAT THERE EVERY NIGHT for ten years now, the people of Canada's Prairie provinces, watching the eleven o'clock TV news, and their nervous systems have been strained beyond endurance. The nightly procession of Canadian newsmakers has been interminably engaged with what Quebec wants and doesn't want, and nobody ever mentions the West. No wonder a farmer in southern Saskatchewan recently fired a shotgun into his TV set as a hapless Liberal MP was trying to explain his government's policy on wheat sales.

The anonymous marksman was expressing in his own way the sense of frustration which has reached crisis proportions across much of Western Canada. Like the meeting and marrying of many drops of rain sliding along a wire to form one huge gusher, the various discontents felt by westerners have combined into a political force that must be taken into account in working out the delicate equation of our national future. The roots of dissatisfaction stretch back to the turn of the century when the western territories struck the bargains that brought them into Confederation. Tariffs, freight rates and wheat sales were the issues then (as they are now), but during most of the first fifty years, the West at least felt that its complaints were being heard and that it possessed the political clout to make Ottawa sit up and listen.

Until the late Fifties, national attention was focussed on the Prairies and British Columbia with discoveries of the huge petroleum and gas fields, the carving out of the aluminum city at Kitimat, the building of the Trans-Canada pipeline, the emergence of giant forest product complexes and discoveries of rich new mineral wealth. But during the Sixties, the focus of national concern shifted almost entirely to Ontario,

234

where the nation's industrial future was being moulded, and to Quebec, where the struggle for national unity was being fought. The West began to feel a deepening sense of isolation from the centres of national decision-making. This mood of irrelevance grew particularly bitter after the defeat of John Diefenbaker and his Prairie proconsul, Alvin Hamilton. Lester Pearson's Liberals never found, or searched very hard for, a Prairie politician who could champion the western cause, and in the four general elections fought under Pearson's leadership, the Liberals won only six of the one hundred and ninety-two Prairie seats where they ran candidates.

It looked for a while as if this estrangement would end when Pierre Trudeau became the Liberal leader, and the three Prairie provinces gave him eleven seats in the 1968 election. But it now appears that the West misunderstood Trudeau's message. Because of his emphasis on the "One Canada" theme, many westerners thought he intended to be tough with Quebec's demands, that his fixation with turning the federal government into a French-oriented technocracy was not really very high on his list of personal priorities. Now, westerners are having difficulty reconciling this impression with the prime minister's actions, and having no familiar framework within which to fit the inexorable impulses of French Canada toward social change, they interpret each Quebec gain as the hot breath of revolution.

This is the great unstated issue across western Canada – the feeling of political abandonment by Ottawa for the sake of assuaging the demands of a militant Quebec. The resultant frustration is made worse by the fact that the West no longer has its own parties of political protest through which it can funnel its demands. All of the Prairie political movements (such as the federal wing of the Social Credit, the Progressive Party, the United Farmers of Alberta) have either vanished or (like the CCF) have been taken over by the unions and eastern intellectuals.

No federal politician now in the House of Commons can claim the personal resonance with the West that would give him the right to be a legitimate spokesman for the western point of view. The Liberals' few western ministers are at best performing a caretaker function for a leader who has yet to emerge.

The other great factor has been the declining importance of wheat in the national economy. Forty years ago, wheat sales accounted for fully one-tenth of our Gross National Product and a third of Canada's exports. (Now, they barely make up one per cent of the GNP and less

235

than four per cent of overseas sales.) The wheat problem is made incredibly complex by the fact that western agriculture has become an industry in which a farmer may have land and machinery worth a hundred thousand dollars on paper, yet live close to the poverty line in terms of cash income. The most absurd and damaging thing Trudeau could have said to the Prairies was, "Why should I sell your wheat?" – whether his remark was quoted out of context or not.

The Prairies have lived for half a century in contradiction. Westerners take pride in individualism, free enterprise, the justice of the free market and the iniquity of tariffs. Yet no other region in the country is as deeply committed to governmental responsibility and administration as are the wheat farmers. What few Ottawa politicians appreciate is that even those westerners who have remained farmers are turning away from the frontier outlook. The impact of television and travel has given them the same aspirations as the big-city dwellers of the east.

What is really happening to the West is that the nature of Canada is changing. This was a country built and developed on an east-west axis, which provided the justification for the colonization of the West. But now, air traffic, rail freight, long-distance calls, magazines, hydro-electric hookups, sports, trade, defence production, taste – almost everything is moving in a north-south direction. None of this means that the Prairies are about to separate. "Separatism in Saskatchewan," says Allan Blakeney, of the NDP, "is something people here feel rather than think about. But there's no doubt that most westerners are concerned that the essential bargain of Confederation has not been kept by Ottawa."

The underlying significance of western separatism is the opposite of what appears on the surface. Its real meaning is a plea for some effective power at the centre.

[1970]

236

Maclean's

L ATE IN THE PAST FIERCE AND DISCONTENTED CANADIAN WINTER, just a week after I took over as editor of *Maclean's,* I was sitting over dinner in a restaurant in the old quarter of Montreal talking to one of the brightest young lawyer-politicians in the country about the nervous state of the national psyche. My friend is an Irish-Canadian, usually given more to ribald laughter than mournful keening, and yet for an hour he elaborated his belief that without some dramatic mobilization of the national will this country might not endure the decade.

I have been hearing this kind of talk for years, put forward in different accents but with similar intent by French-Canadian separatists and English-Canadian continentalists, quitters all, and have always shrugged it off. But somehow that night, after we had gone out in the dark and tried to hail taxis, which could scarcely wend their way through the gloom of the narrow street, I felt a chill of terror that my friend, who has never been a quitter, might be right. In a single instant I realized with greater clarity than ever before just how precious I hold this country's existence to be, and I wanted to shout after him as he drove off, "Listen, there are too many of us who care about this country. We won't let Canada go."

The link between that highly personal moment and becoming editor of *Maclean's* may seem tenuous. But it is not. For *Maclean's* has always echoed that mute shout. This magazine is woven into the dreams and memories of this country; its stated aim for sixty-five years has been to provide a platform that allows the nation to speak to itself.

At no time in our history have we ever been in so desperate a need for just such a platform. Only in a constant interchange between the

237

segments of our fragile society, flung across this unlikely hunk of geography, is there hope of continuing unity. The distinguishing characteristic of *Maclean's* in its best times has been an uncompromising attempt to record and authenticate the Canadian experience for the Canadian reader. It is my intention to renew and embellish that tradition.

We hope to put out a magazine that will paint a monthly portrait of the perceptions, personalities and events that shape the Canadian reality. In a country with ten provinces, five regions, two languages, and no possibility of a truly national newspaper, only a magazine like this one has the facilities, the time, the space and, hopefully, the talent, to pull together for a national audience the essential interpretations of a world that seems to be changing as we walk in it. The Canada that lies out there, magnificently unknowable, is waiting for us to write about, you to read about, and all of us to believe in.

[1971]

Class of '71

OVER THE PAST YEAR, as a visiting associate professor of political science at McMaster University, I went back to college for the first time in twenty years. My own college days are remembered dimly as a grey time of apprenticeship, lacking any unifying generational experience. We were the class of '51, the kids who came along after the war. We published no journals, shared no causes, left no mark; we grew up separately, unaware of each other, drawing out insights unquestioningly from our professors, and if we thought of Canada at all it was as a kind of accidental geographical backdrop, a place to make self-deprecating jokes about.

All that has changed. Whatever Canadian students reject, oppose, or despise, they do not, like many of their American counterparts, despair of their own country. They are excited by the potential of being Canadians. Faced by a contracting job market, they have become gentle desperadoes, anxious to enhance those qualities of life that make Canada unique, but fearful that they won't get their chance. Their open dedication to their country does not mean that they accept all of its values. For many of them the generation gap has become a moral chasm across which they stare at their elders with distrust, convinced that many of the values that make for success in the adult world are fake.

The young today combine irreverence for established ethics with tolerance, spontaneity and the pursuit of raw personal experience. What is trying to be born here – and it may not survive the transition from the classroom to the harsher realities of working life – is a new form of humanism, characterized by a disdain for pomposity and impatience with the pieties of another age.

239

What forms a generation, what provides its perceptions, gives urgency to its expectations and generates its drive for power, is some deeply shared, common experience. It was the soup lines of the depression, the triumphs and agonies of World War II and the smug prosperity of the Fifties that provided the formative influences for most of the adults who now exercise authority in this country.

The climate in today's country of the young is governed by a totally different meteorology of experience. We have yet to see how, if at all, this new breed will alter the social consciousness that determines a society's future. But one thing is certain: long before the end of this century, the generation that now so frightens and baffles their elders will be running every institution in the country. So we had better reach some working arrangement with our successors; we have no alternative.

I don't subscribe to the theory that the young possess any special wisdom, but I salute the spirit of the Class of '71 and hope they'll remain true to the authenticity of their impulses for reform. They will lose their opportunity for making Canada a better place to live only if we force them to abandon their quest.

[1971]

240

Home Country

I N THE EARLY AND MIDDLE SIXTIES, when I was working out of the
Parliamentary Press Gallery in Ottawa reporting on the vagaries of
the Diefenbaker-Pearson years, I would occasionally get a hearty
phone call from someone in the American embassy there, asking me
"as a personal favour" to talk to "this friend of mine, a great guy,
really sold on Canada, up here researching a big take-out on the un-
defended border, all that jazz, you know."

The friend would generally turn out to be some young producer
from NBC or a hardened old hand from the St. Louis *Post-Dispatch,*
baffled by the lassitude of our life-style, impatient with the size of our
snowdrifts, and frustrated by his inability to find a strong focus for the
big take-out. (There is, after all, only so much you can do with an un-
defended border, even if you are a great guy.)

When we met, he would greet me a shade too jovially, and five sentences into the conversation it would become obvious that in the American embassy's catalogue of reliable spokesmen, interesting characters,
and harmless kooks, my name represented a small fringe element; I was
known as a Canadian nationalist. The itinerant luminary and the
embassy official obviously thought this an innocuous pastime, like
lepidopterology or ice-fishing, and I would obligingly mumble my nationalist's set piece over drinks, pointing out as mildly as I could that
Canada as a nation was in danger of drowning in American dollars,
American culture, American know-how, and the American dream.

Eventually, the visitor would take his leave, looking a little glassy
of eye, and when his take-out or program finally appeared, my nationalistic ideas would be reduced to half a paragraph or two minutes on the

screen, the kind of obligatory glimpse that gyrating witch doctors used to command in documentaries about emerging African states.

But times have changed. The American embassy has long since stopped phoning me; all those great guys are reporting on less benign expressions of our nationalism; and along with that small band of Canadians who were nationalists a decade ago, I find myself a moderate voice in a rising chorus of anti-American sentiment. This attitude seems so foreign to the habitual Canadian cast of mind that it almost amounts to a denial of our national character. After displaying for so long the emotional responses of a fearful, immature twenty-year-old who has not yet resolved his adolescent identity crisis, we are experiencing a mood of surging self-assertion. This new aggressive nationalism is strongest among the radical young and the activist intellectuals, but in the past year it has become an issue that even the old-line liberal internationalists, who still form the country's political establishment, have been unable to avoid. It is as though we have come to realize for the first time the true implications of our dependency on the United States. "Little by little," writes James Eayrs, a University of Toronto professor who has come very lately to the nationalist cause, "our independence is seeping southward. It takes place so painlessly that the victim does not notice. But one day he tries to exercise his independence and finds it isn't there – like the decapitated swordsman in the Thurber cartoon who, protesting he's fit to carry on dueling, is told to try and blow his nose."

During the past few years we have been displaying our determination to hold on to our heads in various ways, but nationalism in Canada is still a cause in search of a leader, an issue yet to be joined.

Its historic roots go far deeper than these recent manifestations would suggest. A self-governing colony may sound like a contradiction in terms; yet this has been the underlying theme of our history. Canada moved directly from being a colony of Great Britain to becoming an economic satellite of the United States. Originally, the Canadian nation was a fusion, or rather a living-together, of French-Canadians (following their defeat by the British) and those United Empire Loyalists who left the thirteen colonies after the Revolutionary War because they opted for England and King George. They were joined by waves of Scottish, Irish, and European immigrants fleeing various tyrannies. Born out of many defeats, Canada achieved a form of independence in 1867 (i.e., dominion status within the British Empire), which left its foreign policies to be dictated by Whitehall. Full freedom in inter-

242

national dealings came only in 1931, and it wasn't until 1949 that the judicial committee of the Privy Council in London ceased to be the final appeal from Canadian courts. This prolonged dependence on the mother country caused an impatient generation of Canadian patriots of Lester Pearson's vintage to believe that the umbilical cord with England could be cut only if Canada were aligned with the United States through closer military, economic, and social ties. And so we went directly from being bastard Englishmen to being bastard Americans.

The conquest of the Canadian economy by American businessmen has reduced Canadians to being minority shareholders in their own country. For example, more than 90 per cent of all factories in Canada important enough to have at least five thousand names on their payrolls are controlled by parent corporations in the United States. In addition, some 99 per cent of oil refining, 85 per cent of primary metal smelting, 78 per cent of chemical production, and 77 per cent of the electrical apparatus industry are American-owned. The cliche is that when the American economy catches a cold, we sneeze; the fact is that we develop pneumonia.

When you point out the extent of American economic domination to Americans living in Canada, they become intensely upset, hurt by our failure to remember that American capital has underwritten most of the country's development risks, reducing from generations to years the time required to attain our high standards of living. They had come to regard Canadians as the dullish denizens of their northernmost "state" and are baffled by all of the recent uproar. What they do not realize, and what it has taken us so long to comprehend, is that in exchange for our borrowed American affluence we have been selling out our way of life. In our naive, northern way, we had no idea that allowing the Americans to develop our natural resources implied we were willing to have them pollute our environment, direct our trade unions, deluge our media, bookstores, magazine racks, moviehouses, and even school texts with American ideas and values so that we are in real danger of forgetting who we are and why we are here.

Until recently, any concern with perpetuating the Canadian identity was considered faintly absurd and old-fashioned, since the admired attitude was internationalism and the only real mark of acceptance in every field of endeavour came from the United States. I bought it on Fifth Avenue; he studied at Harvard; she had her hysterectomy at the Mayo; we got our tan in Palm Beach – these were the meaningful accolades. We were the country cousins awed by the new Roman Empire and understood perfectly what Anthony Burgess meant when he wrote: "John Kenneth Galbraith and Marshall McLuhan are the two greatest modern Canadians the United States has produced." All that has changed. The American experience we so envied has become too precious to be entrusted to the new, disturbing America that emerged in the Sixties – the America of the Kennedy assassinations, Kent State, and Viet Nam.

By the very act of confronting our problems of domination from without and dissension from within, Canadians may be able to rework the miracle of their existence. In any case, having survived for a century as an irrelevant hunk of geography – a kind of gullible Gulliver of the North – we have now joined the mainstream of history at last.

[1971]

244